Second Edition

PERSUASION: Reception and Responsibility

CHARLES U. LARSON

Northern Illinois University

WADSWORTH PUBLISHING COMPANY, INC.
Belmont, California

Communications Editor: *Rebecca Hayden*
Production Editor: *Kathie Head*
Art Director: *Katie Michels*
Designer: *Don Fujimoto*
Copy Editor: *Ellen Seacat*
Cover: *Catherine M. Bleck*

PHOTO CREDITS
Chapter 1: *Jerry Berndt/Stock, Boston*
Chapters 2–6: *Steve Renick*
Chapter 7: *Owen Franken/Stock, Boston*
Chapter 8: *Steve Renick*
Chapter 9: *David A. Krathwohl/Stock, Boston*
Chapter 10: *Ellis Herwig/Stock, Boston*

Printed in the United States of America

2 3 4 5 6 7 8 9 10—83 82 81 80 79

Library of Congress Cataloging in Publication Data

Larson, Charles U
   Persuasion.

   Includes bibliographies and index.
   1. Persuasion (Psychology) I. Title.
BF637.P4L36   1979   301.15'4   78–12733
ISBN 0–534–00689–2

CONTENTS

PREFACE

This second edition of *Persuasion: Reception and Responsibility* addresses some of the issues and concerns that have emerged since the first edition was published in 1973. I wrote the book in the first place because I perceived a need for text materials focusing on tools for critical and perceptive reception of persuasion. The context in which the first edition was written was one of social and political turmoil. The voices of reason and moderation were being drowned out by the shouts of militant and violent activists. As I wrote, the war continued in Vietnam; Richard Nixon was winding up his first term and campaigning for his second term. The first edition was published before the Watergate scandal unfolded. Certainly there was a need then to attune students of communication to the unreasoned and perhaps dangerous persuasion of those times.

Many Americans would say, "But times have changed! We no longer see rioting in the streets, presidential abuses of the power of office, violent confrontations of activists and police, and such things." That is true, but other things have changed, too, since the early 1970s. We have been exposed to many kinds of persuasion since 1973. We are seeing as much persuasion today as we saw before 1973. Perhaps even more. The media manipulators seem to be getting more and more skillful. Recent figures indicate that our TV viewing time has increased—apparently by more than 50 percent. We are becoming more and more conditioned to be persuaded by the skillful use of media techniques, which become ever more sophisticated, both technologically and psychologically. Surely there is even more need than in 1973 to prepare students to become responsible *consumers* of persuasion.

More than half the material in this second edition is new, not merely an updating of the first edition. Chapter 1, for example, no longer just traces the differences between persuasion and other forms of communication. Instead an overall analytical tool is presented and discussed, with several demonstrations of how it can help to alert the persuadee. The heavy emphasis on careful analysis of the language of persuasion remains in the second edition as well as the Aristotelean use of enthymemes or premises held by persuadees, which are the targets of a persuader's appeals. The discussion of campaigns and campaign persuasion has been expanded and developed after review and study of several hundred campaigns by myself and my students. An entirely new chapter focusing on the use of media in persuasion is included in the second edition as well as a chapter on becoming a persuader—something that was added at the request of many who used the first edition. Richard Johannesen's updated discussion on ethics reflects some important changes in his perceptions since the occurrence of many of the changes in our context since 1973—Watergate, media manipulation, and so forth.

The organization of the book has remained essentially the same. We begin looking at the smallest and most intrapersonal element in persuasion—the individual persuaders and their choice of language. Then we move to the kinds of psychological or process appeals that persuaders can make and through the kinds of logical or content appeals that persuaders employ. These might be thought of as the interpersonal elements in persuasion—those parts of the process where the interaction is basically between persuader and persuadee. The latter portions of the book deal with broader matters: cultural premises, campaigns, mass media, and ethics. These are matters that involve not only the persuader and persuadee but that take context into account and deal with what might be called the societal or public elements in the persuasion process.

In all of the chapters except the one on becoming a persuader, I have tried to present tools of analysis—ways of investigating the motives and goals that underlie a persuasive appeal. No single tool is presented as a blanket or fail-safe way of looking at persuasion. In fact, there are many situations in which a single tool of analysis just will not work—you will not be able to discover much about the persuasion using that tool. At other times, a combination of tools will be most useful in analyzing where a persuader intends to take you and how he or she intends to take you there. In some instances, use of all of the tools presented in the book will be helpful. The point is not to try to fix on a single formula for creating immunity to persuasion. In fact, we need to be persuaded in a world like ours where there are so many options, brands, ideas, candidates, and so forth. We must learn to use the tools of analysis to train ourselves to be alert when exposed to persuasion—to develop a critical state of mind as a consumer, as a voter, or as a follower. If that can be accomplished to even a moderate degree during one term in a persuasion course using this text, we can all be pleased—teachers, students, and author. Let us hope that we can achieve that goal.

Whenever one writes a book, he has to have help. Many persons— fellow instructors, students, secretaries, critics—have a part in the production of a book. It is impossible to thank them all on an individual basis for their help, ideas, and encouragement. But without them there would be no *Persuasion: Reception and Responsibility.* Some, however, stand out because they went out of their way—often when it was inconvenient—to help this project to completion. Those persons I want to thank specifically: Joann Reconnu and Jeannene Eineke, our departmental secretaries; Arnetha Price, who did most of the typing of the manuscript; Mary Larson, Charles Tucker, Herb Hess, and Dick Johannesen, all fellow teachers who gave me many ideas and allowed me to test my ideas on them as the manuscript was in preparation; and the following teachers who served as critics for the early drafts of the book: Edward M. Brown, Abilene Christian University; Jackson R. Huntley, University of Minnesota, Duluth; Patricia Justice, Mount Hood Community College; June Kable, Midwestern State University; Gerre Price, Mercer University; Stanley Schmidt, Portland Community College; and Robert Varga, Oklahoma City University. Finally, thanks to Becky Hayden and Kathie Head, editors for Wadsworth Publishing Company, who kept me on the right track and on schedule. To all of you and especially to my students past and present, who have sparked ideas, provided examples, and bubbled with enthusiasm: Thank you all.

Charles U. Larson

To
Mary, Martha, and Ingrid—
You light up my life

Persuasion in Today's World 1

W e live in a world of persuasion. The old ways of getting people to do what we want them to are useless. Children no longer take their parents' word as law, so parents must persuade them to do well in school, to look realistically at drug abuse, to help save energy. The church can no longer control its members through fear, and so must persuade them to give more money, to attend services, or to use only certain methods of birth control. Our government, no longer able to rely on the draft to keep the armed services up to strength, must persuade young people that joining will bring them skills, education, security, and travel. Politicians, no longer able to rely on a political machine to get elected or even nominated, must persuade slatemakers and voters that they are best qualified for the nomination or the office.

In marketing, sellers cannot count on brand loyalty or on price alone to sell a product. Instead, they have to persuade consumers of a product's quality, of its ability to satisfy their needs—they may even have to persuade consumers that they have a need that the product can meet.

In education, persuasion has also become important. The days of rote learning or of pounding lessons into the heads of students are gone. Teachers need to persuade students that the class material is relevant and will be useful in years to come. They may even need to persuade students that their mode of teaching is valid.

We could go on and on. Clearly, persuasion pervades our world. Clearly, too, in such a world we need training in persuasion—not only in how to persuade others, but in how—and how not—to be persuaded. Of course, you might try to reject all the persuasion directed at you, but there are pitfalls on that path too. If you rejected all persuasion by politicians, how would you know whom to vote for? If you rejected all advertising, how would you learn about differences between brands or about new products? If you rejected the persuasion of your teachers, how would you know what courses to focus on or which area to major in? You could personally investigate the record of every politician on the ballot in some elections and could personally test every detergent or every motor oil or every ski wax on the market. Maybe you could even take one of every kind of course and study its career possibilities. However, if you did, you would not have time for much else. So, realistic consideration of the world around us tells us that *we need to be persuaded*, at least in some areas, if only to reduce our alternatives before making choices.

The title of this book, *Persuasion: Reception and Responsibility*, suggests the direction we will take. Our focus is on the training of persuadees—those of us on the receiving end of all the persuasion. We need to learn to be critical, to observe and judge the persuasion coming at us.

DOUBLESPEAK IN A PERSUASION WORLD

Even in such a persuasion-riddled world as ours, you would not need persuasion training so much if all persuaders were open rather than hidden, and if all of them talked straight. Far too many "speak with a forked tongue." In other words, they talk in doublespeak. *Doublespeak is the opposite of language: it tries not to communicate; it tries to conceal the truth and to confuse*. For instance, in doublespeak, unprovoked mass bombings could be—and were—called "anticipatory protective reaction strikes." Would these words have persuaded you that the bombings were justified? The Vietnam War, which spawned that particular bit of doublespeak by the U.S. government, is over, but doublespeak goes on.

Government is not the only offender. We always have adpeople and promotion specialists trying to blind us to the defects in their products, their candidates, and their ideas. We now estimate that the average 18-year-old has seen more than 20,000 hours of television, including 350,000 television commercials—about 60 a day since birth.[1] Of course, not all commercials are doublespeak, but enough of them are so that we can scarcely ignore the problem. The pervasiveness of doublespeak is growing and we are becoming more and more numbed by it. Advertisers can tell us the obvious—"V.O. is V.O."—and get results. They can ask us a

---

1.   David Burmeister, "The Language of Deceit" in *Language and Public Policy*, ed. by Hugh Rank (Urbana, Ill.: National Council of Teachers of English, 1974), p. 40.

confusing question—"If You Can't Trust Prestone, Who Can You Trust?"—and can expect that our confusion will lead to increased sales. They can ballyhoo a candidate for office promising "Leadership for a Change" and can expect to influence voters. So how do we go about becoming better at detecting doublespeak? We provide ourselves with analytical tools that will help us to take apart the many sales pitches that confront us. Let us begin by first looking at what persuasion is—how it has been defined at various times and by various persons.

DEFINITIONS OF PERSUASION: A POTPOURRI

In ancient Greece, persuasion was the main means of achieving power and of winning in the courts. The study of persuasion, or *rhetoric*, was central in the education of all Greek male citizens. Aristotle, who was one of the first to study rhetoric in depth, said that it was "the faculty of observing in a given case the available means of persuasion." To him, persuasion could use a man's reputation or credibility or *ethos*. It also included the use of logical argument or *logos* and emotion-stirring appeals, which he called *pathos*.[2] Roman students of persuasion added specific advice on what a persuasive speech ought to include. Cicero said there were five elements—the *invention* or discovery of evidence and arguments; the *organization* of these; the artistic *stylizing* of them; the *memorization* of them; and finally the skillful *delivery* of them. Quintilian added that a persuader had to be a "good man" as well as a good speaker.

Now those kinds of definitions clearly focus on the sources of the messages and on their skill and art in building a speech. Later students of persuasion reflected the changes that have come with a mass-media world. In 1952, Winston Brembeck and William Howell, two communication professors, described persuasion as "the conscious attempt to modify thought and action by manipulating the motives of men toward predetermined ends."[3] There is a notable shift away from the use of logic and toward the internal motives of the audience. By the time Brembeck and Howell wrote their second edition in the early 1970s, they had changed the definition of persuasion too. There it is "communication intended to

---

2.   Aristotle, *The Rhetoric*, trans. by R. Robert, *The Works of Aristotle* (Oxford: Clarendon Press, 1924), p. 1355b.

3.   Winston L. Brembeck and William S. Howell, *Persuasion: A Means of Social Change* (Englewood Cliffs, N.J.: Prentice-Hall, 1952), p. 24.

influence choice."[4] In the mid-1960s, Wallace Fotheringham, another communication professor, defined persuasion as "that body of effects in receivers"[5] that had been caused by a persuader's message. Here the focus is almost entirely on the receiver, who actually determines persuasion. The goals of the source are not even central.(Even unintended messages, such as gossip overheard on a bus, could be persuasion if they caused changes in a receiver's attitude, belief, or action.) Kenneth Burke, literary critic and theorist, defines persuasion as the artful use of the "resources of ambiguity."[6] Here persuasion involves avoiding the specific and creating "identification" (Burke's term) through appeals so ambiguous that no one could object to them.

In the first edition of this textbook, *persuasion* was defined as "a process whereby decision options are intentionally limited or extended through the interaction of sources, messages, and receivers, and through which attitudes, beliefs, opinions, or behaviors are changed by a cognitive restructuring of one's image of the world or of his frame of reference."[7] In that definition, the *process* of persuasion gets the attention. Persuasion only occurs through cooperation between source, message, and receiver. To simplify things and following Burke's lead, in this edition *persuasion* will be defined as *the co-creation of a state of identification or alignment between a source and a receiver that results from the use of symbols.* Once you identify with the kind of world the ad huckster wants you to like— say Marlboro Country—persuasion has occurred. You may never smoke, but you have been changed—for you the world of Marlboro Country has become attractive. You might buy a cowboy hat or just swagger a little. Or you might try to get into the out-of-doors and get a little weathered and tan. You now want to be like the folks in Marlboro Country—there are changes in your attitudes, opinions and behavior, caused by several symbols—like "Come to Where the Flavor Is—Marlboro Country," or perhaps the pictures in the Marlboro ad symbolized the kind of image you wanted for yourself and caused the shift in alignment.

Notice here that the focus is not on the source or on the message or on the receiver but on all of them equally. They all cooperate to make a persuasive process. In co-created meaning, what is inside the receiver is just as important as the source's intent or what is in the message. In a sense, all persuasion is self-persuasion—we are rarely persuaded unless *we* participate in the process.

---

4.   Brembeck and Howell (2d ed., 1976), p. 19.

5.   Wallace C. Fotheringham, *Perspectives on Persuasion* (Boston: Allyn and Bacon, 1966).

6.   Kenneth Burke, *A Grammar of Motives* (Berkeley: University of California Press, 1970).

7.   Charles U. Larson, *Persuasion: Reception and Responsibility* (Belmont, Calif.: Wadsworth Publishing Co., 1973), p. 10.

Other kinds of techniques for changing people—brainwashing or hypnosis for example—usually involve some degree of coercion. However, even then a receiver has to allow the persuader to have influence. The brainwashed kidnapee who is forced to commit crimes at some point cooperated in his or her own persuasion. The person who is hypnotized and told not to eat sweets has to relax enough to let the hypnotist work. The centrality of the receiver is a good reason for each of us to study the process of persuasion from that point of view. We need to watch ourselves being persuaded and try to see why and how it happens so that we can be more conscious of our changes. This will allow us to be more critical and therefore more effective in rejecting persuasive messages when appropriate—and in accepting others when it seems wise to do so.

HOW TO GET TOOLED FOR A PERSUASION WORLD

Little children are often persuaded by TV spots that promote toys—Hotwheels Racetracks, Barbie Dolls, Monster Masks, and so forth. Suppose you wanted to train a child to be more critical of those TV spots. What would you do to make the child a better doublespeak detector? Well, you would point out that the spot is not really designed to help children but instead it is made to sell something. You really are teaching the child to be wary of the source's motives. You are warning that things are not always as they seem; that the announcer really does not mean "Kids, you can have all this fun today with your very own Hotwheels Racetrack!" The real motive is profit. The child may now be able to say, "That's just advertising—they just want you to buy." Next you might try asking what the words in one of those spots really mean. For example, you might say, "What does it really mean when they say, 'You can have loads more fun with a Barbie Beach Bus'?" Here the focus is on the message itself and not on source motives. You would be looking at some of the tactics of persuading. Then you might try to get the child to think about why the toy is wanted. Does the child want the toy for the friends it will attract, or is it the "in" toy this year—everyone has monster kits? Use of questions such as these gets at the motives receivers contribute to the TV persuasion. You might also tell the child that the racetrack is being made to look much larger than it actually is because the camera is tricking our eyes. You may warn your child that the sound effects associated with the toy are not part of the package—the race cars won't screech and roar as they do on TV and the Barbie Beach Bus won't have all that music with it. Thus you would be tooling the child to be critical of the channel or medium that is used for the persuasive message.

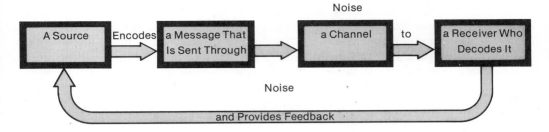

Figure 1-1 *The SMCR Model.*

The simplest model of communication, and the one most widely referred to, is the SMCR model (Figure 1-1) suggested by Claude Shannon and Warren Weaver in 1949 and modified by others such as David Berlo since that time.[8] The model contains four essential elements:

A Source (S), who or which is the encoder of the message. The code may be verbal, nonverbal, visual, musical, or some other modality.

A Message (M), which is meant to convey the source's meaning through any of the codes.

A Channel (C), which carries the message and which may have distracting noise.

A Receiver (R), who decodes the message, trying to sift out channel noise and adding his own interpretation.

These are also the elements in the persuasive process that is the focus of our definition of persuasion. Getting ourselves tooled up involves getting prepared to be critical of all the four elements in the process. You should prepare yourself to be alert to *source motives,* whether they are obvious or disguised. You should pay attention to the *message,* its symbols and its meaning. You would also be wise to think about the *channel or medium* being used to send this message—what kinds of effects does it have? Finally you need to be aware of your role in persuasion—what are you adding to the mix? We will look in depth at these four areas throughout the other chapters of this book.

One of our goals will be to explore various tools that we can use to try to determine a source's motives. Language choice, for example, can tip us off to source intent. The kinds of things a source sees in an audience can

8. Claude E. Shannon and Warren Weaver, *The Mathematical Theory of Communication* (Urbana: University of Illinois Press, 1949). See also David K. Berlo, *The Process of Communication* (New York: Holt, Rinehart and Winston, 1960).

also tell us something about the source's own view of the world. The choice to emphasize certain things can be a tip-off to source motives.

Another goal will be to explore tools that allow us to analyze the message and what it is intended to say. We will look at the organization of the message, its style, and the appeals which it makes. You will learn to look at the evidence contained in the message and at how it relates to the persuasive goal. You may want to look at the nonverbal as well as the verbal elements in the message to see which of these codes has what kinds of effects.

A third goal is to train ourselves to be alert to the kinds of effects that various channels have on persuasion. Does the impact of television, for example, make a message more or less effective? Has TV made us more vulnerable to certain message types? What are the effects of other kinds of media, such as radio and billboards? Are certain kinds of ballyhoo more useful or persuasive than others? Why do some media use certain techniques and other media use different ones?

Finally, you will need to explore ways of looking into yourself to discover why you are more or less likely to respond to some messages and not to others. I was always a sucker for games of chance at carnivals and fairs. Only after looking at what seems to motivate me and others did I begin to understand that everyone works in his own self-interest. I thought that winning would be in my own self-interest and that it would be easy for someone as swift and clever as I am. Later, I discovered that I had overestimated my skills. Games of chance lost their appeal.

The whole idea of identifying doublespeak depends on an understanding of the four elements in communication—source motives, message characteristics, channel effects, and receiver input.

RANK'S MODEL OF PERSUASION

As part of the Project on Doublespeak, sponsored by the National Council of Teachers of English, several persons were asked to suggest ways to train people to be critical receivers of persuasion. Hugh Rank, a researcher on the project, put the challenge this way: "These kids are growing up in a propaganda blitz unparalleled in human history. . . . Will the advertisers and political persuaders of 1980 or 1984 be less sophisticated, less informed, less funded than they are today?" He went on to say that "schools should shift their emphasis in order to train the larger segment of our population in a new kind of literacy so that more citizens can recognize the more sophisticated techniques and patterns of persuasion." Rank outlined a model of persuasion that could help train people to be critical receivers.[9] He called it the Intensify/Downplay Schema and tried to keep it as simple as possible. It can serve as a good overall model for you.

The basic idea behind Rank's model is that persuaders usually use two major tactics to achieve their goals. They either *intensify* certain aspects of their product, candidate, or ideology or *downplay* certain aspects of their cause—often they do both. Like a magician, they want to draw attention away from some things and toward others in order to pull off the illusion. Rank depicted his model and the major ways of intensifying or downplaying as shown in Figure 1-2.

Thus the persuader has four ways to go and six major tactics to use. Let us apply this model to a simple persuasive slogan—"At Avis, We Try Harder." The Avis strategy here is to intensify the good points of Avis and the bad points of the competition, while downplaying their own bad points and the competition's good points. The fact that the slogan is

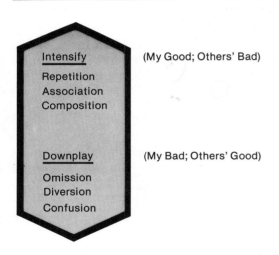

Intensify   (My Good; Others' Bad)

Repetition
Association
Composition

Downplay   (My Bad; Others' Good)

Omission
Diversion
Confusion

Figure 1-2 *The Intensify/Downplay Schema. (Hugh Rank, "Teaching about Public Persuasion" in* Teaching about Doublespeak, *ed. Daniel Dieterich. Copyright © 1976 by the National Council of Teachers of English. Reprinted by permission of the publisher and the author.)*

9. The discussion of the intensify/downplay model in this chapter is based on Hugh Rank, "Teaching about Public Persuasion" in *Teaching about Doublespeak*, ed. Daniel Dieterich (Urbana, Ill.: National Council of Teachers of English, 1976), Ch. 1.

repeated in one form or another on all TV, radio, billboard, and print advertisements suggests that the basic tactic is repetition (if we hear or see something enough times, it sticks). That slogan highlights the persuader's good points while suggesting the possibility of poor service at the other car companies (most of us assume that Avis was aiming at Hertz only, although there are several other such agencies).

Now, there may be disadvantages to going with a second-best company. You might get equipment so continually used that it had not been maintained. You might not have so wide a choice of colors or body styles. Many other potentially bad side effects can go with a second-place supplier. How does Avis avoid bringing those into the consumer's mind? It uses the tactic of diversion to draw our attention away from all of the bad things that could go along with second-placers and focus it on the false issue of *effort*. They try harder, and that is good. At least that is what we are supposed to think.

Let us consider a test case. I've been working with a mechanic to get my engine to stop missing and to get better mileage. He is a bad mechanic, but I got involved with him for the repair work before I knew that. Now I'm stuck with him because of my initial investment. He doesn't charge me double just because I keep bringing the car back; in fact, I've only had the first charge. Although he tries harder and harder every time I return the car, he keeps making it worse and worse. So trying harder isn't always better. In fact, football teams that try too hard often psych themselves out and lose as a result.

Another point lost in the Avis slogan is that the third-, fourth-, and fifth-place firms may also be trying harder. So even if trying harder is an advantage, Avis doesn't have a corner on it. In spite of all of these obvious flaws, the campaign "At Avis, We Try Harder" has succeeded and continues today. Why? Because we persuadees too seldom take the time to explore a candidate's statements or an advertiser's claims very carefully. Just using Rank's Intensify/Downplay device for a short time has revealed the weakness in claiming that trying harder is necessarily better.

Let's look in more depth at the six major tactics Rank outlined in his model. You can try them out on various forms of persuasion you meet each day. Perhaps your class will want to do a team project analyzing an issue on campus and how advocates for one side or the other use the tactics discussed below.

Intensifying

As we noted earlier, we can intensify our own good points or our competition's bad points. The candidate can talk about his stand on the issues and on his opponent's stands on the same issues. Touters of one kind of aspirin can talk about how fast it works without upsetting the stomach and thus can imply that other aspirins are slow and cause stomach upset. The evangelist claims that his way of believing is the only one. The opponent of the Equal Rights Amendment will claim that passage of the amendment will lead to women in combat, pro-football, and so forth. They all engage in the strategy of intensification. How do persuaders carry out this strategy?

Repetition   Repetition can intensify good or bad points about a product, a candidate, or an idea. We all find ourselves humming jingles. Hit radio stations repeat the same ten or fifteen numbers all day. The Trix rabbit is a good example of visual repetition that creates audience awareness of the product. In Chapters 6 and 7, we shall discuss various ways to get such identification in more depth. It is clear that repetition is often used to intensify the good in one's own cause and the bad in the opponent's position.

Association   In defining persuasion as a process whereby receivers aligned themselves with the persuader's image, position, or beliefs we were talking about the tactic of association. Rank cites three steps in association:

1. a cause, product, candidate is linked
2. to something already loved or hated by
3. the audience.

Persuaders engage in careful audience analysis (something we will discuss in more depth later) to identify the fears, wants, and biases of the target audience. Then they set about to mesh their persuasion goals into this set of alignments and preferences. For example, politicians, knowing that we have fears about nuclear power, tie this fear to their own cause by stating that they would put a freeze on all new nuclear power plant building if elected. An advertiser might associate a product—say British Sterling After Shave—with a certain lifestyle. The man who wears British Sterling has a tweedy look, lives in a stately old mansion, sips on a glass of Scotch, and has several gorgeous looking women waiting on his every whim. The persuadee is supposed to identify or align with the lifestyle. The association between lifestyle and product is then made, and the persuadee rushes out to get a gallon or two of the after-shave lotion. Association can be accomplished by verbally linking two ideas or persons or by nonverbally depicting two persons, ideas, or things together, as is often done in visual persuasion. Bruce Jenner, the decathlon winner, is seen eating a breakfast featuring Wheaties. There are also favorable and unfavorable beliefs that are culturally imbedded in members of the culture. We will be looking at some of these in more depth throughout the rest of this book.

Composition   We can intensify goodness or badness by putting it in contrast to something else. For example, the letters U.S.A. have a meaning. If we print the letters this way—U.$.A.—a new meaning emerges. That meaning is a persuasive statement that is made by the composition of the letters. It intensifies a badness that is sometimes attributed to our country. Ads can (and do) place a product in contrast to one or more of its competitors. So we see Coke doing a take-off on the Pepsi challenge by running its own "test," with character actors refusing to try the test since they already know that "Coke is 'The Real Thing.'" Vocally we can create contrast by using pitch, volume, tone, or duration to highlight certain words or phrases over others. You will notice other methods of drawing comparisons as you begin to look at the intensification process in more detail.

Downplaying

Sometimes it is in the persuader's self-interest to downplay certain things. M&M candy has been sold by playing up the fact that it tends to melt not in your hands but in your mouth. There are some disadvantages to the M&M product. For example, you destroy the full taste of the costly chocolate by coating it with the cheap candy coating. However, the advertisers do not focus on that; they downplay the product's shortcomings. A persuader can downplay the competition's advantages. For example, politicians usually do not tell you how good their opponents are. They usually avoid mentioning the success of the person they are running against. What are some tactics that persuaders use to achieve this kind of downplaying?

Omission   Sometimes persuaders downplay their own shortcomings or their competition's advantages by simply omitting key information. After all, in a 30-second or 60-second TV spot you can't tell the whole story, and a billboard should try to promote only a single idea and then in only a few words. Another way to omit key information is to be silent—to avoid being forced to give information that might harm the persuader's cause. A politician accused of under-the-table dealings might refuse to respond to the charges or might dismiss them as mudslinging. Euphemism is another way to omit information or to conceal it. This technique uses word(s) to avoid directly talking about the issue. It is seen quite often in politics. Rank uses the example of the word "bomb" being concealed through the words "nuclear device." As a consultant to the women's apparel industry,

Figure 1-3 *Hagar the Horrible. Hagar is intensifying here by focusing on the good things about his helmet. What are the bad things that he is downplaying? (© King Features Syndicate Inc. 1977.)*

I have discovered the need for euphemisms for the idea of a fat woman. For generations, the industry has used the term "half sizes" to indicate clothing designed for plump patrons (a euphemism for "fat women"), but that doesn't seem to work. One shopowner was successful in talking about "those big, beautiful women out there." The euphemism "queensize" has not been used long enough to measure a payoff.

Diversion   Persuaders can downplay by diverting attention away from key issues or key points. For example, politicians might try to focus away from their deficiencies on the job by pointing to sham issues. One might divert attention from the welfare program by challenging the voters to think about property tax rates. Politicians often divert attention from themselves by pointing to the bad things about their opponents, intensifying the badness in the diversion.

Advertisers have long diverted attention from the negative health aspects of sugar-coated breakfast cereals by loudly announcing that there is a "FREE PLASTIC MODEL INSIDE!" The Federal Trade Commission has compelled companies to run or print ads that are to apologize for earlier misleading ads. The tactic of diversion is a favorite in such "apologies." Wonderbread representatives *quietly* admit that the bread doesn't build bodies in twelve ways as was earlier claimed. Then they *loudly* announce that its new formula guarantees week-long freshness.

Humor is sometimes used to divert attention from key issues. Franklin Roosevelt was once charged with sending a warship to pick up his dog, which had been left behind at a conference in a distant port. He countered the accusations by making a joke of the G.O.P., saying that they had carried dirty politics to the point of attacking "my little dog, Fala." The humor diverted attention and downplayed the costs of the ship and crew to fetch a dog.

Other tactics for diverting attention cited by Rank include setting up a straw man to draw fire; focusing on a false issue or red herring; using emotional appeals based on the opponent's personality; and hairsplitting or nit-picking. Each of these serves to downplay a persuader's weak points or faults.

Confusion   A final tactic for downplaying in persuasion is to create a sense of confusion in the audience's mind. For example, one can shift definitions. An insurance salesman recently tried this on me by shifting the definition of insurance from an emphasis on income protection to a stress on estate protection. Many of us think of insurance as a means to guarantee income for one's family in case of death. Confusion results when we are told that we have protected income admirably, but that there is serious danger that half of the estate will be lost to federal and state inheritance taxes. Some policyholders get so confused or afraid that they jump into a commitment to an overly large and overly expensive policy.

Persuaders use confusion to downplay weak points in their position by using jargon or words with special meanings that are not commonly understood. For example, a persuader trying to get a consumer to buy an expensive home heat pump might use highly technical language about "thermal unit exchange ratios" or "vacuum pulled thermal input" or other words that mean little to the customer. Overwhelmed by words that make them seem (and feel) stupid, homeowners buy the device out of ignorance.

Other techniques for causing confusion mentioned by Rank include faulty logic, talking in circles, being inconsistent, and contradictions. The purpose, once again, is to downplay one's shortcomings while at the same time shifting attention from the opposition's strong points.

Self-protection—A Method

Rank goes on in his discussion of doublespeak to offer some good general advice on how to detect the flaws of persuaders who use various tactics to intensify or downplay.

① "When they intensify, downplay," says Rank. That is, when we recognize a propaganda blitz, we should be cool, detached, and skeptically alert not only to the inflated puffery of advertising with its dreams and promises, but also to intensified attack propaganda, the threats and exploitation of fears by a demagogue or government agent, elected or appointed.

② "When they downplay, intensify," A way to do this systematically is to divide a sheet of paper in quarters as shown in Figure 1-4, then to cite

Intensify Own Good 1. 2.	Intensify Others' Bad 1. 2.
Downplay Own Bad 1. 2. 3.	Downplay Others' Good 1. 2. 3.

Figure 1-4   *Intensify/Downplay Scorecard. (Hugh Rank, "Teaching about Public Persuasion" in Teaching about Doublespeak, ed. Daniel Dieterich. Copyright © 1976 by the National Council of Teachers of English. Reprinted by permission of the publisher and the author.)*

the kinds of downplaying and intensifying that are being done. Simply by seeing these, the persuadee can become more alert to the kind of manipulation that is going on.

Let's try this technique with a brief example. Consider the ad for Smirnoff Vodka shown in Figure 1-5. First let's look at the intensification used in the ad. Remember that the persuader may intensify by repeating, by association, and by shifting the composition of the message.

Notice the number of times the product name is mentioned in the ad. This is a kind of intensification of the product's own good, since there is a folklore belief among consumers that the only true or authentic vodka must be Russian—and the name Smirnoff does seem Russian. Then the ad uses association in its copy. Smirnoff vodka is associated with *Europe's elite*, with *proper food*, with a *delicious evening*, with being *impeccable*, with being *memorable*, and with fine crystal. So association is used to intensify the own-good aspect of the message. There are several ways in which composition is used to intensify as well. Look at the way the picture is organized. The wine glasses are untouched while the highball glasses are in people's hands and have clearly been sampled. Word choice is used to intensify—another example of composition. Then the ad also intensifies the opposition's bad points. The wine just *sat there*. Wine can *ruin* your palate. Again word choice intensifies the bad parts of wine. Notice that wine is made to seem disreputable because it *plays* with your palate, because it is *forceful*. Now, does the persuader downplay anything? Vodka can be potent, especially if you drink it like water during a dinner party. That fact is omitted. Instead we are told that it "Leaves You Breathless"—no one can smell that you've been drinking. There is some faulty logic here as well. Why is it amusing that while the Smirnoff flowed, the wine only sat there? Why is that bit of possible humor not surprising? Was it caused by the food, the after-dinner cigars or the Smirnoff? In all of these references, the ad confuses the reader. By identifying the many tactics at work, the persuadee can become alert and critical to the persuasive messages he sees.

We will discuss a number of other tools of analysis as we proceed, but Rank's Intensify/Downplay tool is a good general one to use at first. You will want to try it with a variety of persuasive messages that you encounter. In future chapters we will discuss the role of language as it is used to persuade. We will also look at how the internal motives and drives in each of us can be used by those who wish to persuade. Our preferences for certain kinds of logic can be used by the persuader who designs the message. Cultural premises that are trained into us from birth are the basis for many persuasive appeals. Finally, we are also affected by the way we respond to various kinds of media used in persuasion.

Figure 1-5 *Intensification and Downplaying in a Persuasive Message. (Courtesy Ste Pierre Smirnoff, a division of Heublein.)*

A REVIEW AND CONCLUSION

If you are now more alert to the possible ways you are being manipulated, you are well on your way to becoming a critical receiver. It is hoped that you are ready to arm yourself with some of the tools of analysis that make wise consumers. It is clear that we must learn to be persuaded in a world like ours, and there is a bonus for learning. In learning how you are persuaded and in exploring the various tactics that other persuaders use, you also can become a more skillful persuader yourself. Seeing what works, in what circumstances, with what kinds of people, will be useful as you prepare to become a persuader. Skillful consumers of messages learn to be more effective producers of messages. As we move ahead, it will be useful to apply the tools of persuasion on your own or through using the study questions and exercises outlined at the end of each chapter.

Questions for Further Thought

1. How would you describe the context in which persuasion occurs? (Discuss briefly in a paragraph or two.)

2. Define persuasion as it occurs for you. Compare that definition with the one offered in this chapter. What differences are there?

3. Beginning with the definition of persuasion offered here, attempt to create a model that reflects all of the important elements of the definition. (*Note:* You might begin with a model such as that offered by David K. Berlo in *The Process of Communication* and elaborate on it or make appropriate adaptations.)

4. Identify three different types of persuasion you have received recently (advertisements, speeches, persuasive appeals in discussions with others, or some other type) and analyze each of them according to the definition offered in this chapter (i.e., what are the symbols? what is the persuader's intent? what does the persuasion "say" about the persuadee's probable frame of reference?).

5. What are the tactics of *intensification*? How do they work? Give examples of them in use on television, in print, on radio, by politicians, and by advertisers.

6. What are the tactics of *downplay*? How do they work? Give examples of them in use on television, in print, on radio, by politicians, and by advertisers.

7. What is a propaganda blitz? Identify one that is presently going on in media or in regard to some political issue. Give an example of one that has been used on your campus or that is being used on campus now (for example, fraternity or sorority rush or a series of investigative news articles focused on some topic like increased student fees).

Experiences in Persuasion

1. Write to an advertiser and ask him to substantiate some of his claims (for example, ask why the product is faster, safer, or better). Compare the answers with the original claims. If your entire class does this, compare your findings with those of your classmates.

2. After having identified the claims of some ad, do an analysis of them, using Rank's Intensification/Downplay system. See if your analysis matches up with the analyses of others in your class.

3. Keep a communication logbook for one day. Count the number of hours you spend reacting to media like television and radio. How many commercials are aired in each hour of television or radio time? Compare your totals with those of others in your class.

4. Listen to politicians. Identify how they downplay and intensify in discussion of themselves and opponents.

Persuasion and Symbols 2

Whenever and however persuasion occurs, symbols are the basic carrier of the message. Imagine a television advertisement for Hamm's beer—and then try to identify some of the verbal symbols (that is, those that employ spoken or written language). First there are the song lyrics—perhaps something like "Hamm's . . . from the land of sky-blue waters; drink to the man who knows the woods; Drink Hamm's!" They call up a mental picture of a prototype—a man who wears woodsy clothes, who can frolic with an 800-pound grizzly bear, who can catch prize-winning fish, and so on. The lyrics also associate the product with a kind of free and exciting lifestyle in a beautiful setting. Superimposed on these verbal symbols might be printed verbal symbols, such as the word "Hamm's" or the slogan "From the land of sky-blue waters," which reinforce the images of preferred lifestyle and the kind of person who drinks Hamm's. In addition, the entire message (for example, the color of the clothing worn by characters and the musical score) can symbolically build and reinforce the brewer's persuasive message.

The study of persuasion from a receiver's perspective requires understanding of the power of the symbolic process in its many dimensions—verbal, nonverbal, musical, and more. We need to know why an advertiser or politician chooses certain words and disregards others. How does *what* is said affect receivers? What might the symbols indicate about the persuader's motivation and intent? The symbolic process is basically artistic as opposed to scientific. We use words, and we choose them carefully because they please us. We hope they will also please our intended audience. Our choices reveal our tastes and our intentions. As responsible receivers, we need to carefully listen to the symbols the persuader uses. We can train ourselves to have a critical ear for persuasive symbols by doing the following:

1. We need to understand the symbol-making process. Why are humans the only creatures that can generate literally millions of sentences by varying a finite supply of words?

2. We need to investigate ways to listen more efficiently and systematically—to develop tools that we can use in analyzing a persuader's style.

3. Finally we have to see how such tools can reveal a persuader's motives and goals.

PART I: THINKING ABOUT LANGUAGE AND ITS ROOTS

The word "persuasion" suggests things like "loaded language" or the emotional words that have persuaded us to vote or to purchase. Jimmy Carter's 1976 campaign slogan is a good example—"Leadership for a Change." The words "for a change" must have been fighting words for Gerald Ford's supporters, who felt that he had been providing leadership during his Administration. The words carried another meaning for those who wanted the political climate and national direction shifted. They voted for the concept of change, not for the idea of leadership. "Persuasion" also suggests eloquence, bringing to mind occasions when men of words were able to turn the day with the artistry of their writing or speechmaking. History tells of many such persuaders—Tom Paine, Jesus, Winston Churchill, Abraham Lincoln, Martin Luther King, Jr., and many more. When language is used eloquently, the persuader and the audience respond to the beauty of the word symbols. The words tend to be repeated. The famous JFK statement, "Ask not what your country can do for you; ask what you can do for your country," has been widely quoted ever since Kennedy voiced it at his inauguration.

Eloquent persuasion is unique and fresh. It strikes us as having caught the moment; it may even prophesy the future. The speech made by Martin Luther King, Jr., the night before he was killed had elements of prophecy. He said that God had allowed him "to go up to the mountain," that he had "seen the promised land," and that he doubted that he would get there with his followers. He concluded, "And I am happy tonight! I'm not fearing any man! Mine eyes have seen the glory of the coming of the Lord!" Though the words were drawn from Old Testament context and "Battle Hymn of the Republic," King's use of them was unique in the context of the movement he was leading. They seemed prophetic after his assassination.

Where did language come from? How did humans discover that they could speak and why did the process progress from simple to complex symbols? Some think that human speech is a result of the babbling stage in infancy. The baby whines and whimpers, advancing to more complex sounds. At some time the little human puts two sounds together—say "da" and "da"—and the child's father is overjoyed with "Dada." He hugs his child, thus rewarding it. Then the child combines other sounds and expands its vocabulary. The child discovers that it can talk *to* its parents and by so doing can control the environment and get others to do things. The child discovers persuasion.[1]

Others explain the development of language by tracing it to certain stages in the development of the brain and its many cells. By the time the child reaches age two, the brain is ready to learn language. The two-year-old talks almost nonstop, sometimes making mistakes, sometimes being cute, and sometimes managing to use new and varied words.

A useful view is offered by philosopher Susanne K. Langer in her book *Philosophy in a New Key*. Langer argues that of all the things that have been suggested as making humans unique among the beasts, it is not their ability to make tools (chimpanzees use "tools" on occasion) or to use a language (porpoises have quite extensive vocabularies).

Even the honeybee communicates through a "dance" signaling the location of flowers, their type and their distance. The story is told of a researcher who made an electric bee that could do the honey dance. The problem was that the bees in the hive answered the electric bee with a dance of their own—something like "Okay, we're on the way." The electric bee, however, didn't receive messages. Like so many persons, the bee just sent them. So the little machine continued the message of "lots of roses, 100 yards northwest of the hive," over and over. The real bees were angered and attacked the electric bee, finally ruining it. Communication, even in bees, is two-way and fairly complex. We could probably learn something from the bee about how to handle compulsive talkers. Many dog and cat owners are certain that their pets can "talk." Their language consists of simple signals to other animals and to their owners.

Langer says that one part of human behavior that no other creature has is the ability to *make symbols*.[2] Even the earliest cave dwellings show this impulse. Long before we had written language, we humans painted on cave walls and made charms to ward off evil or to bring luck. These early humans were busy with symbols. We cannot help making symbols.

---

1.   Roger Brown, *Words and Things* (New York: Free Press, 1958).

2.   This notion (use of symbols as uniquely characteristic of human beings) is also seen in *A Grammar of Motives* by Kenneth Burke (Berkeley: University of California Press, 1970) and *A Rhetoric of Motives* by Kenneth Burke (Berkeley: University of California Press, 1969) and several other works, such as *The Presence of the Word* by Walter S. Ong, S.J. (New Haven, Conn.: Yale University Press, 1967). Susanne Langer refers to it throughout her book, *Philosophy in a New Key* (New York: New American Library, 1951).

Just look at what we do with our symbols. We use them to control others. We use them to create works of art like poetry. We use symbols to reject, to cajole, to seduce, to comfort, and to anger others. Sociologist Hugh Duncan ties every society to its symbols. They provide the clearest image of a culture, as the title of his book suggests—*Symbols and Society*. We can produce a wide variety of symbols—music, painting, dance, advertising, speech, architecture, and politics. Langer says that the need to make symbols is akin to a biological drive—it is instinctive. Even handicapped persons create symbols—Renoir demanded that paintbrushes be taped to his arthritic hands in his old age; he *had* to paint. Mentally retarded children often spend hours painting, drawing, and humming. The process of making symbols drives us to action.

An example of the power of symbol-making was reported by Helen Keller in her autobiography. Blind and deaf from age two, Keller had been deprived of an outlet for her symbolic drives. Then Anne Sullivan, her private tutor, began to teach her sign language through the sense of touch. Keller could not speak but now could ask for simple things. The scene in which Keller discovers that a word can stand for a thing (a symbol) is the most dramatic. She describes the event:

> As the cool stream gushed over my hand she spelled into the other the word water, first slowly, then rapidly. I stood still, my whole attention fixed upon the motion of her fingers. Suddenly I felt a misty consciousness as of something forgotten—a thrill of returning thought; and somehow the mystery of language was revealed to me. I knew then that w-a-t-e-r meant the wonderful cool something that was flowing over my hand. . . . I left the well-house eager to learn. Everything had a name and each name gave birth to a new thought.[3]

We all felt the same thrill as we learned the power of word symbols as children. Anyone who has listened to a three-year-old knows that the impulse to create and use·words is continuous almost to the point of driving the parents out of their minds.

Language Use as an Art Form

I once bought a set of oil paints and a canvas in a sort of delusion that I could be an artist. The result was pitiful, and my picture was finally given away as a white elephant. I rationalized my failure away and went back to talking and teaching. Since most of us are not artists, we seek other outlets

---

3.   Helen Keller, *The Story of My Life* (New York: Doubleday, Doran & Co., 1936), pp. 23–24.

for our creative impulses. Some choose gardening; others try sewing or home decorating. All of us use our verbal language to release some of our creative needs and drives.

Even with as few as 20,000 words (pocket dictionaries usually cite more than 50,000), the number of possible combinations is almost infinite. Mathematically, the number would be found by multiplying 20,000 times 19,999, times 19,998 and so on down to times one. Language use can be considered the one art experience that almost all humans share. If you have ever been alone at a party or in a house for a short while, you know how hard it is to be isolated from words. You probably turned on the radio just to have words near you or talked to the closest klutz at the party. Most of us are so tied to the language-filled world that we cannot exist normally if we are long deprived of language. That is what makes solitary confinement such an effective punishment and one that most prisoners dread. Stories of torture techniques often include communication deprivation as one strategy to break a person's spirit.

What does all of this have to do with persuasion? As persuaders and as persuadees, we should care about our artistic impulses because our artistic symbols reveal our motives, our hang-ups, and our personalities. We usually like the sound of our own voice, and we all know how wise our own thoughts are—at least sometimes. Language makes us all egoists. The receiver of persuasive messages can learn to pay careful attention to not only what persuaders say but to the particular words they use. Consider the Jews in Nazi Germany during the 1930s. Most of them surely knew the language used by Hitler and others in references to Jews. What motives could be assigned to those who referred to Jews as "vermin," "sludge," "garbage," "lice," "sewage," "insects," and "bloodsuckers"? Those red-flag words and others foretold Hitler's "ultimate solution." The words are symbols for *things* not people. No one should be surprised that more than 6 million Jews were treated like *things*: they were ruthlessly, methodically, efficiently exterminated; their hair was woven into rug pads; their gold teeth were pried out; and finally even their bodies were rendered into soap. Alert receivers of those days should have been able to foresee what was coming; some did realize, but not many were able to escape.

Even in less dramatic and less obvious situations, persuaders reveal their motives and beliefs in their choice of words. Women's liberation advocates object to sexist language use. For instance, take the example "lady doctor." Does the term reveal sexist motives or attitudes? It is something like the term "gentleman farmer," isn't it? How seriously should we take his interest in farming? Will he be a financial success in agriculture? Probably not. So a "lady doctor" is probably not to be taken seriously. . . that is what the phrase suggests.

In another example, Oster Corporation has a "Food Crafter" instead of a "food chopper," the choice of words telling us of Oster's gourmet approach to food preparation. Or how about "What America Wants, America Gets at Goodyear—Hassle Free Service"? When you go to a Goodyear dealer, you won't get the homey treatment of Joe's service station—but you won't get all of Joe's sad stories either. Product names are sometimes revealing about their producers' attitudes toward the public. In the status-conscious 1950s and 1960s cigarettes had classy names like Viceroy, Carlton, Tareyton, Marlboro, and Benson and Hedges. If you were status-minded those were brands for you. Quite a different attitude is suggested by the names of brands more recently introduced—Fact, True, Merit, Vantage, and More.

For persuadees, knowledge of the artistic aspect of language symbols is useful. It enables us to look beyond the surface and to delve deeper into the meaning of the message and motives of the source. This knowledge is also useful for persuaders. Receivers will be more affected by artistically crafted words and phrases than by more emotionally loaded words. Of course, persuaders cannot always know for certain whether their word choices will match with those of the audience. If persuaders analyze audiences beyond mere demographics, they can discover audience word preferences. In the business world, for example, the term "self-starter" is persuasive. If a job seeker wants to persuade an employer that he or she is the best candidate for the job, using words like "self-starter" may be persuasive. When Burger King advertising says, "Have It Your Way!" it hooks into audience feelings of insecurity. The attitude toward us consumers of hamburgers is that we feel NOT OK. The promotion experts were listening to their audience. Not only can persuaders shape messages in the most artistic way possible, but also they can "listen" to the audience for cues as to what the receivers need and want to hear. How do we learn to listen in this critical way?

Some Characteristics of Language

Try to think of language within a globe with three axes running through it (see Figure 2-1). Along one axis are the *functional characteristics* of language—the jobs it can do (naming things and connecting ideas, for instance). Along the second axis are the *semantic or meaning characteristics* of language—the various meanings and shades of meaning that words can represent. Along the third axis are the *thematic characteristics* of language—the flavor or texture or feeling of various words or combinations of words (for example, the slithery smooth feeling you get from slogans like "Feel Black Velvet" or "Black Velvet Is Smooth"). With this globe, we can chart *function, meaning,* and *texture* or *theme* of any set of words. Let us begin with these three dimensions and study them in an extended example. As you train your receiver's ear, you can add other dimensions.

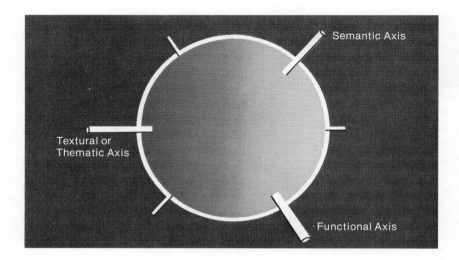

Figure 2-1 *This figure is based on a description of a model for meaning suggested by Charles E. Osgood, George J. Suci, and Percy H. Tannenbaum in* The Measurement of Meaning *(Urbana: University of Illinois Press, 1957). They suggest that semantic meaning can be located for any word or concept by charting it in "semantic space" using the Semantic Differential, a tool whereby receivers respond to a word, phrase, or concept along several polar scales. Each end of a scale represents an adjectival description (for example, "good-bad" or "heavy-light"). The globe here expands such charting to include two other attributes—function and "feel," or motif, of words. An investigator could add other axes to chart the sexuality, the aggressiveness, the dialectical, or other qualities of a particular symbol.*

Consider this line of copy from a magazine advertisement: "Sudden Tan from Coppertone tans on touch for a tan that lasts for days."[4] On the functional axis the words "Sudden Tan" name a product. Semantically, however, much more is involved. The word "sudden" indicates that the tan is almost instantaneous, and indeed this is a major advantage for the product—it dyes your skin on contact to look tanned. The headline on the ad is reinforced by the semantic meaning of the word "sudden," as is the photo over which the words are printed. The headline is "Got a minute? Get a tan." The photo shows before and after pictures of an attractive blonde who has been dyed by the product. On a textural or thematic level, the words that name the product do even more. The word "sudden" sounds or feels like the word "sun," so the product name sounds like the word "suntan." There is a repetition of the sounds "s" and "t" in the line

---

4.   *House and Garden,* June 1977, p. 31.

of copy as well. This reinforces the notion of *suntan*. Try to describe how the message would make you feel if the meanings of the words disappeared and only their sound remained.

The functional axis: what do the words do?   Words have jobs they can do. We have traditionally grouped these jobs into grammatical classes— nouns, verbs, adjectives, adverbs, prepositions, conjunctions, interjections, and so on. We have all memorized some of the definitions of these—for example, "a noun is the name of a person, place, thing, or idea." It would be impossible for us to diagram all the sentences we hear. Diagramming might show a preferred pattern of sentence structure or a tendency to use certain words or word classes more frequently than others. Such preferred patterns are normal for most speakers and really would tell us little about the source. We need a way to answer the question "What are the words doing in this message?" On this level, we are interested in the form of the message, not the content.

Persuaders want words to do one of at least three things: (1) to identify or locate an issue or topic; (2) to assign a cause or a cure for a problem associated with the issue; or (3) to motivate the audience to take action. These three functions—location, identification of cause, and motivation—are served by language or words. Look at them as you are being persuaded. Where is the persuader taking you? How is the issue located? What words assign cause? What is the motivational technique used?

The semantic axis: what do the words mean? The semantic axis tries to answer the question "What do the words mean in this message?" This second axis focuses attention on why certain words are used instead of others. Take, for example, the slogan of the Kennedy Administration— "The New Frontier." Why is the word "frontier" used? The word "vista" or "future" might have been chosen as well. Most would agree that the word suggests challenge, effort, adventure, and discovery. Those synonyms are different from the synonyms for a word like "future." Listing synonyms is a useful way to determine what words mean. Comparing the chosen word with the possible alternatives can tip us off as to a persuader's intent. We will look at several other tools of semantic analysis later.

The thematic axis: how do the words feel?   There is a third kind of question we can ask: "What unites the words used in this message?" "What underlying theme is suggested by them?" Answers to these questions depend on the textural qualities of language—the flavors or "feel" of the words used. This characteristic of language analysis relies on intuition or feeling. We probably would find only minimal agreement among observers on the "texture" of language, but that is not crucial. The problem facing persuadees in our information age is not how to make the *best* choice, but how to make a choice at all. What is important is that we become aware of the various qualities of persuasion that tempt and sway us. Persuadees should be attuned to the tone or texture of the language used by persuaders.

Richard Weaver, in *The Ethics of Rhetoric*, notes that style is a process of accumulation. We really discover a persuader's style only after listening to it over time. A single word, sentence, or paragraph is not enough to give us the full story. Winston Churchill was one of the best known persuaders of the first half of the twentieth century. One of the thematic qualities of Churchill's persuasion was to cast light-dark images,[5] or pictures related to day and night. The Nazis were always pictured as thugs or "gangsters" engaging in monstrous acts in dark places; on the other hand, the English were bright, sturdy, and capable of overcoming this "darkness" with the "light of their resolve." His light-dark metaphors were a trademark.

There are other metaphors that have meanings transcending time and even cultures. Blood metaphors suggest sacrifice, heroism, and purity. They have been used in these ways by such different groups as the Vikings, historic and modern Christianity, and Nazism. Water metaphors often have meanings connected with fertility, life, or purification. As we consider messages of persuaders across the ages, the trends of their word choices indicate some universal patterns.

During his political career, Richard Nixon frequently used the words "let me make myself perfectly clear"—often, it seemed, when he intended to be anything but clear. His favorite pronouns were "I" and "me," a preference indicating a person concerned with self. It seems less than surprising that he was willing to do almost anything to save himself in the Watergate scandal. He blamed his aides, his long-time personal secretary, the Congress, the media, even a sinister force for his downfall, but never himself.

Consider the semantic, functional, and thematic or textural qualities of some words in the following portion of a speech delivered by Jimmy Carter during the 1976 primary campaigns when he was trying to capture the Democratic nomination.

> *I have been accused of being an outsider. I plead guilty. Unfortunately, the vast majority of Americans are outsiders. We are not going to get changes by simply shifting around the same group of insiders, the same old tired rhetoric, the same unkept promises, and the same*

---

5.   For a more detailed discussion and case study of the use of light-dark images, see Michael Osborn's "Archetypal Metaphor in Rhetoric: The Light-Dark Family," *Quarterly Journal of Speech*, Vol. 53 (April 1967), pp. 115–126.

divisive appeals to one party, one faction, one section of the country,
one race or religion or interest group. The insiders have had their
chances, and they have not delivered. Their time has run out.[6]

Some of the words have done a semantic reversal. It is usually bad to
be an outsider—generally, we don't like to be considered outsiders. As
Carter used the word, he set a different frame of reference. It became good
to be an outsider; in fact, most of us became outsiders. The same thing
occurs with the word "insider," which usually refers to someone in the
know who has savvy. In the Carter context, the word implied "political
hack." Functionally, the words create identification between Carter and
his audience in the case of "outsiders"; they debunk with the word "insider." Another word tied to insiders is the word "same." Notice how
many times it is used in just a few lines. Through repetition, Carter re-
called the feeling we get with a line like "The same old thing, day in and
day out." This feeling colors our whole image of those insiders—they are
boring, plastic, and disgusting.

These examples should have alerted you to one of the abilities you
already have, an ability based on your years as a language user. Because
you sometimes use words artistically, you can identify artistic uses of
words. Your judgment may differ from mine, but you can profit from
merely listening more critically. However, we all need to be able to
analyze a persuader's style systematically. The goal of Part II of Chapter 2
is to provide you with some sample tools that you can use as you consider
the various persuasive appeals that bombard you daily. They are not the
only ways to analyze persuasive style, but they should get you started;
you can add to your defensive arsenal as you go. As responsible receivers,
we should be continually arming ourselves with tools that can identify a
persuader's motives and goals.

PART II: TOOLS FOR ANALYSIS OF LANGUAGE

Consider the language used in each of the following presidential campaign slogans or catch phrases:

1960: The New Frontier (John F. Kennedy)

1964: A Great Society (Lyndon B. Johnson)

---

6.   "Jimmy Carter: Not Just Peanuts," *Time*, March 8, 1976, p. 16.

1968: Bring Us Together *and* Nixon's the One (Richard M. Nixon)

1972: Re-Elect the President (Richard M. Nixon)

1976: I'm Feeling Good about America (Gerald Ford)

How would you go about interpreting each of these slogans, considering what they seem to mean? Would you look at who was the ghostwriter for them? Would you look at the situations that gave rise to them? Or would you look at all of these? The problem is to choose a method of analysis that allows you to proceed objectively. Many methods can be used to psych out the style of a persuader. You should experiment with several of these methods and then work out your own. Your goal is to take apart the persuasion directed at you and to look behind the words for some indication of what the persuader is like, how messages affect you, and why you should be alert and interested in what is said.

Return to the presidential slogans. Offhand, what can we say about any of them? Well, we can first describe their structure and form—the functional axis. Kennedy used a three-word descriptive phrase: a definite article (the word "the"), an adjective (the word "new"), and a noun (the word "frontier"). Johnson also has a three-word descriptive phrase with an article, adjective, and noun. It differs from the Kennedy slogan in that its article is indefinite (the word "a" depicts one of several, whereas the word "the" refers to the only one). One 1968 Nixon slogan has self-centered qualities similar to those mentioned earlier—"Nixon's the One." The other 1968 Nixon phrase is not descriptive—it is an imperative (it gives an order for action, not a description of a situation). It begins with a verb, "bring," followed by a pronoun, "us," and ends with an adverb, "together." This pattern was again followed by Nixon in 1972. Again the word order is imperative—"Re-elect the President." This imperative too shows a concern with the self. This time there is no collective pronoun, and the order has shifted direction. In 1968, it was an order from the people to the candidate. By 1972, the order is from the candidate to the people. The 1972 slogan provides a tip-off as to the persuader's attitude and motivation: He *is* the President and the people are beneath him, subject to his commands. The Ford slogan is the longest. It describes a personal feeling. The winning slogan for that year was "Leadership—for a Change," which we have already discussed.

Now that the structure of these slogans is clear, so what? There is little we can say with certainty, but even this simple action of describing the structure of the slogans has alerted us to some of their differences. Perhaps the framer of the phrase "*The* New Frontier" was more definite than the framer of "*A* Great Society." Perhaps the Nixon imperatives indicate that he is authoritarian. The Ford slogan may indicate that he tends to be wordy and that he deals with situations on a highly personal level. In fact, that was the judgment of many persons who analyzed the

1976 campaign—Ford was often too homey and too personal and not "presidential" often enough. Of course, all these judgments (whatever their validity) are made after the fact, and it is easier to see implications now than it was for the voters at the time. Even so, such judgments are better than the passive buying of the slogans. Looking at the make-up of the slogans activates our receiver antennae and forces us to ask the question "What if . . .?" about the framer of each slogan.

We can do more than look at word order and grammar. On the semantic dimension, we can speculate about the meanings of some of the words. For example, take the adjectives in the Kennedy and Johnson word strings. What does "new" suggest? What kind of word is it? Could other words have been used? Which ones? Initially, I would say that the word "new" suggests innovation, progress, and an orientation to the future. There are not many words that could have been substituted for it without a loss of the flavor. "The Innovative Frontier" would not have worked well. The slogan also has links with "The New Deal" of Franklin D. Roosevelt and "The New Freedom" of Woodrow Wilson; in addition to its thrust toward the future, it has historical roots. It is an exciting word when we look at it in this context.

What about the word "great" in Johnson's slogan? It seems oriented more to the present than to the future; it describes a state of affairs at hand. It, too, could not easily be replaced. "Grand" might have been used, or "proud," with less lost than a Kennedy replacement for "new," but neither of these two words works well. Then, the word has an egotistical smack to it. It sounds like bragging.

What about the nouns in the slogans? Kennedy's "frontier" could be replaced with "vista" or "horizon" with little loss of meaning or texture. It is also future oriented and dramatic—we think of the challenges of the old frontier, the tests of ability, the discoveries, and the heroes. Johnson's word "society" seems less exciting and less flexible. He might have used "country" or "culture" or some other word, but again it would not have worked well. The word is not exciting and does not stir the imagination as the word "frontier" does. Neither does it call attention to the future. (You can see a frontier and can imagine it, but a society seems less concrete.) Let us draw these word characteristics together:

Kennedy: Definite, future oriented, flexible noun, inflexible adjective, rooted in the past, dramatic

Johnson: Indefinite, somewhat inflexible in both adjective and noun, present or status quo oriented, static, perhaps egotistical

Take the gist of the 1972 Nixon slogan, "Re-elect the President." It suggests that there is no longer a candidate who is to be elected—or defeated; instead there is an office to be verified. The candidate has become the office, somewhat as Hitler came to be known as Der Führer (The Leader), and has ceased to have an individual personality. This tendency to personalize his presidency typified Nixon the officeholder;[7] it is also clearly indicated in the symbolism of the 1972 campaign slogan.

Symbolic Expression

What we have been doing with presidential slogans is admittedly amateur psychoanalysis. However, given the power of persuasion in our times (remember that the average eighteen-year-old has watched about 20,000 hours of television programming and more than 350,000 TV spot commercials), it is better to be overly skeptical about the persuasion we encounter than to painfully discover its implications too late. Given the power of symbols to motivate peoples and cultures, it is wise to look for the motives that the symbols carry.

We know, for example, that the kinds of symbols that a person uses and responds to can affect his health. Persons who use words like "I can't stomach it" or "I'm fed up" or "It's been eating away at me now for a year" have more stomach ulcers than other persons. The symbols (stomach words) become reality (ulcers) for these persons.[8] Symbolic days like birthdays can also have dramatic effects. In nursing homes, more persons die during the two months *after* their birthdays than do during the two months *before*. Thomas Jefferson and John Adams both died in 1826, precisely on the Fourth of July,[9] a date of tremendous significance for both of them. Jefferson is even reported to have awakened from a deathlike coma on July 3 to ask his doctor if it was the Fourth yet. The human body responds in highly symbolic ways to events like death. Some widows begin the menstrual cycle again after the death of their spouses. Some persons die soon after the death of a loved one—and from the same disease. In other words, symbolic sympathy pains can be real. In the mid-1970s, Dr. Arnold Mandel, a psychiatrist, reported on an in-depth study of a pro-football team. Hired to try to find out why the team was losing, he found instead that the various players symbolically acted out their on-the-field roles while they were off the field. Wide receivers were narcissistic and always groomed themselves carefully, while defensive linemen and linebackers—the destroy boys—had the most run-ins with the law for barroom brawling and unpaid parking tickets. Quarterbacks saw them-

---

7.   Dan F. Hahn and Ruth M. Gonchar, "The Rhetorical Predictability of Richard M. Nixon," *Today's Speech*, Vol. 19 (Fall 1971), pp. 3–14.

8.   "Fed Up? It May Lead to an Ulcer," *Chicago Daily News*, November 24, 1972, p. 30. For a more detailed discussion, see Howard Lewis and Martha Lewis, *Psychosomatics: How Your Emotions Can Damage Your Health* (New York: Viking Press, 1972).

9.   Peter Koenig, "Death Doth Defer," *Psychology Today*, November 1972, p. 83.

selves as saviors of the team on the field and were most likely to hold strong religious beliefs.[10]

Not only do symbols have great impact on individuals, but also they serve as a kind of psychological cement for holding a society or culture together. The central symbol for the Oglala Sioux Indians was a sacred hoop representing the four seasons of the earth and the four directions from which weather might come. In the center of the hoop were crossed thongs that symbolized the sacred tree of life and the crossroads of life. Shortly after the hoop was broken during the massacre of the battle of Wounded Knee in 1890, the tribe disintegrated. An Oglala wise man named Black Elk explained the symbolic power of the circle for his tribe:

> You have noticed that everything an Indian does is in a circle, and that is because the Power of the World always works in circles, and everything tries to be round. In the old days when we were a strong and happy people, all our power came to us from the sacred hoop of the nation and so long as the hoop was unbroken the people flourished . . . . Everything the Power of the World does is done in a circle. The Sky is round and I have heard that the earth is round like a ball and so are all the stars. The Wind, in its greatest power, whirls. Birds make their nests in circles, for theirs is the same religion as ours. The sun comes forth and goes down again in a circle. The moon does the same, and both are round.
>
> Even the seasons form a great circle in their changing and always come back again to where they were. The life of a man is a circle from childhood to childhood and so it is in everything where power moves. Our tipis were round like the nests of birds and these were always set in a circle, the nation's hoop, a nest of many nests where the Great Spirit meant for us to hatch our children.[11]

Black Elk felt that the Sioux had lost all of their power or medicine when the whites forced the Indians out of their traditional round teepees and into the square houses on the reservation.

What are the central symbols of our society and how are they used by persuaders who are marketing their products or ideas to us? Certainly success in its many symbolic forms is the basis of appeals like the name of Sears' inexpensive mattress—it is called the "Sears-O-Pedic Imperial."[12]

---

10.   This study has been reported in several places: CBS's *60 Minutes*, January 5, 1975, which featured an interview with Dr. Arnold Mandel; "Psychiatric Study of Pro-Football," *Saturday Review/World*, October 5, 1974, pp. 12–16; and "A Psychiatrist Looks at Pro-Football," *Reader's Digest*, January 1975, pp. 89–92.

11.   Black Elk, *Touch the Earth*, edited by T. C. McLuhan (New York: Outerbridge and Dienstfrey, 1971), p. 42.

12.   *House and Garden*, June 1977, p. 43.

Another message that is sent to the members of our culture in a number of ways is that we are extraordinary in the world; so we hear that the United States is a superpower and we invented Superman and Sears offers a "super big, super thick, super thirsty, super soft, super plush towel" and at "super sales prices."[13] The importance of the law is noteworthy in American culture. The symbols that we print on our money refer to our legal system and laws; the courthouse or city hall is the symbolic center of many towns and cities; and in reaction to many perceived problems Americans tend to say, "There ought to be a law about this."

The power of symbols is enormous; they not only can reveal motive but also can affect our health, our self-image, and our national character.[14] Let us turn now to consideration of some of the tools that are available to persuadees for analysis of the functional, semantic, and thematic axes of language. Remember that these tools can overlap from axis to axis. In developing listening skills, the important thing is to apply them when and where you can.

Tools for the Functional Axis

We shall consider three functional tools: (1) the "rhetorical aspects of grammatical categories" suggested by philosopher Richard Weaver, (2) the ways in which word arrangement or syntax affects persuasion, and (3) how ambiguity helps in persuasion.

Grammatical categories   Weaver said that the grammatical form used by persuaders may indicate their intentions. He argues that sentence structure, for example, may reflect a person's method of using information and of coming to conclusions. The person who uses simple sentences does not see a complex world. As Weaver puts it, he "sees the world as a conglomerate of things . . . [and] seeks to present certain things as eminent against a background of matter uniform or flat."[15] The simple sentence sets the subject off from the verb and object; it sees *causes* that *act* to

---

13.   *Ibid.*, p. 33.

14.   Those who wish to explore the relation between symbols and human expression should consult Hugh D. Duncan, *Communication and Social Order* (London: Oxford University Press, 1963); Kenneth Burke, *A Grammar of Motives* (Berkeley: University of California Press, 1970); or Mircea Eliade, *The Myth of the Eternal Return: or Cosmos and History* (Princeton, N.J.: Princeton University Press, 1971).

15.   Richard M. Weaver, *The Ethics of Rhetoric* (Chicago: Henry Regnery Co., 1953), p. 120. For a discussion of the Platonic idealism and political conservatism underlying Weaver's conception of rhetoric, see Richard L. Johannesen, Rennard Strickland, and Ralph T. Eubanks, "Richard M. Weaver," in Johannesen, ed., *Contemporary Theories of Rhetoric* (New York: Harper & Row, 1971), pp. 180–195.

have *effects* upon objects. When a persuader uses this form, the persuadee ought to look at what is being highlighted, at what affects what, and at how action occurs.

The complex sentence features a more complex world—several causes and several effects at the same time. Weaver says that it "is the utterance of a reflective mind,"[16] which tries "to express some sort of hierarchy."[17] Persuaders who use this kind of sentence express basic principles and relationships, with the independent clauses more important than the dependent clauses. For example, consider the following paragraphs from an advertisement run by the Mobil Oil Company in its campaign to get the public to force Congress to grant more offshore oil leases to the major producers:

> *Economic obstacles: It defies all logic to raise the price of already-discovered oil through taxes, while denying the oil companies a share of the resulting revenues. The producers will be forced to sell oil from existing wells at far below its replacement cost. Ignored is the fact the today's petroleum exploration and development is growing ever more costly because of the need to explore in remote frontier areas like Alaska or in deep water offshore, and to resort to expensive recovery methods to squeeze more oil from reservoirs. How long could any businessman stay in business if he must sell his inventory at prices substantially lower than he will have to pay to restock?*
>
> *What America has, in short, is a "Catch 22" policy toward developing its oil and gas resources. The President indicates we need to develop more domestic energy. The U.S. Geological Survey says the oil and gas is probably there. The oil companies want to look for it. But the government not only is making it harder and harder to explore the most promising offshore locations but insists on keeping price controls which deny the industry the needed capital. And then along come those who tell us the oil companies can't do the job of increasing domestic supply. How's that for a self-fulfilling prophecy?*
>
> *We urge that the national energy debate focus on the paramount issue: development vs. non-development of U.S. energy supplies. We believe that the social and economic consequences of development are being grossly overestimated by many in Washington and that, as subsequent messages in this series will point out, the social and economic consequences of non-development are being grossly underestimated.*[18]

---

16.   Weaver, p. 121.
17.   *Ibid.*
18.   *1977 Mobil Current Energy Series #3* (New York: Mobil Oil Corporation, 1977) reprinted in *The Chicago Tribune*, July 28, 1977, Section 1, p. 8.

Examine each complex sentence. Look at the first sentence. The clause stating the principle is independent—it can stand alone. The dependent clause (". . .while denying. . .") states the minor message elements. The independent material is higher on the source's ladder of values than the dependent material. It is probably more important to Mobil corporate management that people realize the undesirability of imposing taxes to raise prices on oil already discovered than that profits be questioned. Most people realize that Mobil has a vested interest in getting a share of profits from high-priced oil. Identify some of the other complex sentences in the excerpt and see if Weaver's prediction doesn't hold true. The major premise being sold in a complex sentence is usually the one stated in the independent clause; the minor premise is usually stated in the dependent clause.

Remember what Weaver said about the use of the simple sentence to depict "the world as a conglomerate" in which certain facts were to be highlighted against a rather flat background? Note what Mobil does in the second paragraph. With one exception, all the sentences of that paragraph are simple. The tactic is to rattle off a series of assertions as if they were absolute truths. This rat-tat-tat style is convincing.

Weaver says that the compound sentence sets things either in balance (for example, "He ran, and he ran fast") or in opposition (for example, "He ran, and she walked"). It expresses some kind of tension—whether resolved or unresolved. Weaver says it "conveys that completeness and symmetry which the world *ought* to have, and which we manage to get, in some measure, into our most satisfactory explanations of it."[19] Persuaders who use this sentence type see the world divided into polar opposites or similarities—totally against one another or in concert with one another. The union leader, for example, says, "You are either against us, or you are with us!" and thus oversimplifies a complex world by using the compound sentence.

Weaver also had some observations about types of words. For example, nouns, since they are thought of as words for things and as labels for naming, are often reacted to *as if they were the things they name*. They "express things whose being is completed, not whose being is in process, or whose being depends upon some other being."[20] Thus when someone calls a policeman a pig he makes the policeman into an object—a thing. It is easy to spit on a pig. The pig is an object; the policeman is a person with a family and feelings. One of the functions of a noun is to label something as we want it to be. Looking at persuaders' nouns may clue us as to their perception of things. They may reveal what the persuader intends to do

---

19.   Weaver, p. 127.
20.   Weaver, p. 128.

about those things. When persuaders reduce persons to things or objects, they do it for a reason. They indicate that the persuader wishes to deal with them as things and not as people.

The function of an adjective is to add to the noun, to make it special. To Weaver, adjectives are second-class citizens. He called them "question-begging" and said that they showed an uncertain persuader.[21] If you have to modify a noun, Weaver would say you are not certain about the noun. In Weaver's opinion, the only adjectives that are not uncertain are *dialectical* ("good" and "bad," "hot" and "cold," "light" and "dark"). Examination of adjectives used by persuaders may reveal what they are uncertain about, what they want to be sure about, and what they see in opposition to what.

The adverb, to Weaver, is "a word of judgment."[22] Unlike the adjective, it represents a community judgment—one with which others can agree and which reflects what the persuader thinks the audience believes. For example, adverbs like "surely," "certainly," or "probably" suggest agreement. When persuaders say, "Surely we all know and believe that thus-and-such is so," they suggest that the audience agrees with them.

By looking at sentence type and word choice we can get a handle on a persuader's motives and beliefs.

Syntax as an analytical tool　Another functional characteristic of language is revealed in the way words are ordered in a sentence. The persuadee can take note of persuaders' syntax and be alert to the way in which they order their thoughts.

For example, suppose a persuader said, "There is no greater hypocrite than the dedicated environmentalist who preaches clean air and drives home in a 350-horsepower gas guzzler!" The word order of the sentence alerts us to the theme: hypocrisy. However, we are left wondering until the last phrase why hypocrisy is involved; then the large car is revealed. The persuader could as easily have said, "Environmentalists who own 350-horsepower gas guzzlers while they preach clean air are the kind of hypocrites we don't need to have around!" The second version lacks the drama of the first. It does not get the listener involved with the task of trying to discover the cause of the hypocrisy. It has a preachy quality about it—as if the persuader knows he is right. It may reveal a certain closed-mindedness or dogmatism about the persuader.

Consider the following sentence from an editorial by Robert Shrum of *New Times* magazine. Shrum was lamenting the swing to conservatism that seemed to be occurring in the late 1970s. "The House has approved

---

21.　Weaver, pp. 129–130.
22.　Weaver, p. 133.

the neutron bomb, the ultimate weapon of a dehumanized capitalism; it will kill people but leave the real property standing."[23] Word order here also signifies something about its author. His first clause stands as an indictment of the House of Representatives. His second phrase elaborates upon the indictment, expanding on it in highly accusatory terms. His last clause explains his indictment. It gives us his reasoning for making the judgment. The order of the argument reveals a deductive thinker waiting until the conclusion to offer his specific pieces of evidence. He tends to move from the general to the specific. That persuasive syntax is quite different from the following copy from an advertisement for a Rita Coolidge album: "Her clear voice, perfect pitch, and instinctive emotional delivery takes the greats and makes them greater. Because Rita was born to sing."[24] The persuader could have reversed the order here, beginning with the general conclusion that Rita was "born to sing" and then giving us the reasons with something like "and you will know it when you hear her clear voice, her . . ." but this style is inductive and assumes that the reader wants to think the same way.

A number of questions can be asked about a persuasive message if the receiver takes a few minutes to examine the syntax of the proposition. Why didn't the persuader do it differently? Does the word order suggest anything about a view of the world? of the audience? Does it indicate a certainty about judgments? Is the audience lured into the sentence? Does the source let receivers do a search for meaning and relationships? These questions and others can tell us how the message is working—that is, what its functions are.

Ambiguity as a functional device of style   Another element in style is the degree to which the words are specific or ambiguous. At first thought, the most effective persuasion ought to be that which is simplest. Yet if you think about it a little longer, and especially if you think about the fact that no two people will ever see the world in exactly the same way, the simple might not be best. Let us suppose that I were trying to persuade you to buy a certain kind of automobile. If I told you the reason why I thought you should buy the car, I might antagonize you. I would never be able to really touch the key strings of motivation that might cause you to actually make the purchase. For example, suppose I said that the car was dependable and sturdy in construction. If the key motivation for you is sex appeal— how the car symbolizes potent sexuality, for example—I would lose the sale. Dependability and sturdiness seem more tied to vehicles like tractors, Jeeps, or family station wagons than to sexy sports models or hatchbacks. A better strategy for me would be to be less specific. The strategy

23.   Robert Shrum, "Party Lines," *New Times*, July 22, 1977, p. 4.

24.   *New Times*, July 7, 1977, p. 57.

THE BORN LOSER   **by Art Sansom**

Figure 2-2 *The Born Loser. Ambiguity arises when a word like "term" can have several meanings. (Reprinted by permission of NEA.)*

should let you sell yourself on the sexy body style, color, or interior design. In other words, by being ambiguous I allow you to enter into the persuasive process. I let you define the terms (and a good salesperson carefully listens to customers and reinforces their statements). Furthermore, the same strategy will work with diverse sets of people if the message is ambiguous enough. Most politicians are judged by media reporters as being fuzzy on the issues at one time or another. Perhaps they are just being ambiguous in hopes of persuading as many of their constituents as possible and alienating as few as possible. Although this may not result in the most intelligent votes or in the best person being elected, it probably does result in more winning and less losing for the skillful politician—which gives us another reason for being responsible persuadees.

Tools for the Semantic Axis

There are several ways in which persuaders can create persuasive ambiguity. One way is *semantically*. Here the persuader carefully chooses words that can be interpreted in many ways, often in contradictory ways, depending on the receivers. For example, a politician favors "responsibility in taxation and the education of our youngsters." Those who think teachers have been underpaid and need substantial raises could hear this as a call for *spending* tax dollars. Those of a reverse view could as easily interpret the statement as saying that educational spending needs to be *cut*. There are other possible interpretations. The key word that increases the ambiguity is "responsibility." It sets up the rest of the sentence.

The term "black power," which emerged in the late 1960s as part of the Civil Rights Movement relied on semantic ambiguity. The key word there was "power"—what kind of power? Economic? Political? Social? There could be many interpretations. The term was striking in its time, in the use of the word "black," a term that the National Association for the Advancement of Colored People (NAACP) had been fighting for years.

The group hated "black" almost as much as the more derogatory "nigger." Given that context, use of the term by the black militants rejected the leadership of existing groups. The term is unsettling and thus attracts attention.

Another way that persuaders can create ambiguity is structural. That is, by altering such things as syntax or sentence/phrase/clause structure, meaning is affected. Take the term "moral decay," which has frequently been used to describe developments in our society tending away from strict morals. The term refers to the decay of morals, but by putting the word "moral" as the first word in the pair, meaning grows. We respond to "moral decay" in the same way we respond to "tooth decay." We recall the ads showing microscopic views of bacteria squirming around on teeth, the social rejection when we forget to brush, and so forth. The term also gains meaning because a positively loaded word—"moral"—is paired with a negatively loaded word—"decay." This plus/minus conflict is tension-producing and thus involves the persuadee emotionally. The words "child pornography" operate in a similar way. The plus of the first word strikes the minus of the second word and creates tension, meaning, and ambiguity. Is it pornography involving children or aimed at children or what?

The number of syllables in the words in a phrase can create a kind of rhythm that also affects our responses to the term. For example, they could have named Virginia Slims the Sue Thins or the Betty Slims, but the 4:1 syllable ratio of the words gives a kind of image to the product name that the 1:1 or 2:1 options do not. Furthermore, the state of Virginia is a prime growing place for tobacco. Rebecca Slims would have come closer. Hildegarde Slims would have flopped—structural and semantic dimensions interact with one another.

In addition to these dimensions of the semantic axis, other approaches are being suggested. General semanticists aim at developing a tool to increase semantic meaning by asking people to add more descriptive qualities to their language. For example, the semanticists recommend that instead of saying "car" you ought to say "station wagon" or better yet "blue Ford station wagon" or even better "1977 blue Ford Country Squire station wagon with a dent in the left front fender." Thus, the semanticists argue, you can sanitize language by reducing ambiguity. This tactic may not have persuasive impact though, if ambiguity persuades. Kenneth Burke in his book *A Grammar of Motives* suggests a better tool. The title of his book gives a clue to his purpose. He wants to present a set of terms or a grammar for identifying motives. Burke should be helpful to us. He calls his device the dramatic pentad.[25]

---

25.   Burke, *Grammar* (cited in Footnote 2). See the introduction especially.

The Dramatic Pentad

The basic premise put forth by Burke is that human beings see the world in terms of drama. Each person focuses on one of these terms as most important or as most essential to him or her. This focus is seen in how each of us talks about the world. We can infer the world view of persuaders from the focus they take. There are five elements of drama we need to consider. Burke says that the five are comprehensive and include all the possible parts of dramatic action. You may add other terms, but to start there are these five:

Memory

Scene—or place where action occurs (perhaps the persuasive situation). (Persons who focus on the scene are _materialists_.) They believe that changing the scene or environment will change people. They would support urban renewal, for example.

Act—or the action that occurs. Persons who focus on the act are _realists_. They process and record information and believe that a mixture of causes directs human affairs.

Agent—or the actor who acts out the action or plot. Persons who focus on the agent are _idealists_. They believe that people control their own destiny. Persuaders who focus on the agent would support self-help programs.

Agency—or the tool the actor uses to accomplish his ends. Persons who focus on the agency are _pragmatists_. They search for the most speedy and most practical solutions. They might support gas rationing, for example.

Purpose—or the reason why a person does what he does. Persons who focus on purpose are _mystics_. They believe a power or focus beyond them directs human destiny.

Consider the following description of a dramatic situation:

> _A young man and a young woman are standing in front of an altar rail in a church. They are dressed for the sacrament of marriage (he in tuxedo, she in a white dress). A young and handsome minister is preparing to conduct the "Repeat after me . . ." portion of the service, when he suddenly turns from the altar rail, walks swiftly back to the altar itself, takes down a massive brass candlestick, and bludgeons the bride to death as the groom smiles._

Which element of this drama is most intriguing to you? The tension between the act of murder and the setting of a church? The character of the young minister? The use of a holy object to kill? The reason why the groom does nothing to stop the murder and even smiles about it? Burke would argue that your interest in one particular element over others may reflect how you see the world operating—what you think prompts action and gives meaning. Further, Burke would predict that you would choose to talk about the world according to what struck you as most important; your words would reflect your preference. If you thought that men control their own destiny, you would focus on the agent. If you felt that circumstances compelled action, you would focus on the scene. If you felt that high principles and ideals carried even weak men through trying times, you focus on the purpose.

Persuaders tend to center their topic around one of the terms of the pentad. They choose their evidence in relation to this term, and they devise metaphors drawn from it. Persuadees can use this tendency to predict what persuaders are likely to say and do. Further, knowing people's *key terms* helps us analyze their weak spots if we want to persuade them. Of course, persuaders may draw on the other four terms, but they emphasize one or another of the five terms—that is Burke's proposition. Thus, if you are interested in the agent you react differently from someone whose focus is on the act, and you will each choose different language to discuss the same problem.

Consider the following:

> *Over the past few years the image of politics that has taken shape for me is that of an immense journey—the panorama of an endless wagon train, an enormous trek, a multitudinous procession of people larger and more confused than any of the primitive folk migrations.*
>
> *There—ahead—lies the crest of the ridge, and beyond it perhaps the plateau or the sunlit valley—or danger. The procession stretches out for endless miles, making its way up the tangled slopes through strange new country. . . .*
>
> *Up there, at the head of the advance column, the leaders quarrel bitterly among themselves, as do the people behind. From their heights they have a wider view of the horizon . . .*[26]

The scenic quality of the quotation is clear. The author has a vision of a setting and a background. What is important is the panorama—the view from the ridge—the scene. The author sees the setting as powerful, drawing people and leaders on, forcing them onward, even in ignorance of what lies ahead.

Another person might view things quite differently:

> *Some wobbly thinkers think that laws will stop you from hating, laws will make you generous. But when I read about street crimes,*

---

26.   Theodore H. White, *The Making of the President: 1964* (New York: Atheneum, 1966), p. v.

about hatred with blood, I ask what's happening to the land of the free; what's happened to the principles these men died for . . .?

. . . and the fault is not only in government, but in us. Ask yourself before going to bed tonight: Did I live today with hate? Did I steal, cheat, hate, take shortcuts? If you answer "yes," you haven't been a good American. . . .

I deplore those far-out partisans of principles that are trying to tear the American people apart, trying to tear the home apart, trying to assume they can do such things . . . .[27]

This persuader sees the agent as most important. Consider the number of personal pronouns used (for example, "us," "I," "we," and "you"). Problems are caused by agents—"wobbly thinkers" or "partisans of principle." This persuader sees people acting to do wrong by cheating, hating, and stealing. There is a focus on principle as well. Some important principles are lost or overlooked while there are clever "partisans of principle" who substitute other principles that are ruining the country and its people. Thus there is a focus on the agent and on the purpose. This person will probably seek solutions in different ways from the scene-oriented persuader. The agent-oriented persuader might try to bring individual action to bear on problems. The scene-oriented persuader would try to change environments in response to problems. The purpose-oriented persuader may preach repentance.

The same sort of analysis can be done with the act and the agency as key terms. A persuader who was convinced that means were more important than ends might be an agency-oriented persuader. Phone company persuasion often focuses on the means (long distance) over scenes (home), for example. They advertise that "Long Distance Is the Next Best Thing to Being There" or that "Home Is Wherever There Is a Telephone."[28] An act-oriented persuader would probably describe an action that has taken place and then imply that another action can remedy or improve the situation. Take, for instance, this ad copy: "Overdone by the sun? When the sun burns you up and makes you sizzle, when you're overdone by the sun, stop sunburn pain fast with Solarcaine . . ."[29]

The dramatic pentad of Kenneth Burke can be used in these ways—to discover the persuasive focus and hence the underlying beliefs or key elements of an advocate and also to discover and to label a persuader's characteristic symbols and rituals. By looking at what persuaders say and at how they use language (what kinds of words they use frequently), their

---

27.   Shrum, p. 4.

28.   *House and Garden*, June 1977, p. 81.

29.   *Ibid.*, p. 78.

underlying symbols and preferences become clear. Those preferences usually tell us something about the persuaders' motives and their interpretations of the motivation of others. Receivers need to isolate the persuaders' key terms, determine if they agree with the persuaders' analysis or if the key term is reasonable and attractive, and then decide whether or not to be persuaded by what is said or implied.

Tools for the Thematic Axis

The thematic axis of language refers to a quality that is not really functional (syntactic) or semantic. It is not concerned with word order or the referent for particular words. Rather, it refers to the "texture" of the language. A classic example is shown when we try to rewrite Lincoln's Gettysburg Address—"Eighty-seven years ago the signers of the Declaration of Independence started a new country designed to have liberty and equality for everyone. . . ." We find a semantic correspondence between this set of words and Lincoln's version, but there are obvious thematic differences.

Sometimes thematic differences come from a repeated sound. (Burke argues, for example, that his childhood prayer: "God love me/Guard me in sleep/Guide me to Thee" relies on a G—d or "God" form.) Sound repetition is one of the textural qualities of language. Onomatopoeia (or phonetic sounds that resemble their referents—for example, "swish" or "rustle") is another example. We will now look at three thematic or textural tools in some detail: (1) the use of motifs and metaphors, (2) the development of God and Devil terms, and (3) the pragmatic versus the unifying style. Beyond these, there are other tools you may want to explore.

Motifs and metaphors   Persuaders can establish a great deal of their message by setting the mood for the persuadees. They can depict a setting appropriate for the message by repeatedly using certain sounds and certain images. In a study on the use of archetypal metaphors (or universal and primal images consistent within and even across cultures), in particular the light-dark comparison, Michael Osborn maintains that, traditionally, we identify light with the sun, warmth, growth, comfort, and so on; while we see dark associated with mystery, night, cold, and other uncomfortable and troubling things. Osborn points out that persuaders often use repeated reference to this dichotomy.[30] John F. Kennedy, in his Inaugural Address, used this archetypal metaphor when he talked about passing a torch from one generation to another and predicting that the light from

---

30.   Michael Osborn, "Archetypal Metaphor in Rhetoric: The Light-Dark Family," *Quarterly Journal of Speech*, Vol. 53 (April 1967), pp. 115–126.

this symbolic torch could illuminate the world for freedom—the light was viewed as good, warm, friendly, and virtuous. Elsewhere the world was filled with darkness and poverty.

There are other archetypal metaphors. For example, the power of the sea and the life-giving power of water may explain the holy or magical powers that are given to water (for example, the fountain of youth or baptism). Mircea Eliade is convinced that there is an archetypal metaphor of "the center." We repeatedly look for a central point—a symbolic navel for our world. For some groups it is a specific place (Mecca for Moslems, Munich for Nazism, Jerusalem for Jews and Christians).[31] For some students, a certain place on campus may be the symbolic center—their dorm room, the student center, or a fraternity house. On some campuses there is a "free-speech area," often a focal point for protest speechmaking or other gatherings. The White House is a sacred center for many Americans.

Associated with these motifs or repeated references to images that set the stage for persuasion, we also seem to be strongly drawn to myths or dramatic metaphors. A good example is the American fascination with the concept of savior. Persuaders often use this image of the savior or man of power. Take, for example, TV commercials featuring The Man from Glad, who swoops down out of the sky to save the day by bringing a package of Glad Bags to the lady in distress. The thought of it is stupid; yet people have been persuaded by this image. The savior comes in various versions: Mrs. Olson must have saved hundreds of young couples from the divorce courts by whipping out her ever-present can of Folger's. Kojak saved the world week after week, using ingenuity and in the nick of time. In other situations, a wizard or a genie arrives on the scene to save the day (for example, the Mr. Clean figure).

There are other archetypal metaphors that set the stage for persuasion and can be used as persuasive premises. Some mythic patterns seem to recur: the search or the hunt, the ritual of passage or initiation, the wisdom of the rustic, the trial by fire, the power of the machine, and the sacrifice. Each has its own characteristics, and each may be used in various ways and places—advertising, political persuasion (see Chapters 5 and 6), or interpersonal communication. We all use these molds at one time or another, but we are reluctant to recognize and label them as tactics in the persuasion of others.

God and Devil terms   Another thematic or textural characteristic of style—often used in persuasion—is the development of families of terms. Persuaders, like the rest of us, like to see the world as divided into neat categories. They also use these categories to try to persuade others and are often successful. One of these category sets is the creation of God terms

---

31.   Eliade (cited in Footnote 14).

and Devil terms, as noted by Richard Weaver. Weaver said that terms or labels are really only parts of propositions. However, they are often linked with other terms or labels to shape a message or a persuasive sense. He defines "God term" as an expression "about which all other expressions are ranked as subordinate and serving dominations and powers. Its force imparts to the others their lesser degree of force . . . ."[32] Weaver sees a God term as an unchallenged term that demands sacrifice or obedience in its name. He uses three terms as examples of God terms: "progress," "fact," and "science." Though these were God terms for the 1950s when Weaver wrote, their force has changed. We do not now attach high positive values to "progress"—counter terms have identified it with waste, war, pollution, and a series of other ills. "Science" has lost some of its credibility, for science has produced, along with constructive marvels, nuclear weapons and technology that may destroy the earth through pollution.

Recently, other God terms seem to have emerged—"individuality," "concern," "sincerity," "communality," and others. Over time, they, too, will probably fall out of vogue. It is important that persuaders and persuadees have attachments for families of related terms and that each persuader designs discourse to highlight those terms that are seen as having high value. For example, the human-potential movement uses the following God terms: "tenderness," "loving," "openness," "trust," "letting go," "acceptance," "touching," "love," and "together." Many of these terms may have negative. value to certain persons; for example, some persons see "touch" as a bad thing. For the human-potential movement, however, they are God terms. They set the mood or the motif for a message: "Be yourself; tell others that you love them; don't worry about the future; and be open with yourself and others."

At the same time that persuaders devise God terms, they may also devise sets of terms expressing negative values—Devil terms. Weaver defines Devil terms as "terms of repulsion," which group together and have great potential in arousing emotions. Weaver says that though "they defy any real analysis . . . they generate a peculiar force of repudiation. One only recognizes them as publicly agreed-upon Devil terms."[33] As examples, he uses some terms from the 1950s: "prejudice," "communist," and "ignorance." More recent terms like "military-industrial complex," "restrictive," "establishment," and "waste," all have negative connotations. Each Devil term has helpers that make up a Devil family. *Waste* is something that *depletes* resources and causes *pollution* and *exploitation* by the *haves.*

In an interview concerning the problems facing blacks, Reverend Jesse Jackson of Operation PUSH said:

---

32.   Weaver, pp. 211, 212, and 214.

33.   Weaver, pp. 210–215.

It is futile for us to think about ending racism; that is a psychologi-cal problem that seems beyond our attempts to affect it. We are fighting to end colonialism—oppression and exploitation. That requires power. The civil rights movement is a lifetime struggle for power. A man who is impotent, no matter how courteous and pleasant looking he is, is told to wait in the lobby. But if you have power, you can be an illiterate boor with tobacco juice running down your face and they will open the door for you.[34]

Notice the development of a set of Devil terms that come into opposition with one God term. "Racism," "colonialism," "oppression," "illiterate boor," and "exploitation" all form the Devil family, which is met by the single potent God term—"power." This term can defeat the entire Devil family. There is a minor Devil family here also. It is associated with the Uncle Tom image: "courteous," "impotent," and "pleasant," all describe qualities that will get you nowhere. Again, "power" is in opposition to these words. The development of these terms is a drama in itself—the two sets of terms do battle, and one emerges victorious.

Weaver points out that, on occasion, terms with a clear positive or negative load can be turned around to reverse their connotation. His example is the value placed on certain terms used by soldiers, words that symbolize death or killing. Defecation words or words referring in one way or another to the sex act or to sexual perversion are death words. They take on acceptable values to the soldier living a lifestyle that em-phasizes death. The Marine private visiting home after boot camp may slip at the family dinner table: "Please pass the f— peas." He ties a negative death symbol with the life symbol of food. This makes the contrast even more emphatic. There are other times when terms have their value rever-sals. "Military" seems to be in disrepute in the late 1970s (though in the 1950s it was a God term), as do "status quo" and "progress" and "Negro," while other previously negative terms such as "black" have assumed positive values.

Weaver describes another kind of term. He calls it the charismatic term, or "term(s) of considerable potency whose referents it is virtually impossible to discover. . . . Their meaning seems inexplicable unless we accept the hypothesis that their content proceeds out of a popular will that they *shall* mean something."[35] His example is the word "freedom," which has no direct referent but which seems, even a quarter of a century after Weaver wrote about it, to have potency for many persons. The word "power," though it has plus loadings at times, may have minus meanings

---

34.   "*Playboy Interview: Jesse Jackson*," *Playboy*, November 1969, p. 85.

35.   Weaver, p. 227.

at other times. Power has no real referent but derives its meaning from those who submit to the power.

The development of sets of words with high positive or negative value loadings for their user—God and Devil terms—is one of the tactics used by persuaders to lend texture or a thematic quality to their discourse. Things seem to be consistent and to "go" with one another. The persuadee can learn much from identifying a persuader's sets of positive and negative terms, for they signal the kinds of relationships he sees operating in the world—what he sees in opposition to what.

Pragmatic versus unifying style   A final characteristic that builds a thematic wholeness or gives a kind of texture to persuasion is the reliance of a persuader on one of two kinds of styles—the pragmatic style or the unifying style.[36] These styles can be thought of as signifying two separate strategies; and persuaders can utilize the tactics of either strategy, or they can choose some tactics of both extremes.

Pragmatic persuaders are usually in the position of having listeners who do not necessarily support their position. As a result, they must try to change minds, as opposed to reinforcing beliefs, and must choose appropriate tactics. The unifying persuaders are faced with a much more comfortable position. They talk to persons who, in large measure, already believe what is going to be said. They do not need to change minds; they only need to reinforce beliefs—to whip up enthusiasm or to give encouragement and dedication. These two styles demonstrate two opposing situations, and they describe the problems facing the persuader in these situations. The problems for the pragmatic persuader are very practical—he must change opinion before he can expect action. The unifying persuader can be much more idealistic—can be more bombastic and probably not offend the audience. These persuaders can be more emotional and less objective than the persuader faced with a questioning audience. What are the stylistic devices of these extremes?

The unifying persuader can afford to be idealistic and will focus on the then-and-there—on the past or on the future, when things were ideal or when they can become ideal. The position of these persuaders is that things look better in the future, particularly if we compare them with the present. Language choice, since the audience will fill in the blanks, can be abstract. It is usually poetic and filled with imagery; these attributes (imagery and abstractness) excite the imagination of the audience. Though there may be little that is intellectually stimulating (or that requires careful logical examination) about what unifying persuaders say, there is

---

36.   For examples of speeches illustrating these styles, see Wil Linkugel, Ron R. Allen, and Richard L. Johannesen, eds., *Contemporary American Speeches*, 3rd ed. (Belmont, Calif.: Wadsworth Publishing Co., 1972).

much that is emotionally stimulating to the audience. The words and images offered by such persuaders are precisely the words listeners believe they would have said if they were talking. The unifying persuader is thus the mouthpiece or sounding board for the entire group, providing them with the cues, but not the details, of the message. They can participate with the persuaders in the creation of the message; in fact, they sometimes actively participate by yelling encouragement to the unifying persuader or by repeating shibboleths to underscore his words—"Right on" or "Amen, Brother" or "Tell it like it is."

Pragmatic persuaders, because they must win an audience, cannot afford to take the risk of appealing to abstract ideals. They must be concrete, focusing on facts instead of images, emphasizing that which cannot be disputed or interpreted so easily. They will not try to depict an ideal situation in subjective there-and-then terms. Instead they will have to focus on real aspects of immediate problems familiar to the audience— problems of the here-and-now, which are realistic, not idealistic. Their orientation is toward the present instead of the future. Since pragmatic persuaders are forced into a position where they must be concrete and realistic, their language is concrete and prosaic. Lofty thoughts are of little value, especially if they are expressed in equally lofty words. The persuader tends to focus on facts and statistics instead of imagery.

Clearly, these two extremes are not an either-or proposition— persuaders may, on occasion, utilize the tactics of both perspectives. When they do this they are probably responding to their audience's level of doubt or overly favorable initial position. Let us examine a few examples of these two differing styles.

The following excerpt is from an editorial discussing the controversial neutron bomb that was developed in the late 1970s. Its major advantage was that it would kill people and animals by radiation shortly after being dropped and would not damage buildings or other property. The advancing army could then wait until the radiation had cleared (a short time with this weapon) and claim the territory, machinery, buildings and so forth. This kind of topic tends to polarize people and to generate unifying persuasion.

> At no time in history have two such major powers been at peace so long even though they faced each other "eyeball to eyeball" with pikes in hand. We haven't killed each other yet because we know we'd be killed in the process.
>
> Terror has maintained the peace; and the terror has to get more terrible with each passing year. . . .
>
> I'm still scared by the neutron bomb—I guess because it emphasizes the paradoxical lunacy of peace being maintained by ever-increasing terror. I don't buy the pacifist suggestion that we should therefore put away our weapons and let the Russians move in. I'm skeptical about

> *disarmament because it has never worked in human history and be-*
> *cause I don't trust the Russians and I don't think anyone in his right*
> *mind should trust them.*
>
> *Of what nature is human nature that it does not kill because the*
> *weapons for killing are becoming ever more destructive—and we even*
> *need computers now to tell us how destructive? There is something*
> *terribly wrong somewhere—did I hear someone say sin?—but all the*
> *quick and easy ways out seem even more wrong.*
>
> *Then where does that leave us?*
> *Scared.*[37]

Notice the use of several metaphors. There is the personification of the superpowers standing "eyeball to eyeball" like ancient knights with "pikes" for weapons. The world is seen as an insane asylum governed by terror and there is the reference to sin. The speaker is referring to a there-and-then—the future when the atomic war will start. He does not use lofty words as some unifying persuaders do, but he does use poetic syntax (for example, "of what nature is . . ."). There are few statistics or concrete facts cited. The speaker seems to be speaking for the audience. The speaker is their mouthpiece in objecting to the new weapon.

Compare that style with the following example of a pragmatic persuader citing facts that he hopes will turn a doubtful audience around to his point of view. The excerpt is from a report on the rising costs of professional baseball due to the decision by the courts to allow players to become free agents and auction off their talents to the highest bidding baseball club.

> *A salary of $100,000 a year for five years; a bonus of $125,000 for*
> *signing; an investment account with a value of $250,000; a $200,000*
> *payment to his agent; an off-season job with the team owner worth*
> *$50,000; deferred payments of $450,000; and a new car every year—*
> *all this to be paid even if he never gets another base hit.*
>
> *That's what Gary Matthews, who earned $46,000 with the San*
> *Francisco Giants last year, was given by the Atlanta Braves to come*
> *and play ball for them.*
>
> *One hundred thousand dollars is the most Mickey Mantle ever*
> *made. According to UPI, the average regular this year is getting*
> *$95,149.*
>
> *It kind of makes you wonder: are baseball players worth it?*[38]

---

37.   Andrew Greeley, "Death Plays in the Real World," *Chicago Tribune*, August 2, 1977, section 1, p. 7. Copyright 1978, Universal Press Syndicate.

38.   James S. Kunen, "Slow Down: Are Baseball Players Really Worth It?" *New Times* (New York), June 10, 1977, p. 12.

Notice the number of facts, each more overwhelming than the last. Then all of them are rounded off by the surprising revelation that the pay is there even if the player flops totally. The language is clearly "here-and-now." It refers to what the going price of ball players was at the time of writing. Certainly the language is prosaic; no lofty sentiments here nor any imagery, just plain talk. The persuader here sees a chance to influence those who are neutral or even some of those who feel that players deserve to be paid for what they think they are worth or based on market conditions—what the traffic will bear. Even an audience polarized against the persuader would have a problem dismissing his evidence. His comparison with Mickey Mantle, who was a greater star than Gary Matthews, would bother even the most staunch players' advocate.

These persuaders have probably used both styles. These two styles are a function of the audience, not of the persuader. They reflect the persuader's view of the audience. Persuadees can gain insight into how they are being seen by the persuader by looking at the unifying or pragmatic styles used in messages.

TUNING ONE'S EAR FOR CUES

Persuadees—to be aware and critical—ought to tune their ears for the various clues to style and motives already discussed. What are some ways in which you can tune your ear? Trying to use some of these tools is one way. If you have thought about these tools, if Langer's theory about self-revelation through symbols has sparked your imagination, or if you have tried to apply these tools to the persuasion around you, you have already started the tuning process. Applying the study questions at the end of this and other chapters is another good way to continue the process. There are at least three other things you might do to make yourself more critical of style and to "read" or "psych out" persuaders:

1. *Role-play the persuader.* Assume that you are the persuader or a member of a group with a persuasive cause. How would you have shaped the persuasion you hear? For example, if you were favoring high salaries for ball players, how would you go about framing a pragmatic message for half-hearted believers, those who are neutral, or others who are only moderately opposed? You would mention things like the shortness of most players' careers (hence a low overall salary across a lifetime in spite of high yearly salaries). You might compare ballplayers to entertainers who make several million dollars per year for relatively little actual work time. You might cite overall profits made by ballclubs and the rather meager retirement programs in pro sports. If your audience was the annual meeting of Association of Professional Baseball Players, you could afford to bypass the numbers and use highly emotional and abstract language to motivate the audience. You might create images of club owners as filthy rich bloodsuckers who mindlessly use up the best years of a man's physical life as the strip-miners ravage the landscape. Your language would probably be there-and-then—referring to new goals of the group or talking about past abuses. So your style would show your view of the audience.

2. *Restate a persuasive message numerous times.* Instead of pretending that you are the ghostwriter for the persuader, just try to restate what has been said in several different ways. Ask yourself what the options were (as we did sketchily with the three presidential slogans earlier in this chapter). Then try to determine how these options would have changed the intent of the message and its final effects. This process should lead you to draw some conclusions about the persuader's intent. You might want to determine what the persuader's pentadic emphasis was and then try to restate the persuasion from the viewpoint of the other four elements of the dramatic pentad.

For example, take the following slogan for Grand Marnier Liqueur: "There Are Still Places on Earth Where Grand Marnier Isn't Offered after Dinner." The slogan is printed on a photo of a deserted island. The appeal is scenic. The product goes with almost any setting. That is the gist of the message. An agent-oriented version of this slogan might be "People with a Taste for the Good Things of Life Offer Grand Marnier." Here the focus would not be on setting but on the kind of actors who are likely to use the product. A purpose-oriented version might read something like: "When You Want to Finish the Conference, Offer Grand Marnier." An agency-oriented version might say, "From a Secret Triple Orange Recipe," stressing the method of production. The act might be used by saying "Do the Right Thing Now, Offer Grand Marnier." Of course, these slogans should be used with appropriately matched visuals depicting elegant people, an important business conference, a view of the distillery, or a couple about to snuggle up in front of the fireplace at a ski lodge.

3. *Attend to language features in discourse.* Don't allow yourself passively to buy into any persuasive advice that is being hawked. Instead, get into the habit of looking at the style of messages. Analyze messages on billboards and in TV spot commercials, the language used by your parents in discussions with you, the wording on packages you purchase or in discussions between you and your friends, enemies, or salespersons. In other words, start listening not only to *ideas*—the thrust of the messages aimed at you—but to *words* or the packaging of those ideas. Try it on me. What kind of words do I use? Why? What do you think I'm like? How does my style differ from Richard Johannesen's (see Chapter 9)? From other persuasion textbook writers? From the way you would have said it? Focusing on these features in as many situations as possible will give you an intriguing pastime in which you operate as a kind of amateur psychoanalyst. Further, you will develop an ear for stylistic tip-offs, a skill that will prove valuable in your inter-personal relations—it allows you to predict and respond to the com-munication of others.

A REVIEW AND CONCLUSION

In conjunction with Susanne Langer's suggestion that artistic activity is uniquely characteristic of human beings and that language as a symbol system offers most persons their entry into artistic activity, this chapter has tried to present several tools for analyzing the stylistic aspects of language activity.

There are at least three stylistic axes we can look at: the functional characteristics of style, the semantic aspects of style, and the thematic or textural qualities of style. Though there are numerous tools one might use to critique these elements of style, Richard Weaver's use of word classes, syntactical characteristics, and the nature of ambiguity all relate to the functional axis. At the same time, persuadees can explore the semantic nature of persuasion by using the dramatic pentad suggested by Kenneth Burke, as well as subsymbols or metaphors, such as the rite of the kill, that emerge when one looks at the dramatic qualities of persuasion. Finally, we can attempt to get a notion of the textural or thematic trends in persua-sion by looking for families of God and Devil terms, by exploring motifs and metaphors, and by looking at the unifying as opposed to pragmatic characteristics of the persuasion.

All these critical devices are, of course, enhanced in their potential by role-playing, restating, and developing awareness of the words and style as well as the ideas in a persuasive message, be it a speech, a TV documentary, a film, a candidate, a social movement, a package designed to sell a product, or a friend's entreaty.

Questions for Further Thought

1. What are the three axes of language activity? Give examples of them from your own writing or speaking. Give examples from the speaking or writing of a parent or friend.

2. Transcribe the lyrics of a popular song. Now analyze them according to the functional tools presented here. Is there a preference for a cer-

tain word type? A certain sentence structure? Is the message ambiguous or concrete? Explain.

3. What are the semantic tools suggested here? What do you think is the pentadic perspective of the author of this book? Why? Give examples. What do you think is the pentadic favorite of your instructor?

4. What kinds of rituals do you go through in a given day? Give examples (for example, in eating, in sleeping, in relating to roommates or classmates or teachers). Are they symbolic? In what ways? What are you trying to communicate?

5. What are the tools for a thematic or textural analysis of language? Use some of these to analyze the persuasion occurring in a recent political campaign. What do these analyses tell you about the candidate? Explain.

6. What are the God terms held in esteem by your parents? What are their Devil terms? Shape a request for something from your parents, expressed in terms similar to God terms. Now do the same thing with Devil terms. Try them both out as an experiment.

7. How does a unifying persuader differ from a pragmatic one? Find examples of each type of persuader in your class, in some persuasive attempts of the past, or in some persuasive issue being discussed on campus or in your community. Are there other differences between these two types? What are they?

8. What are three ways to tune your ear to the symbolic and ego-revealing aspects of language use? Give an example of where you have done this. Make a prediction about a persuader, based on your analysis of him, using the tools of this chapter and the three suggestions offered at the end of the chapter. Present the reasons for your prediction in an essay or speech.

Experiences in Persuasion

1. Attend a film with a persuasive message (that is, one that does more than merely tell a story). Analyze the words of one or more of its characters, using the tools of this chapter. Do you think the tools work in other symbolic media like film? Why or why not? Why is the film persuasive to you? Analyze your own reasons for saying that it is or is not persuasive. What in the film made you react that way? Was that thing a scenic phenomenon, or did it focus on actions, agents, principles, or methods (for example, someone might say that Hitler's propaganda film *Triumph of the Will* was persuasive because of the spectacle it presented—tens of thousands of people, huge flags, and the

like—all scenic items, while someone else may have found *Rocky* persuasive because of the power and charisma of its star.

2. Analyze the persuasive impact of a particular show on TV—it may be a talk show or a dramatic show. Does its persuasiveness come from a particular part of the pentad? Which one? Give examples. Now look at each of the characters in the episode. Explain how each of them tries to persuade others. Refer to the kinds of words they use, the sentence structures they use and so on; use the tools of this chapter.

3. Catalog the uses of obscenity you find in popular literature or reported as being used by persuaders for certain causes. What word classes are they (see the discussion by Weaver)? Which element of the pentad do they represent? Why are they called profane? Who gets bothered by these words? What are they responding to in the words? Refer to the tools of this chapter.

Process Premises for Persuasion 3

A well-known luggage manufacturer recently spent thousands of dollars to produce a very impressive and clever TV ad. The spot opened on luggage being handled roughly as it was loaded into the cargo bay of a huge airliner. The central piece of luggage was made by the sponsor. The plane is next seen in flight. We are shown a slight problem—someone has failed to latch the cargo bay door. As the plane banks, our star piece of luggage falls out of the now open bay door. The camera follows the suitcase as it falls through 30,000 feet of space and lands with a huge thud on some rocks. The case is opened to reveal no damage to the contents. Now that ought to be pretty convincing as to which kind of luggage to buy. However, airing of the commercial was followed by a tremendous drop in sales. Why? Using in-depth interviews, researchers found that most people, even regular airline travelers, have some fear that the plane may crash. They resented the implication that their luggage would survive them in event of a crash and so rejected that brand.

This example dramatizes the focus of Chapter 3—the presence of needs in all persons. These needs make us all vulnerable to persuasion, and professional persuaders effectively tap into our needs. Needs are also the catalysts for persuasion boomerangs, as the luggage manufacturer discovered. These needs are *process premises* because most operate in some kind of psychic sequence or process. For example, take the need to feel loved. This need is partially met by pets, parents, siblings, friends, spouses, children, mistresses, fraternal groups, and so forth. The key is the word "partially" because we probably all feel the need to be loved more than we are, in spite of all those sources of love noted above. Even if we feel totally loved today, there is a good chance that tomorrow we won't.

Both as persuaders and as persuadees, we need to become aware of these needs. For us as persuaders, they are useful targets to aim at as we shape persuasive messages. As persuadees, our needs make us open to persuasion. We need to guard against making foolish decisions in response to deceptive messages that are really aimed at our deep-seated needs. Let's explore some of these premises that can be so important in the process of persuasion.

THE ASSUMPTION OF SIMILITUDE

We all like being individuals in this world, but most of us do not want to be thought of as too different from the norm. At the same time, it gives a feeling of security to know that others like us the way we are. We need to convince ourselves and the rest of the world that we are all similar to one another in at least some important ways. That basically is what the assumption of similitude is all about—we want others to be like us, and we twist and weave until it looks that way to us. Take me, for example. I am just plain gullible. I have been slicked out of more dollars, favors, and good faith than most. Usually there is no big problem tied to this characteristic, and I can go along my merry way thinking that I am like everybody else. However, two or three times a year, I get fooled. Those are disturbing moments because they remind me that I am not totally like other people. I don't tell about my blunders because people might laugh. I try to convince myself that, since I am falling for fewer con jobs each year,

THE BORN LOSER   **by Art Sansom**

Figure 3-1 *The Born Loser. Our hero in this cartoon strip has just experienced a breaking of his assumption of similitude—the whole world is not like him. (Reprinted by permission of NEA.)*

I am finally maturing. I can always fall back on that old reliable folk wisdom: "It was a good lesson, and no one was really hurt." You can probably identify some similar problems you have. However, when things like that happen, you are brought up short and realize that others don't behave as you do. As a result, maybe you lose your temper, go into gray and sullen moods without warning.

This need to explain away our foibles is one on which persuaders can and do build. We can get assurance that we really are like others by purchasing a popular product, by attending the *in* film, or by voting for a well-known candidate. Knowing that persuaders are going to appeal to this need can alert us to their strategy and help us make more rational, objective, and less emotional judgments when we do encounter persuasion.

The assumption of similitude is but one kind of need. We could cite many others. It will be more useful to search for tools to help us to identify those needs in us that persuaders so often target. As in Chapter 2, we are looking for models that will be flexible from one context to another.

NEEDS: THE FIRST INTRAPERSONAL PREMISE

Human beings, like other organisms, have needs—some weak, some strong—that must be met from time to time. The problem is to identify these needs, for they often serve as the first premise in persuasive argument. For example, a person dying of thirst can easily be persuaded to take drastic action in order to get to water to fulfill the need for liquid. The need for H_2O is an important premise in persuading that dehydrated person.

Maslow's Pyramid

Abraham Maslow, a noted psychologist, offers us a starting point for examining gross need levels.[1] He notes that people have various kinds of needs that emerge, subside, and emerge again as they are or are not met. For example, the need for food or drink emerges and then recedes as this need is met. Maslow argues that these needs have a *prepotency*—that is, they are tied together in such a way that weaker needs, like self-respect, emerge only after stronger needs, like the need for food, have been filled. We probably could not persuade our dehydrated desert wanderer to clean

---

1.   Abraham H. Maslow, *Motivation and Personality* (New York: Harper & Row, 1954).

up a little before going to the well. We had better fulfill the need for H_2O first. Our need to slake thirst is prepotent; Until it is fulfilled, it is literally impossible for us to consider other topics.

Maslow arranges the various needs in a clear and understandable model. He says that needs are arranged in pyramid fashion, with lower levels having the stronger needs and higher levels having the weaker needs (Figure 3-2). Remember that the pyramid is only a model and that the lines between needs are not as distinct as the picture suggests. It should also be noted that the higher needs are not any better than lower ones. They are just different and, in all likelihood, weaker and less likely to emerge until stronger needs are met.

Basic needs   On the bottom level are the strongest needs we have— basic needs. These are the physiological needs of each human being. We need regular fufillment of our needs for air, food, water, sex, sleep, and elimination of wastes. Until these needs are met, we cannot concern ourselves with other, higher needs. The basic needs are too strong to be forgotten in favor of other needs.

Security needs   The second level of Maslow's pyramid contains our needs connected with security. There are several ways one might look at our need for security. We may want to feel secure in our ability to get basic needs. If we feel that our job may end shortly, we have a strong need to get income security. We may want to get another more secure job. Or we might want to save money for hard times. This is one kind of security. At the same time, we might look at this need level in another light. Let us suppose that we have job security—our boss assures us that we will be the last to be let go. We may still feel insecure because of the rising crime rates

Figure 3-2   *The Maslow Pyramid of Needs.*

in our neighborhood. We might take drastic action to ward off thieves. We might install a burglar alarm system, or we may sleep with a loaded pistol under the pillow. Even when we feel secure about home, we may still feel insecure about world politics. We may feel that our country needs more missiles or antimissile missiles. A person may have social insecurity and as a result spend money on self-improvement classes, deodorant, hair transplants, and mouth wash. In other words, this need for security emerges and reemerges as various threats to our security become evident and must be met. Once the need is met, it redefines itself and thus is always present to some degree.

Belonging needs   Once we feel that security needs are met at least in part (we know we will have a job in the future and that thugs will have problems robbing us), we become aware of other needs on the third level. These are belonging needs. Persons who feel fairly secure, like the horse who looks at the field of clover across the road, look to other things which they now feel are needed. We have a number of options open to us in meeting the need for association. We may choose to fulfill these needs in our immediate family. We all know of people who relate to no group other than at the job and in the family. This way of meeting belonging needs is the exception rather than the rule, however. Usually the individual seeks groups with which to fill this need. Suburbia is filled with persons who seem to have a strong need for belonging—they are the joiners of our society. They become members of dozens of groups like the PTA, bowling leagues, churches, golf clubs, or service groups. Usually we keep the number of groups we join small, and though we may be members of a number of groups, we are active members in only a few. Regardless of how many groups we join or of how active we are in any of them, we only partially meet our belonging needs. We will continue to join groups throughout our lives, for this need is also a reemerging one.

Love or esteem needs   Once we satisfy belonging needs, we will feel the emergence of other needs. This is level four of Maslow's model, the need for love or esteem. Once we are part of a group, we want to feel that the group—be it family, lodge, or bowling team—values us as a member. As human beings we want to feel wanted and valued. We are happy when our families understand and admire the things we do. This need is also a reemerging need. That is, if we find that we are needed and esteemed and loved by our family, the need for esteem does not fade away. Instead, its focus shifts. We want now to feel needed and loved by our coworkers and our boss or by our friends. Once we get this kind of esteem, the need becomes less compelling. However, it is never fully satisfied, and we try to seek other circumstances in which we can achieve status and rank that will help meet our need for love and esteem by others. Many product pitches rely on this need. We are told that we can be well liked if we own a sports car or a Bionic Man set or a new style of clothes.

Self-actualization At the top of Maslow's model is the need for self-actualization. Stated in another way, this need might be called the need to live up to what we think is our own true self-potential. Although this need is weaker than the other need levels, there are instances in which lower needs are displaced to fulfill the need for self-actualization. We have all heard of artists who have gone cold and hungry just so they could continue painting or composing music or writing poetry. Such behavior is unusual among human beings; these persons define their self-actualization level as a basic need. To the artist, creative activity is as basic as breathing or eating or sleeping. As W. H. Auden describes it, this is genius—the man who wants to do what he must do. Late in his life, Maslow renamed this level, calling it a *peak experience.* (He came to believe that we live for these peak experiences. They are the mileposts of our developing human potential.)

We are not geniuses, so for our purposes this need is not a strong one, and it is not likely to emerge until or unless the four lower and more prepotent needs have been met. Again, this need reemerges and, even when partially met, is seen again. For example, let us suppose that we worked our whole life on a single project or toward a single goal—the curing of cancer, for instance. If we achieve this goal, do we petrify? Some persons kill themselves after reaching their life's goal or die on skid row or fade away when they retire. In most cases, though, such self-actualizing persons define a new goal for themselves so that they can continue to reach toward their own potential. So even at the top of Maslow's hierarchy there is a continuing reemergence of needs.

Packard's Eight Emotional Needs

Somewhat related to Maslow's model of human needs are eight needs identified by Vance Packard in his bestselling book *The Hidden Persuaders.* Although based on research that is now more than twenty years old, Packard's list of needs seems to still describe the kinds of appeals we see today on TV, in magazines, and in the world of politics and ideas.[2]

Need for emotional security In today's world of insecurity (for example, the possibility of war, sickness, economic or natural disasters, and so forth) people need to acquire or embrace symbols of a more secure life.

---

2.   Vance Packard, *The Hidden Persuaders* (New York: Pocket Books, 1964).

These symbols may be in the form of products like home freezers that keep one safe from starvation or cosmetics like deodorants that keep us socially safe or in the form of political persons whom we can trust. Politicians vow never to lie. A 1970 poll showed that while only 8 percent of respondents felt it was important for a candidate to be a man who perceived vital issues, 47 percent thought that it was important that he be "honest, a man of conviction."[3]

Reassurance-of-worth needs   We live in a highly competitive and impersonal society in which we feel like mere cogs in a machine. Packard noted that people need to feel valued for what they do. This need was particularly important for many housewives of the 1950s and 1960s who saw themselves as mere drudges doing the dirty work of the family for no real payoff. Product advertisers who could promise that their brands would lead to appreciation were usually successful in gaining new adherents. Sta-Pruf starch promises that hubby will succeed on the job with a crisp white shirt and will kiss wifey when he comes home with the raise she helped him get. Politicians often promise to return us to our earlier national greatness. Many social service agencies promise that volunteers can do something "worthwhile in the world" if they give several hours of time per week. So the need to be valued (like Maslow's esteem needs) serves as a powerful persuasive premise.

Need for ego gratification   One step from worth needs are needs to stroke one's own ego: "Not only am I worth something, I am really pretty special." Packard refers to a heavy road-equipment manufacturer who increased sales by featuring in magazine ads the drivers of the machines instead of the machines themselves. Operators have major say-so in purchase decisions. Persuaders often identify a group whose members feel they have been put down for some time—teachers, police, or social workers, for instance. It is easy to sell products, ideas, or candidates by hooking into the out-group's ego needs. In the late 1970's, one candidate promised a "pro-family" emphasis. For years, the family idea had been out of vogue in favor of living together, communes, gay marriage, and rising divorce rates. The appeal worked. Factory safety campaigns often have a scoreboard to record the number of accident-free days achieved by workers, thus gratifying their egos.

Need for creative outlets   In our age, few products can be identified with a single craftsman. Many of the earlier outlets for creativity have been

---

3.   Tony Schwartz, *The Responsive Chord* (Garden City, N.Y.: Anchor Books, 1973), p. 102.

bypassed. For instance, take the increase of prepared foods, microwave ovens, and eating out instead of creatively cooking a meal from scratch. There still seems to be a need for people to demonstrate their own handicraft skills. Given this need, macramé, gourmet-cooking classes, bonsai gardens, home improvement tools, and other hobby-type activities are bound to succeed. Even in prepared foods, where the art of cooking has been almost totally removed, manufacturers are finding that creativity still sells. Hamburger Helper leaves room for you, the cook, to add your own touch. Noodles Romanoff makes you a chef worthy of the Czar. Even Old El Paso taco dinner reminds you of all the creative toppings you can put on a taco shell. In our town, a high-status thing for young mothers is to be the Picture Lady at the grade school. Picture Ladies bring works of art to one of the grades and give question/answer type lessons on them. You can cite many situations in which persuaders are using the need for creative outlets to get you to buy their product or idea.

Need for love objects   This need is particularly important for persons whose children have grown up—the empty-nest syndrome. These persons have the need to replace the child love object. For some the replacement is a pet; for others it is a child met through the organization Foster Grandparents. It may be a childlike entertainment personality such as Liberace, who always said, "Goodnight, Mother" at the end of each TV show. Perhaps persons who are not yet in the childless years are motivated by the need for another kind of love object to replace the parents whom they left or the lover who has never appeared on the scene. This could account for the recurring emergence of stars with great sex appeal—for example, Robert Redford or Jacqueline Bisset. The major audience for pro wrestling is elderly women; the wrestlers may serve as love objects to these women.

Need for a sense of power   If you have ever driven a motorcycle on the open road, you know what it feels like to have this need. We, more than members of any other culture, seem to be programmed to buy potency and power and also to gratify this need symbolically more than others. The bigger the auto engine, the better. Sno-mobiles and their counterparts for summer fun are marketed by the sense of power they give. Almost any automotive product will feature the words "heavy-duty" to convince you that you are getting a powerful replacement part. Although some of our politicians are short or have slight builds, the big powerful types seem to win more frequently.

Need for roots   The increasing interest in genealogical research intensified by Alex Haley's novel *Roots* testifies to the continuing importance of this need. Perhaps the fact that most persons move several times during their lives and many times to locations far from home explains this need to find roots. At your age, you will move once a year for ten years. Persuaders can and do appeal to this need in a number of ways. George McGovern's 1972 campaign slogan "Come Home, America" has a roots appeal. The homey appeal of Pepperidge Farm bread products probably relates to a need for roots. You can think of many other situations in which what is being "sold" is not a product, a candidate, or an idea but instead a sense of roots.

Need for immortality   None of us believe in our own mortality. We like to think that life will go on and on in much the same way as at present. This fear of dying or need for a sense of being around as an influence on the lives of others lies behind many insurance appeals, according to Packard. The husband and father needs to feel that he will have impact on his family forever. Insurance makes this possible. In buying it he buys some life. If he does not die at an early age, the insurance will provide a tidy extra for those endless retirement years. Lifetime guarantees sell the same symbolic immortality.

Some Uses and Conclusions

Thus, one given at the process level is the need state. Persuaders may capitalize on need levels if they know that the audience has certain needs or drives that must be fulfilled. Relying on this process, the persuader shapes messages directed at particular needs. The idea of a need state is like a premise in an argument; the argument runs like this: "Since you have within you a need for X, I will show you how to get X. You will get X by following my advice." Success in persuasion largely depends upon the ability to assess need states accurately.

We may wish to relabel our needs in terms other than those of Maslow or Packard, but their categories serve as good general descriptive devices of human needs. We ought to consider the requests persuaders make of us from the perspective of our own need states. For example, if a persuader asks us to use a new brand of soap because it pollutes less, we ought to ask if our security is really threatened to the degree that we ought to change brands of soap at extra cost and with little hope of its reducing pollution.

As persuaders, we ought to examine the current needs of those we wish to influence. If we do that, not only are we more likely to succeed, but also we are more likely to do our audience a service by giving them a means to satisfy their needs.

A good way to train yourself to evaluate appeals from this critical perspective—as persuadee or persuader—is to try to restate existing pieces of persuasion, such as TV commercials, while considering the five need levels of Maslow's hierarchy or Packard's list of needs.

Take for example, an advertisement for mouthwash. The ad suggests that if your breath is bad, you will not have a happy love life. Clearly, the ad attempts to present a threat to your esteem or love needs, but it has potency at other levels too. Critical persuaders and persuadees can restate this request in other terms. The mouthwash for lovers will also make it easier for the user to belong to certain groups, so there is also an appeal to the belonging need. This kind of testing of appeals and playing with variations of appeals encourages a critical awareness on our part. We are able to observe and identify various persuasive techniques—an ability that ought to serve us in our roles as persuaders and as persuadees.

Maslow's pyramid can be used in many everyday persuasive opportunities. When we want to persuade a teacher that a certain grade or method of evaluation is unfair, we must analyze what kinds of needs the professor has. Is he or she likely to feel insecure? Is he or she in need of esteem? Is he or she trying to self-actualize? Or suppose you were trying to persuade your roommate to take a trip to Florida with you instead of working over the break period. You want to know what kinds of needs were being fulfilled by the potential trip or by the plan for work during the vacation. Many marital quarrels are rooted in differing motivations—a wife may want to take a trip to San Francisco for the vacation, while a husband is interested in going to fishing country, with each trying to fulfill different needs. Ultimately, one side or the other will agree to give up his or her plans. The insurance sales representatives who plague college students offering special rates are also appealing to needs (probably security needs) they assume operate in the students.

What kinds of needs might the professor, the roommate, or potential purchaser of insurance be exhibiting if we used Packard's listing? How might particular appeals be restated, in terms of several of Packard's needs? For instance, the appeal to status that lies behind many ads for luxury cars could be restated in ways that would make the ads appeal to potency or the need for ego gratification. Try restating such persuasive appeals from several perspectives.

In conclusion, people seem to be motivated by the desire to be similar to others and by their need states. This first process premise operates on the belief that people have drives that need to be reduced by meeting them. The drives probably reemerge from time to time and thus motivate us throughout our lives and probably throughout the life of our nation. Persuaders can take advantage of this by directing their messages toward audience needs, promising or perhaps only hinting that by following their advice, the need can be filled or reduced. As persuadees, we can take advantage of our knowledge of this first process premise by being alert to the goal of persuasion aimed at us and by restating messages that aim at our needs. This will make the persuader's strategy clearer and will also alert the persuadee as to the hidden reasons for choosing to buy a certain toothpaste, to vote for Senator Fogbound, or to join the "End Nuclear Weaponry" protest group.

ATTITUDES: THE SECOND PROCESS PREMISE

Another building block for persuasive messages is the existence of certain attitudes in each person's mind. These attitudes may exert force on behavior. For example, suppose you have a positive attitude toward rural life. Persuaders would be most successful in getting you to follow their advice if they could tie their appeal into that attitude. Politicians might want to dress in clothes that suggest the land. They might wear jeans or work shirts or they might get pictured working on their own hobby farm. They might refer to a country heritage and helping with the harvest or with chores. All these messages as well as the many media messages that could accompany them (for example, a musical score) would align with your positive image of country life. Given an alignment, you would be likely to vote for the candidate—at least that is what most attitude theories predict.

Really, attitudes are only part of a kind of family of influences on behavior. Probably the most easily changed factor of human behavior is opinion. We have opinions about the President's competence based on what was said during the campaign and on what he has done since entering office. These opinions can change, however, especially if the President makes a few key errors—a foolish statement, fighting the Congress on a particular issue, or choosing to support a friend who turns out to be corrupt. The Gallup and Harris polls record such shifts of opinion on a regular basis. It should be remembered, however, that opinions may not influence the behavior of persons who hold them. Take the examples just discussed. Though our opinions about the President may slip toward negative across a few months, we may still vote for him in the next election. This is not to say that opinions are not related at all to behavior—only that they exert very weak influence.

Given a large enough change in opinion we may not support the President in the next campaign; or, given enough small shifts in our opinions, we may change our overall *attitude* toward him. Thus attitudes become the second level of internal pressure on behavior. We have an attitude toward smoking composed of many opinions. It is our opinion that it is costly; that it is unhealthy; that it is dirty; that it bothers others; that it destroys the body's supply of vitamin C, and so on. Opinions are verbal statements of part of the attitude. Philip Zimbardo, a prominent sociologist, puts it this way when he notes that attitudes are "either mental readiness or implicit predispositions that exert some general and consistent influence on a fairly large class of evaluative responses."[4]

---

4.   Philip G. Zimbardo, Ebbe E. Ebbesen, and Christina Maslach, *Influencing Attitudes and Changing Behavior* (Reading, Mass: Addison-Wesley Publishing Co., 1976), p. 20.

Notice that Zimbardo features the enduring quality of attitude shifts. There is even a school of advertising research that goes under the acronym DAGMAR. The philosophy is that ad agencies ought to Design Advertising Goals so they can be Measured by Attitudinal Response. In other words, the goal of advertising is *attitudinal change* toward the company or product and not purchase behavior. It is hoped that if we have an improved image for a product—say Rice Chex—there will be an increase in purchase of the product. Unfortunately, this attitude/behavior linking has been very difficult to demonstrate, perhaps because of the many intervening variables that might also cause purchase of a product. Simply being aware of a product's name, its packaging, where it is displayed in a store, what kind of background music is being played may cause purchase. Other factors like time of day or sex of purchaser may be the key. Even in carefully controlled experiments with many of these causes filtered out, the attitude/behavior link-up does not consistently occur. Researchers blame this on poor design in research studies or a weak measuring instrument.

Thus what we know about attitudes is not how or if they determine actions, but instead we know about how they change and which of them are most likely to change. In the early studies done by psychologist Carl Hovland, he found that attitudes that changed were usually not ego-involving, not central or they were based on previous experience or commitment of the subjects studied. Hovland studied these, he said, because otherwise his research team would "run the risk of no measurable effects, particularly with small scale experiments."[5] Later research did use socially significant and ego-involved topics. Until recently, most research measured attitude shift as Hovland did—caused by short, one-time messages, measured by pencil and paper tests. Remember that, as Zimbardo pointed out, a verbalized attitude is really an opinion statement. Opinions are the most easily changed and most fickle of the family of internal knowledge on which we base our actions. It was no surprise that such research found that attitudes were easy to change, and debate raged as to which theory could best explain the changes.

One of the more recent advances in the study of this second process premise is the work done by Martin Fishbein.[6] He substituted the term "behavioral intention" for the concept of attitude. He then measured what people say they intend to do and not how they feel about a particular product, candidate, or idea. Thus more recent research has moved from looking at a general feeling toward a topic to the more concrete—what people think they will do about that topic, object, or person. This makes

5.   Zimbardo, p. 92.

6.   Martin Fishbein and Icek Ajzen, *Belief, Attitude, Intention and Behavior: An Introduction to Theory and Research* (Reading, Mass.: Addison-Wesley Publishing Co., 1975).

sense, for given any attitude toward or image of a politician, for example, there are several things that a voter might do—vote for the candidate, stay home from the polls, donate money to the campaign, work for the opponent, and so on. To discover overall attitude toward the politician does not tell us much about the probability of any of these behaviors.

Probably attitudes and opinions are social tools as well as internal states. They help us to get along in various social situations. We can sound slightly conservative when talking about gun control with good old Uncle Harry who is the president of the local National Rifleman's Association. In other circumstances, we can use our opinion statements to sound outraged that the local discount store is selling the deadly AR-15, which can easily be converted to a machine gun, or takedown rifles, which can be packed neatly into a briefcase or umbrella. Uncle Harry would rage against our complaints, but when he is not on the social scene, we can use such data to align ourselves with persons we believe are like us.

What does all this mean to the persuadee who is in the business of critically listening in a world of doublespeak? In other words, what can we do to uncover the persuader's intentions and beliefs about the audience? One of the advantages of at least being aware of attitudes is that we can second guess about our image in the eyes of the persuader. For example, what kind of attitude is the customer presumed to have in the ad for a grandfather clock shown in Figure 3-3? The persuader obviously believes that members of the target market have high status needs. They have strong attitudes about the importance of success. They are somewhat snobbish, and they cultivate taste. Are these the people who read *House and Garden*, the magazine in which the ad appeared? If you read the ad would you be persuaded to go in and look at the clock? How would the company advertise in another kind of magazine—say *Playboy* or *Outdoor Life*? By seeking out the attitude that persuaders assume we have, we can become more critical receivers. Philip Zombardo explains that attitudes have a consistency to them. We do not often act inconsistently. A given attitude will operate the same way in similar situations. Furthermore, Zimbardo tells us that attitudes have effect over not just one action but several sets of action.

Beliefs are similar to attitudes but are probably harder to change. This is because we have had some real-world experience that has confirmed our belief. For instance, most persons believe that success is better than failure. As a result, they act in certain ways—they go to school to get an education so they can succeed. They get jobs and try to improve their job slots. They try to show their success through the display of some signs of success—a trophy, a house, well-behaved children, an attractive spouse, and so on. We might change their attitudes about playing the stock market as one road to success, but it would be difficult to change their core belief about the value of success. They might drop stocks in favor of real estate, but their goal would still be financial success. Our experience in the

If you have to ask the price you can't afford it.

On this Howard Miller clock, the famed cathedral chimes of Westminster, Winchester and St. Michael are reproduced by nine chromium-plated tubular bells. All are housed in a superb case 87 inches tall. A case made of oak and rare Carpathian elm burl veneers. This is set off by a brass and silver plated dial and ornaments of brass fretwork. A great lyre pendulum sedately measures every hour. If you crave the excellent—and have its price—ask for the President.

From the Howard Miller Golden Collection

Figure 3-3 *The company (persuader) reveals its attitudes toward potential customers (persuadees) as well as assumptions about their attitudes toward such things as spending, status, and quality. (Courtesy Howard Miller Clock Company. All rights reserved.)*

world from earliest childhood has verified the value of success over failure—in the classroom, in sports, with friends, in child bearing, in careers, and elsewhere. Thus the belief tends to endure even longer than the attitude.

Unfortunately, much research done on attitudes has dealt with attitudes as if they were beliefs, which do have this kind of potent, long-lived influence over what we think and do. As a result many assume that true persuasion occurs if we can measure the overall impact of a message—say, in a poll. This is not always so. For example, H. R. Haldeman, Richard Nixon's chief aide in the White House, watched Nixon try to explain Watergate in the six hours of televised interviews conducted in 1977 by David Frost. Nixon tried to persuade Frost and the TV audience that the Watergate scandal was caused in part by his own sense of loyalty to his top aides who, he indicated, were the real culprits. After the interviews were aired, Haldeman announced that he would reveal his version in his book, *The Ends of Power*, which was published in 1978. Although the Haldeman book contributed little that was new about Watergate, it did reveal some unattractive Nixon character traits. Nixon did not intend for this response in the interview. He missed the attitude of at least one viewer and triggered an unexpected result. Listening not only for the attitude that persuaders assume we have but also for their attitude toward us as receivers can be a powerful tool for responsible persuadees.

BALANCE AND CONSISTENCY: THE THIRD PROCESS PREMISE

At least most of human existence revolves around successfully adapting to the world. For example, take new college freshmen. They are not aware of all that is going on in the confusion of registration, grades, book buying, using the library, finding buildings on campus, and other activities that will affect their lifestyle. What do they do in response to this unknown world? As a general rule, they observe and search for patterns that will help them to adapt. Among many things, they learn that you can study at the library without interruption. They find that dorm food is fattening and that parking is available before but not after 10:00 A.M.

Much the same holds true for teachers who cope with their classes and students through predictions. Unless the lectures they prepare lead to discussion or feedback, they will abandon their notes and shift to something else. Unless the students relate to the class in meaningful ways (that is, absorbing and applying the concepts instead of sleeping through class), the instructor will be forced to change the class or leave it.

These examples show the basis for the third kind of premise that humans respond to—the *need for predictability*. This premise relates to the good feeling we have when our predictions about the world are on target. Humans want a resolution of psychological conflict. We cannot tolerate confusion in our world. This desire for resolution provides a potent process premise to which persuaders appeal.

Two ways of looking at this problem of resolution of incongruity are found in Fritz Heider's balance theory and Leon Festinger's theory of cognitive dissonance.

Heider's Model: Balance/Imbalance

Heider's theory is relatively simple.[7] It reduces incongruity to its simplest instance—one person talking to another person about a single topic or idea. Attitudes between the two persons (we could call one the persuader and the other the persuadee) can be represented by positive (+) signs or by negative (−) signs. Thus, the two persons could like (+) or dislike (−) one another; they could agree that the idea they are dealing with has bad (−) or good (+) values. They might disagree with one another so that one felt good (+) toward the topic while the other felt bad (−) toward it. Notice in Figure 3-4 that both the receiver and the source have good feelings about one another. Since they agree on the topic and relate posi-

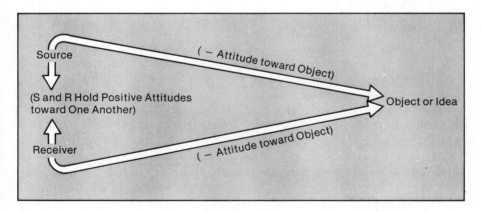

Figure 3-4 *Heider's Model: Balance.*

7.   Fritz Heider, "Attitudes and Cognitive Organization," *Journal of Psychology*, Vol. 21 (January 1946), pp. 107–112.

tively toward each other, there is a feeling of comfort—in Heider's words "balance."

There are three ways in which a person can feel this balance.

1. The source and receiver can both have a negative attitude toward the object or idea and can have a positive attitudinal set toward one another, as in Figure 3-4.

2. The source and receiver can both have a positive attitude toward the object or idea and can have good feelings toward each other. (You and I can like the same idea or object and like one another, thus experiencing comfort or balance.)

3. The source and receiver can disagree about the idea or object and can dislike one another. (Since you and I are not alike and since we dislike one another, it is comforting to know that we disagree about the values of certain things or ideas.)

It is nice to know that those we respect and like have the same values and ideas as we do. It is also nice to know that those fools whom we dislike don't agree with us.

The persuader who tries to strengthen preexisting beliefs in an audience can do so by creating a *balance* or comfortable situation for the receiver. As persuadees, we need to be aware of this strategy. When a persuader deals with you on a face-to-face basis and tells you what you already know or believe (for example, that living in a suburb is bad, that the price of food is skyrocketing, that you are a wise person), you ought to realize that creating balance is the strategy.

Suppose that the persuader wants to *change* beliefs and attitudes. It will be foolish to try to create balance for the persuadees. Instead, the persuader will try to throw their view of the world out of whack by creating imbalance in which their beliefs are shaken. Consider Figure 3-5. In this situation, someone whom I do not respect dislikes the same things that I dislike. I am bound to feel uncomfortable or in a state of imbalance in such a case. How can such an idiot agree with me?

Suppose you want to persuade your parents to let you go to Europe this summer and to help finance your trip. You might already know that they oppose the trip. They are afraid you will be "led astray." They may also feel that they cannot afford to pay your way. They will feel the pinch of your not earning your own keep for the summer. Obviously, you will not get far telling them that you are grown up enough to handle yourself. Instead, you need to create imbalance in their beliefs. You might say getting involved with drugs is more likely at home when people are bored than while getting college credit on a European art tour. Or you might point out that you have done well in the past when given some freedom.

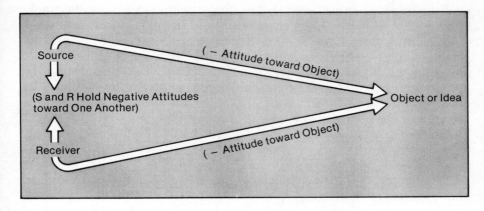

Figure 3-5   *Heider's Model: Imbalance.*

Or you might remind them that there will be no cost for food while you are gone. All of these tactics aim at creating imbalance in order to change minds.

There are probably only two ways in which to create imbalance in persuasive situations:

1. If the source and receiver favor one another but disagree about an object or idea, imbalance will be experienced.

2. If the source and receiver disfavor one another but agree on attitudes toward an object or idea, imbalance will be experienced.

Again, a principle we already know is operating. We want the world to live up to our expectations of it. If it does not, we experience imbalance; if it does, we experience balance.

Persuaders who want to get receivers to change their minds about an idea or object can create feelings of psychological imbalance or discomfort. When persuaders destroy your beliefs (for example, they prove that joining a fraternity or some other group will detract from your social life, not add to it), you ought to realize that they create imbalance for you. They want to change your opinion by relying on your need for psychological balance or comfort.

Festinger's Model: Consonance/Dissonance

Heider's theory is, of course, fairly limited. Not often do people hold beliefs that are simply positive or negative. Beliefs have magnitude as well as direction. We can have strong positive opinions toward a topic or relatively weak positive feelings. The theory proposed by Leon Festinger in his book *A Theory of Cognitive Dissonance* attempts to deal with some of the shortcomings in Heider's theory.[8] Festinger calls imbalance *dissonance*, which he defines as a feeling resulting from the existence of two nonfitting pieces of knowledge about the world: "... considering the two alone, the obverse of one element would follow from the other." Consonance, Festinger's pair term for balance, exists when "considering a pair of elements either one does follow from the other." The degree to which one of these elements may or may not follow from one another can vary, which is not true in balance theory. Though I may greatly dislike door-to-door sales representatives as a group, my weak positive feelings toward a certain salesman may create only slight feelings of dissonance or imbalance.

As in balance theory, there are times when things fit or "go together." This is *consonance*, or, in Latin derivation, "sound at the same time, harmonize, agree." Festinger says that any two beliefs could be shown as two parallel lines (see Figure 3-6). The solid line shows belief A, and the X on the line marks an attitude toward that belief. The broken line represents other information about A. The Y on this line represents our position on the new information, which we might call belief B. The distance between these two points—X and Y—is the amount of *dissonance* we feel when the two beliefs are not congruent. We feel psychic discomfort—the world is not acting as it should. The feeling comes from the dissonant cognitions. The dissonance must be reduced. This is the basis for many actions. Some persons change their beliefs by moving them closer to one another. Others rationalize the problem away; one way is to discredit the source of the cognitions. Others escape from feelings of dissonance by the processes of selective perception, selective retention, or selective expo-

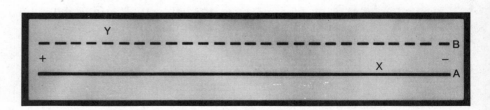

Figure 3-6   *Festinger's Model: Dissonance.*

8.   Leon Festinger, *A Theory of Cognitive Dissonance* (Stanford, Calif.: Stanford University Press, 1962). See also Shel Feldman (ed.), *Cognitive Consistency* (New York: Academic Press, 1966).

sure; in other words, they choose to forget or not to receive/perceive or not to be exposed to the information.

Let's look at a real case. Suppose that you smoke cigarettes—assume, for the sake of argument, a pack or more a day. Now assume that you hear that the odds of lung cancer are seventy times higher for smokers. Under Festinger's theory, you will be uncomfortable because of these two sets of information or beliefs (your smoking habits and the information relating to the danger of these habits). You may try to reduce this discomfort. You might cut down to fifteen cigarettes a day; you might quit; you might ignore the information and switch to some other more comfortable message; or you might rationalize (for example, hope for a cancer cure soon, discredit the source of the message).

Psychological discomfort is caused by inconsistency between our beliefs and information inputs. The tension created must be relieved in some way. Festinger suggested several ways by which people try to relieve the tension:

1. They devalue initial beliefs.

2. They devalue the information by labeling it as biased, unproven, or untrue.

3. They perceive the input as a hatchet job. Researchers call this selective perception—seeing what we want to see.

4. They may try to forget about the new information. This is called selective retention or selective remembering and forgetting. (Parents are good at this one sometimes.)

5. They may rationalize by saying something like "Oh, well, things are like that all over."

In some cases, people may use more than one of these ways at the same time. They may change their attitude about a topic in general while devaluing the information and rationalizing. This combination is familiar among smokers who, after hearing of the dangers of smoking and its links to fatal diseases, devalue the research and rationalize that you have to die of something anyway. At any rate, this experience with dissonance is common, and persuaders often try to create it to get the persuadees to feel psychologically uncomfortable and thus to nudge them to change.

Though Festinger does not deal very deeply in his book with the notion of consonance, it seems clear that most persons seek it. We listen to the candidate of our choice, and more often than not avoid listening to the person we will not vote for. A good deal of research shows that we seek information that fits with our beliefs and we avoid data that conflict with our beliefs. Conservative persons read conservative newspapers; liberal

Figure 3-7   *Snoopy is clearly experiencing dissonance. The world of tennis does not live up to his expectations. He chooses to use the tactic of rationalization to decrease his dissonance. What might the cartoon have looked like had he chosen one of the other tactics? (© 1977 United Feature Syndicate, Inc.)*

persons read liberal publications. Suppose you have a low opinion of Billy Graham. Now suppose you see a film like *Marjoe*, which tells the story of a child evangelist who was coached by his parents to deliver revival sermons at the age of seven. He would respond to cues from his mother like "Praise the Lord," which might have meant that it was time to take up the collection or to ask for the converts to come forward. This input fits with your initial belief, so you experience comfort or consonance. These feelings confirm what you always knew. They are related to the assumption of similitude mentioned earlier—we like to have our view of the world confirmed by other persons and by other information.

With such confirmation there is no need to resolve any inconsistency or any psychic discomfort. This experience is common; we find information confirming our position, and that makes our belief stronger. There are many actions we can take as a result of feelings of consonance:

1. We can revalue our initial beliefs, making them stronger in all likelihood—now we know for sure that at least some revival conversions are faked.

2. We can revalue the source of information input. We may view the story of Marjoe as a typical and highly unbiased documentary.

3. We may perceive the information as stronger than it actually is and focus on the strongest parts of it.

4. We may remember the most negative parts of it and choose to high-light those that best support our belief.

5. We may expose ourselves to more negative data by reading novels like *Elmer Gantry* or newspaper exposes.

6. We may do several of the above at the same time.

The tactic of creating consonance, then, is used to create stronger attitudes, to undergird existing cognitions, and to increase one's source of credibility. Consonance negates the old saying that "flattery gets you nowhere" and turns it around to "flattery gets you everywhere." People enjoy exposure to consonant information—it proves that they are right!

A REVIEW AND CONCLUSION

One kind of premise to which persuaders appeal arises out of psychological processes that occur in all of us. One is the presence of certain need states. There are many ways of labeling need states; but, for the receiver, the set of labels is not so important as is the process of identifying the need states to which persuaders are appealing in their messages. So it does not matter if you realize that a persuader is trying to appeal to your belonging needs or to your reassurance-of-worth need. The important thing is that as a receiver you do not fall blindly for a message that plays on your weakness. The same principle holds true as we examine attitudes. Knowing that a persuader is trying to appeal to attitudes that we hold or values that we have helps to reveal the persuader's purposes. Though not clearly linked to behavioral change, attitudes and opinions are important to mass persuaders, advertisers, and politicians. Whether attitudes affect behavior or not, these persuaders think that they do and build their messages accordingly. The critical persuadee can turn this strategy into a potent tool of reception. By identifying the attitudes that persuaders presume to be foremost in our minds, and by speculating about source attitudes toward the audience, we can discover much of a persuader's purpose. This can aid us in making the choices presented to us by various persuaders. Finally, looking at our states of balance/imbalance or dissonance/consonance can identify our vulnerabilities. Knowing where we are weak can help alert us to persuasive appeals to those weaknesses.

In short, in Chapter 3 you have been offered several more tools for knowing what is happening when you are confronted with persuasion, whether it is the appeal to buy Pepperidge Farm bread because it is like the bread that grandma used to make or the appeal of the "down home" candidate or the appeal of a Moonie recruiter. Training yourself to "listen" for the process premises being appealed to can help you to detect unwise advice. As we look ahead to other kinds of premises to which persuaders appeal, let us carry what we now know about language and psychological premises with us.

Questions for Further Thought

1. What other needs (aside from those listed in Maslow's hierarchy) do humans experience? Which of them could be translated into Maslow's terms? How? Give examples.

2. What is the difference between a *process* premise and a *language* premise? Cite several examples where these have operated in your life recently.

3. If a person favored more lenient marijuana laws and then heard that a favorite politician opposed such a change, would the person experience consonance or dissonance?

4. What about a person who opposed more lenient marijuana laws?

5. Describe a consonant situation and a dissonant situation for person X who has an initial attitude favoring energy conservation.

6. Cite examples of the following methods of reducing dissonance:
    a. Devalue the source of inputs or information causing the dissonance
    b. Selectively expose oneself to nondissonance-producing information
    c. Selectively forget information that causes dissonance
    d. Selectively remember information that reduces dissonance
    e. Change attitudes or beliefs
    f. Selectively perceive the world in order to reduce dissonance

    You may wish to follow a single case through these methods of reducing dissonance (for example, your parents facing a dissonance-producing problem, such as letting their "baby" have an apartment off campus), or you may cite several different examples.

7. Cite examples of the following methods of increasing the feelings of psychological comfort experienced in consonance; follow the directions given for question 6:

   a. Revaluing the source of the consonance-producing source

   b. Selectively exposing oneself to consonance-producing information

   c. Selectively remembering consonance-producing information

   d. Selectively perceiving things that are consonance producing

   e. Changing one's attitudes or beliefs

   f. Selectively forgetting things that do not lend themselves to feelings of consonance

Experiences in Persuasion

1. Select newspaper and magazine advertisements for a certain product or type of product (deodorant, for example). When you have a good selection (ten to twenty), analyze them according to the needs on Maslow's hierarchy to which they appeal. The ads may be doing several things at once and may appeal to more than one level. Discuss this concomitance of appeal. Argue for the effectiveness or ineffectiveness of one of the ads in particular.

2. Write a letter to the editor of your campus paper or your local paper, couching it so that it would appeal to the *security* level of Maslow's hierarchy. Rewrite it so that it appeals to the *belonging* level; the *esteem* level; the *self-actualization* level. Determine which of the four ways would be the best; discuss how and why it might be the best. (If you do this as a group, one person might write the message aimed at *security,* another at *belonging,* and so on; then the group would determine which was most effective.)

3. Trace the history of research concerning dissonance (try speech communication journals such as *Quarterly Journal of Speech* and *Speech Monographs,* as well as journals in other fields such as the *Journal of Abnormal and Social Psychology*) and report to the class on your findings. What do we know about dissonance? Self-persuasion? Belief discrepancy?

4. Do the "letter to the editor" assignment (see number 2), but this time write a letter answering an editorial in the paper. Do it in a way that will cause dissonance for the editorial writer and then in a way to cause consonance. Submit both letters using your own name on one and the name of another person on the other if he is agreeable. What happened? Explain to the class what you did and what were the results.

Content Premises
in Persuasion 4

T **here** is another kind of premise that can be the raw material of persuasion. This type of premise does not rely on personal preference for certain language choices or styles or on the internal or psychological premises we have just discussed. Instead the content premise is one on which there would be a good deal of agreement from persuadee to persuadee and which would not change much from situation to situation. For example, a group of persuadees believes that symptoms usually have causes. When causes are removed, a reduction in the symptoms will follow. In this case, we will bite on cause-to-effect reasoning. Draw a strong link between the cause (say, the over consumption of petroleum fuel in this country) and the symptoms or problems coming out of this cause (for example, high rates of inflation, a poor export/import ratio, national apprehension over the future, and so on). Persuadees need to be alert to persuasive appeals that rely on these premises. We all try not to appear contrary or out-of-step with those around us. This encourages us to accept certain persuasive advice just because everyone else seems to think it is the totally logical thing to do. For instance, take the debate over the controversial anticancer drug Laetrile, which is made from peach or apricot pits. Those who favor the use of the drug argue that since the cancer victims are going to continue with the disease unchecked by use of the available medically approved drugs and therapies, they might as well be allowed to experiment with their own bodies and the drug. Opponents to the drug argue that the problem is that it often deters the ill person from seeking medically accepted drugs or therapy that might slow or even stem the disease. Both positions are trying to use content premises to win the day. The proponents believe that the persuadees will buy a "last-ditch" argument while the opponents hope they will buy an argument that relies

FRANK AND ERNEST   **by Bob Thaves**

Figure 4-1 *Content premises are ones that most people would accept. What about Frank's line of reasoning in this cartoon? Would most people agree that owls are probably dumb, based on it? (Reprinted by permission of NEA.)*

on full and scientific proof being necessary before administering drugs. Who wins the day depends on which content premise is more acceptable.

There are four dimensions of content premise persuading:

1. *The nature of content and proof:* What causes us to believe or not believe a persuader who is appealing to our intellect? Why do we sometimes believe with very little evidence presented and at other times demand much detailed evidence? How much proof is enough?

2. *The nature of evidence and reasoning:* What is evidence? What is reasoning? What are the basic modes of drawing conclusions or of linking information to action?

3. *Strategic and tactical levels of content premises:* What is the difference between the *overall* organization of content-oriented persuasive messages and the *internal* steps used to get agreement with this overall thrust of the message? Are there easy ways to describe and analyze both levels?

4. *Proving a point:* Does *self-persuasion* operate in all persuasion? If so, how? Is one kind of *evidence* better than another for the purposes of proof? Is one kind of *proof* better than another? Why do some methods seem more successful than others? Why is emotional or empathic evidence so persuasive?

With these questions and others in mind let's look at persuasion as it occurs around us—on TV, in the newspaper, in the classroom, on campus, and in our homes. We know that we are persuaded many times each day and that we need to be persuaded in order to make choices in this confusing and complex world. But *how* are we persuaded?

WHAT IS CONTENT?

Suppose that you are confronted by a Campus Crusade evangelist on campus. He wants you to join the group and hopes to get a new convert. He tells you that you must go to the informational meeting in the student center lounge at 7 P.M. tonight. You have three options: you can do as he asks; you can reject him out of hand; or you can ask for good reasons for going to the meeting. The first two options are likely to be prompted by some kind of emotional response you have to the speaker and the topic. You might hate "holier than thou" evangelists and thus reject the persuasion. You might be a true believer already and so will warmly follow the advice. The last option, however, is the one that seeks further information. If you said, "Give me three good reasons," you would be asking for proof in the form of content premises—arguments or statements that would be convincing to most reasonable persons. The crusader could say, "Well, because you are attending the philosophy of religion class with me. This is a good way to add to your knowledge about that subject. You may even get information useful in writing that term paper we have to do." This would be a good enough reason for many people to give the informational meeting a try. You might be a little more demanding and say to the persuader, "That's one good reason, two more to go." If the evangelist hoped to persuade you, he or she would have to come up with more information that would be reasonably acceptable.

So the value of the content premise for persuaders is not in its ability to prompt an emotional or psychological response but rather to elicit a logical or rational response. This response relies on the nature of the evidence presented in the argument and on the logic by which the evidence fits with the "widely accepted" content premise held to be reasonable or true by receivers.

WHAT IS PROOF?

It is clear that adequate proof varies from situation to situation and among receivers as well. Further, there are numerous forms of proof or evidence. Aristotle identified at least three general classes of proof. *Ethos* was taken to be a persuader's reputation or image, which could be improved or impaired by things done while speaking. In other words, knowing that Walter Cronkite is widely respected as a news commentator will be a kind of proof when he speaks at a convention of the National Association of Broadcasters. If he is articulate and stimulating in his address, his ethos will improve, hence making him even better proof. A second kind of proof discussed by Aristotle was called *pathos* or appeals to the passions or will. We can think of this kind of proof as being related to emotions. We hear of the horrors of one person's experience with being raped and our emotions may cause us to be persuaded to support a death penalty for rapists. One might think of pathos as a kind of psychological proof in which experience is often a primary component. Finally Aristotle dealt with *logos*, a kind of proof that relies on intellect and reason.

According to Aristotle, there are several ways to talk about logical persuasion, the foremost being syllogisms. A classic syllogism is usually expressed in three steps: a *major premise*, a *minor premise*, and a *conclusion*. For example: All men are mortal (major premise); Socrates is a man (minor premise); hence Socrates is mortal (conclusion). Since the time of Aristotle, the task of the persuader using logical persuasion has been to identify major premises that would be generally acceptable and then to offer minor premises *substantiated by evidence* that would lead to conclusions that would imply action or belief changes. That is also the focus throughout this book—to identify the stylistic, process, and content premises that are generally held by audiences and to which persuaders often appeal.

Most contemporary theorists agree that *proof is comprised of two things: reasoning and evidence.* In the proper mix, these two will lead persuadees to adopt the changes advocated by the persuader. Sometimes more evidence is needed. Sometimes very little reasoning is involved. For instance, in the musical comedy *The Music Man*, Professor Harold Hill sells an entire town on a need for a boys' band complete with uniforms (which he, by chance, happens to sell) on the flimsiest of logical appeals. He points out numerous symptoms of trouble in the town (kids are smoking, reading dirty books, cursing, dressing outrageously, and so on). He then concludes with these words,"That's trouble and that starts with T and that rhymes with P and that stands for 'pool.'" He goes on to point out that with a band to be busy with, the boys will make no more visits to the pool hall where the bad habits are all learned. In this example, an overkill of evidence enables the persuader to short-circuit the reasoning process. His "proof" relies on a rhyme scheme—P rhymes with T, therefore pool means trouble. Usually the "mix" between evidence and reasoning is not so extreme as in Harold Hill's case. More often there is an evidence threshold that might be met, given consistency in reasoning. Let us look closer at these two components of proof.

EVIDENCE AND REASONING

There are several ways to look at evidence and reasoning. The way in which information is linked (that is, reasoned out) is the strategic element in discourse using content premises; and the information that is combined and the choice of it (that is, evidence) are the tactical elements in content premise persuasion. We are interested in *strategic* effect. By examining what the persuader does—how he operates—we can infer motives and discover what he is ultimately up to. For example, suppose I wished to persuade you that smoking causes lung cancer. The thrust of my message—the strategy of it, so to speak—is to create a cause-effect argument. I want to prove to you that a given effect—lung cancer—has a given cause—cigarette smoking. Along the way I might engage in a variety of *tactics* (for example, I might show slides of infested body cells; I might give vivid testimony of the pain and suffering involved in cancer deaths; I might offer statistical correlations; or I might do a variety of other things), but they are all related to my general strategy, belief, motive, or intention. These tactics are the "stuff" from which proof will ultimately emerge for you as persuadee; somewhere along the line, I will reach the threshold for you and will have "proved" to you that you must stop smoking. In other situations, other elements will persuade you to stop— the key may not even be planned by a persuader but can still be the threshold for change.

By looking at the traditional rule-governed ideas about evidence and reasoning as the *strategic* level of persuasion, we are able to consider various kinds of "proof," ranging from direct experience to emotional description to intellectual consideration of data and statistics—all under the label *tactics* or *evidence*. When coupled with the notion of a threshold for persuasion, the set of terms suggested here for analysis offers the persuadee a maximum amount of flexibility in examining not only what kinds of content premises persuaders utilize in the persuasive attempts but also the ways in which they present these. The rationale behind these moves can indicate motive or intent and can again provide the persuadee with a powerful tool for critically examining and reviewing persuasive information before making a decision.

TYPES OF EVIDENCE

Earlier, brief reference was made to the varying strengths of bits of evidence: In some situations, statistics are strong; in others, pictorial evidence is most powerful; and in yet others, experience is the best evidence. In all these instances, persuasion relies on an assumption that one can learn and act on the basis of information gained indirectly and vicariously.[1] Even

---

1. A good discussion of this premise (that we learn much of our knowledge vicariously) is presented in Mark Abrahamson's *Interpersonal Accommodation* (New York: Van Nostrand-Reinhold Co., 1966).

experiential evidence relies on the assumption that the same experience need be enacted only once to have persuasive potency. For example, the jury of men and women who listened to the trial of Adolf Eichmann, the architect of Hitler's mass extermination of Jews, heard Eichmann say that he had never committed murder but that he had "exterminated" and "relocated" Jews. Having heard this pronouncement once, the jury did not need to repeat that experience to realize that *renaming* an activity changed it in the Nazi mind. From that point on, words from Eichmann's mouth became much more important and double-edged than before. When he talked about words like "solution," "experiment," or "protection camp," they knew that the words did not mean what they might normally mean.[2]

Given this assumption of vicarious learning, the problem for the persuader is to determine how best to get the audience to change or to "learn" new activities, and it is here that the nature of evidence becomes important. What kind of evidence is most effective and efficient in retraining persuadees? How much evidence is enough? How much is too much? How should the evidence be presented? All these questions face the persuaders as they prepare messages. Generally, evidence falls into two categories: the emotionally laden, which appeals dramatistically to the imagination and emotions of the persuadee, and the rule-governed, which appeals to the intellect. Let us look at these types more carefully. They are related to two of the ancient categories—pathos and logos—now viewed as parts of content premises.

Dramatistically Oriented Evidence

Imagine the following situation in your class: a student stands and announces that he is going to give a speech on abortion. As an introduction to this speech, he turns on a cassette tape recorder, and you begin to hear an interview with a young girl who is dying in a hospital as a result of an illegal abortion. The testimony is being taken by a hardened policeman, and the young girl is weakly gasping for breath. Her voice rattles in her throat as she recounts the abortion scene, the amount of money paid, the instruments used, and so forth. She is clearly in pain, as indicated by her voice, and she is also obviously frightened and in need of comfort. As the details unfold, you feel yourself becoming sick to your stomach. When recorded this way, the bare facts are almost unbearable. The persuader is

---

2. Hannah Arendt, *Eichmann in Jerusalem: A Report on the Banality of Evil* (New York: Viking Press, 1964). See especially p. 22, where Eichmann is quoted as saying " . . . I never killed a Jew or a non-Jew, for that matter I never killed any human being"; and p. 84, where Arendt cites some of the "code names" for extermination, such as "evacuation," "special treatment," and "resettlement," and discusses the "language rules" of the Third Reich.

utilizing what most persons would call "emotionally laden" proof—some call it psychologically oriented. Clearly aimed at deep-set fears and dislikes, its purpose is to cause revulsion in the listeners—and to persuade them that illegal abortions are horrible. Although the evidence is emotionally oriented, it is certainly not "illogical" to conclude, as a result of it, that illegal abortions are not desirable; in fact, it is *totally* logical to draw such a conclusion. Instead of labeling this evidence and reasoning as "irrational," "nonrational," "illogical," or "nonlogical," we call it *dramatistically oriented* evidence.

The point is that emotional responses to problems are often as logical as intellectual responses. One does not need to sift systematically through mounds of statistics on abortion. The conclusion is not based on intellectual ability but on human emotional response. This reality has been one of the points made by critics of today's American culture—that we do not respond emotionally often enough, that we rely too often on "intellectualized responses" to problems, thus neglecting human situations and feelings in favor of hard cold facts. Perhaps a single example of illegal abortion *is* enough evidence to convince any *reasonable* person that legalization of abortion is needed to prevent human suffering. If the evidence is dramatic or emotional enough, persuadees will not ask for more; they will not engage in philosophical discussions about first premises relating to the sanctity of human life. Instead, by vicariously suffering with the victim of the illegal abortion, the persuadees become convinced.

Perhaps it is that word "dramatic" that really is important here. Dramatistically oriented evidence invites and encourages vicarious experience on the part of persuadees in an attempt to persuade them to a certain course of action.[3] Such persuasion relies upon the persuadees' ability to project themselves into a context or situation described by the persuader—to "feel" what others feel, to live the problem vicariously.

If we were to look at historic persuasive speeches or at highly successful speeches of the present, we would undoubtedly find a great deal of emotionally oriented and dramatic evidence. The persuader presents a dramatic situation to the audience and then "invites" the listeners to participate in the drama—in their imaginations, to become actors themselves. There is no intellectualizing here; at the same time, one would be hard put to say that the audiences reacted "illogically" or "irrationally."

---

3.   Several good discussions of the importance of the dramatic structure can be found in literature from various fields. For example, see Kenneth Burke, from the perspective of literary criticism, on the power of the dramatic to cause *A Grammar of Motives* (Berkeley: University of California Press, 1970); Robert F. Bales, *Personality and Interpersonal Behavior* (New York: Holt, Rinehart and Winston, 1970)—see especially Chapter 7, "Describing Fantasy Themes," pp. 136–155; Ernest G. Bormann, "Fantasy and Rhetorical Vision: The Rhetorical Criticism of Social Reality," *Quarterly Journal of Speech*, Vol. 58 (December 1972), pp. 396–407.

They merely responded to dramatic evidence. This type of evidence encourages the persuadee to co-create proof with the persuader. The result is powerful perusasion, which is probably long lasting.[4]

Intellectual or Rational Evidence

One might use dramatic evidence to persuade listeners to conserve fuel (for example, describe a cold, desolate North America with most of its population dead from exposure and those who are left huddled together in our southernmost states without electricity, conveniences, and so on). With topics like this, however, we are more likely to hear evidence that appeals to our intellect and not to our emotional needs. Most appeals urging conservation point out that we can save money by insulating, for example, or by avoiding jack-rabbit starts and speeding. The persuaders assume that there is in us a major premise, which is that it is good to avoid waste and hence to save money. By giving us a minor premise—that insulating or slow driving saves money—and by backing it up with numerous examples the persuaders create a kind of syllogism:

Major premise—saving dollars is good.

Minor premise—conserving fuel saves dollars.

Conclusion—hence conservation is good.

This appeal is based on data that we can verify and not on imagining some distant setting or time. In this sense, intellectually oriented evidence relies on the ability of persons to generalize. The persuader using this tactic asks them to draw conclusions from the evidence. Dramatistically oriented evidence, on the other hand, relies on the ability of persons to use their creative imagination and empathy; this ability is usually related to specific situations. To say that one is more or less logical than the other clouds the issue. It may be totally logical to respond to highly dramatic material or events. It may be totally illogical to stick to only advice that is intellectually oriented. Both methods work, but at different times and in different ways with different sets of persons. They both rely on the persuadee's matching data with beliefs or laws of reason which he holds to be true.

---

4. Good examples of the use of dramatistic invitations can be found in a number of speeches in recent times as well as in the history of public speaking. Some examples are Clarence Darrow's defense of joy killers Richard Loeb and Nathan Leopold, which "invites" the judge to join in the high drama of humanitarian change; John F. Kennedy's Inaugural Address, which invites the listeners to do something for their country; and others.

Figure 4-2 *Bermuda. The evidence presented here is very dramatistic—it invites you to visualize yourself in Bermuda. Following the persuader's advice may be totally logical even though the evidence doesn't demand that the persuadee generalize, categorize, or sift evidence. (Courtesy Bermuda Department of Tourism.)*

TYPES OF REASONING

In our discussion of evidence types, we have touched on reasoning to some degree. Whenever we begin to talk about "reason" or "rational" processes, we inevitably talk about the kinds of ways in which people *link* the conclusions they make to the evidence given and to other conclusions or courses of advised action. Consider this example:

Suppose I come up to you on the street and say that it would be worth your while to prepare to meet your Maker since the world was about to end and that I would therefore suggest that you sell all you have, give it away, and go to a church and pray. If you don't dismiss me out of hand as another religious fanatic, you might ask me why I thought the world was about to end and perhaps even why giving away possessions made any sense in the face of impending doom. What you would be doing would be asking me for evidence to support my request or advice.

Now suppose I answer, "Why, the world will end because I dreamt that it would, and I also had a car accident on the way to school today and an upset stomach when I got up." If you were patient with me, you still might not totally dismiss me as a lunatic, and you might ask what those three things possibly had to do with the end of the world. What you would be asking for is the *relationship* or *linkage* between my proof and my conclusions. How in the world does a car accident or an upset stomach have anything to do with doomsday? A dream about the end of the world is at least related to the claim that tomorrow is the end of time, but accidents and gastrointestinal problems seem at best to be totally unrelated to my request.

Until I can demonstrate the relationship to you adequately, you would not, in all probability, sell off your belongings or go to church to pray. In other words, until some *reasoning* could be demonstrated, persuasion would not occur. You would have been an astute and aware persuadee in choosing not to follow unsupported or undemonstrated advice. In this case, the choice *not to follow* advice would be easy; at other times it is more complex and less clear.

Let us look at the ways in which linkages or reasons for following advice work. First, we need to examine the problem of consistency between evidence and conclusions; then, we need to see the ways linkages can be formed; and, finally, we need to study the basic factors in rational linkages. In a sense, we need to look at the raw material of reasoned persuasion (consistency between evidence and conclusions), at the method of reasoned persuasion (the ways in which linkages are crafted), and at the end product—the linkage itself.

Consistency between Evidence and Conclusions

Let us return for a moment to the argument concerning the end of the world—on the surface of the argument or advice to sell all your belongings and prepare to meet the end, there seems to be little consistency between the evidence offered (dream fantasy, bad driving luck, and stomach problems). Even so, there is a sort of "evidence hierarchy" at work. Clearly, the dream is the most powerful bit of evidence offered; the bad omen associated with the car accident is probably the next most powerful piece of evidence; and the upset stomach is probably the weakest evidence for the advice being given.

Interestingly though, even with this clearly foolish and ridiculous argument, there is a shred of consistency between at least two of the pieces of evidence and the action requested. If one were mystical, he could see a reason to pray in the face of disaster on the basis of the dream fantasy about the end of the world. Even if he were not particularly mystical, he might be partially persuaded by this piece of evidence if we could demonstrate that I have a good track record on dreams—that I am psychic. The persuadee in this argument might be even more persuaded if it were also demonstrated that every time the psychic dream was followed by a bad omen and an upset stomach, the dream came true. In other words, as the consistency between evidence and conclusion increases, receivers begin to label the argument as more and more "logical," "reasonable," or "rational." It has currency and can be cashed—we "buy" what the persuader is saying.

Rational Linkages

Having looked at what evidence and reasoning are, at the types of evidence one can use, and at the nature of rational or reasoned discourse, we find the next most logical question to be "What are the ways in which one can link evidence to conclusions?" Stated in another way: "How do persuaders try to get compliance with their advice vis-à-vis reasoned argument?" The ancient rhetoricians talked about the *topoi* of argument, or "topics" that could be argued or seats of arguments. What they were looking at were the kinds of linkages a persuader might employ in a persuasive attempt.[5] Behavioral scientists have investigated the same kind of issue from different perspectives by looking at such things as

---

5.   Aristotle, *The Rhetoric*, trans. by Lane Cooper (New York: Appleton-Century-Crofts, 1932), pp. xxiv, xliii, and 159–176.

primacy versus recency[6] or the presence of emotional arguments as opposed to rational arguments.[7] Though we shall investigate both of these perspectives in more detail later, it should be noted that the findings or theories of both groups of communication scholars deal with what we have been talking about—"What makes some pieces of persuasion work while others don't?" or "Where do persuaders find the stuff of persuasion?"

There are probably only three types of linkages: (1) *cause-and-effect* linkages, (2) *correlational* linkages, and (3) *congruency* linkages. As we examine each of these types, keep them in mind for later discussion since, on both the strategic level of reasoned persuasive communication and on the tactical level, these three categories can serve to link evidence to conclusions.

Cause-and-effect linkages   Cause-and-effect linkages rely on a temporal relationship between two things—a time frame is important in relating cause to effect or vice versa. For example, we might take the advertisement shown in Figure 4-3, which seems to appeal to our belief in the cause-to-effect linkage. The persuaders are trying to sell their product—fiberglass insulation for homes. The ad makes a cause-and-effect claim—in fact two claims that interrelate. First, the advertiser claims that a cause (your bringing a copy of the ad to your home building contractor) will have a certain effect: He will follow some of the energy-saving tips included in the ad. This effect then becomes the cause for another set of effects—the savings of from $1,000 to $5,000 over the length of a mortgage. Notice the time span necessary to make the argument. You must bring the ad to the builder *before* he finishes the house in order to give him ample warning to order and install the energy-saving windows, insulation, and ventilators; and they must be installed *before* the savings can occur.

There is a danger, however, in reversing the logic and concluding from a set of effects to a cause. This error is called the *post hoc ergo propter hoc* fallacy—"after this, therefore because of this." For example, one might conclude that, since the introduction of the oral contraceptive

---

6.   The most complete discussion of the primacy-recency issue available under a single cover is *The Order of Presentation in Persuasion*, ed. Carl I. Hovland (New Haven, Conn.: Yale University Press, 1957). See also Ralph L. Rosnow, "Whatever Happened to the 'Law of Primacy'?" *Journal of Communication*, Vol. 16 (March 1966), pp. 10–31.

7.   See for example, the discussion included in Gary Cronkhite's *Persuasion: Speech and Behavioral Change* (New York: Bobbs-Merrill Publishing Co., 1969), pp. 40–43; Edward Z. Rowell, "The Conviction-Persuasion Duality," *Quarterly Journal of Speech*, Vol. 20 (November 1934), pp. 469–482; Gary Cronkhite, "The Relation of Scholastic Aptitude to Logical Argument and Emotional Appeal," Master's thesis, Illinois State University, 1961; and Gary Cronkhite, "Logic, Emotion, and the Paradigm of Persuasion," *Quarterly Journal of Speech*, Vol. 50 (February 1964), pp. 13–18.

1. Blankets of Fiberglas‡ insulation, with reassuring NAHB Research Foundation label. (Not all insulations have the label; it shows you're getting every cent of insulating power you pay for.) Insulation installed to recommendations on map, below.
2. Double-glazed windows, or equivalent.†
3. Storm door and standard door used in combination, or an insulated door properly weather-stripped.
4. Use of vapor barriers (1.0 perm or less) in walls, ceilings, floors, and crawl spaces.
5. Perimeter insulation (slab-on-grade).

6. Adequate ventilation of air and moisture.
7. Windows weather-stripped.
8. Caulking, sealing of doors, chimneys, etc.
9. Certain air-handling ducts insulated.
10. Correctly sized heating/cooling plant.

Show this ad to your builder.
It could save you thousands on future
heating and cooling costs.

Minimum insulation recommendations for ceilings/walls/floors.

Announcing the energy-efficient home

Here it is—an answer to one of the biggest problems of our times.

That house above is no particular *style*. It can be a ranch, contemporary, or any other design you might want.

But it's a complete *system* for saving energy—and fuel bills.

The thermal experts at America's leading manufacturer of insulation, Owens-Corning Fiberglas, have developed it, based on experiments of the last decade.

Right now, such energy-efficient homes are being tested *and metered* to determine the exact size of savings you can expect. All indications are that homes built to Owens-Corning's 10-point specs could save you from $1,000 to as much as $5,000* over the life of your mortgage, depending on where and how you live.

And construction costs can be comparable to those of conventional housing!

Take the first step toward an economical, energy-efficient home now. Show this advertisement to your builder.

‡Reg. T.M. O.-C.F.
†In certain geographic areas.
* Savings based on 6" (R-19) insulation added to a 1,000-sq.-ft. uninsulated attic; 7% yearly rate increase for gas heat, electric cooling.
©Copyright 1977 O.-C.F.

Owens-Corning is Fiberglas

Figure 4-3 *Cause and Effect Linkages in Home Insulation Advertisement. (Courtesy Owens-Corning Fiberglas, © 1977.)*

preceded the advent of sexual freedom and gay rights, it caused these two developments. Perhaps other causes were responsible for the effects, including the disenchantment with traditional values that developed during the war in Vietnam. So while a carefully observed cause-and-effect linkage can be persuasive, there is danger in trusting in its obverse unless all possible intervening causes have been ruled out.

Correlational linkages   Correlational linkages do not rely on time sequences or the "before-after" mode of connecting ideas; instead, they deal with *association*. For instance, suppose I were to try to persuade you to purchase a small economy car. I would probably tell you how much less pollution is emitted by the small car engine, and I might point out to you the economy of repairs and the decreased likelihood of getting into an accident because of increased maneuverability. In all of these arguments, I try to *correlate* two things: owning a small economy car and certain advantages (savings, safety, ecological values, and the like). In other words, I say that the two phenomena are associated with one another—that they occur together—that they are "symptoms" of one another. Although this example is fairly simple and straightforward, most correlational linkages are not nearly that simple and clean. They usually are more complex and difficult to analyze.

For example, we sometimes hear people talk about inflation. Since inflation and pay raises seem to occur together or seem to be correlated, then they must be symptoms of one another. As a result, inflation and recession logically cannot occur together. Yet that is precisely what happened in the period starting in 1974. The inflation was due at least in part to skyrocketing fuel costs for imported oil. The recession was related to our inability to sell our products overseas to a world also trapped by high costs for energy. Americans could not make their dollars stretch to buy new products when gasoline for their cars was doubling in price along with any other products that relied on oil. Believing that inflation and recession occur or do not occur together also has its traps, again in the form of the intervening cause.

Congruency or analogical linkages   Congruency or analogical linkages are not concerned with a time scheme (before-after) or with an associational model (characteristic A is associated with or symptomatic of characteristic B); instead, they rely on a model that shows the extent and limit of *similarities and differences* between two phenomena. In a sense, this method of linking conclusions and evidence is like what we have traditionally thought of as the analogy. In the analogy, two different objects, phenomena, or ideas are compared with one another in an attempt to persuade the audience that what is characteristic of the one is also characteristic of the other (for example, government is like a spider web—dangerous, delicate, and complex). Several theorists have argued that this form of proof is not very effective and that it is vulnerable[8] while others argue that it is at the root of human thought and human symbolic activity and is therefore the strongest method of linking proof to conclusions. This method of linking evidence and advice is typified by this hypothetical argument:

> *The problems with getting along at school this year are like the problems of getting along there last year—dorm costs are rising; the price of food is skyrocketing if you cook for yourself; books are incredible; and there seems to be an ever-shrinking job market.*

Notice that several pieces of evidence are offered for the conclusion or premise that last year resembles this year (for example, price trends). The assumption underlying the argument is that since a number of the limits or characteristics of one are also characteristic of the other, then the two instances are similar in other ways and can be understood in reference to one another. In a classic case of analogy, A is an analog for B and is therefore predictive of B. Some argue that this form of linkage is vulnerable, because there are other characteristics that may be different. For instance, in the preceding example, it is possible that this year there are more scholarships or better summer job opportunities.

In any case, the congruency argument differs from both the correlational and the causal linkages in that it is not dependent upon association or time but rather operates on a *spatial* kind of level. That is, the argument depends on the degree to which one incident or case is *congruent* with another, or the degree to which a boundary of one matches up with a similar boundary of the other. In all likelihood, this is the way we learn—by matching situations and attempting to predict. Persuadees ought to ask themselves whether congruency linkages reflect all possible factors and whether the situations being compared have fully congruent parameters.

CONTENT PREMISES: THE STRATEGIC LEVEL

Having considered the theoretical nature of proof, evidence, and reasoning, we now face the task of seeing how these operate in practice. We will do that by looking at content premises on two levels: (1) the overall

---

8. The belief in syllogistic reasoning as the appropriate format and the belief that analogy is a weak form of argument can be repeatedly seen in Elton Abernathy, *The Advocate: A Manual of Persuasion* (New York: David McKay Co., 1964), pp. 48, 49, 64, 86, 112; Glen E. Mills, *Reason in Con-*

thematic level, or *strategic level,* and (2) the more particular and specific, concrete level, or *tactical level.* In so doing, we must continually take the notions offered here and compare them with the persuasion presented to us every day. We ought to look for the strategic moves made by persuaders in editorials in the campus newspaper, in advertisements on TV, or by politicians trying to capture our support.

Again, we assume that the way a man uses symbols is indicative of his world view, his likely intentions, and his probable actions. This assumption applies not only to language use (see Chapter 2) and to how those language choices are organized and put together—but also to our interest here. One way to look at the strategic level of content premises is through the use of the syllogism as an organizational device, which is discussed in this section. Another way is through the system for argument analysis proposed by Stephen Toulmin, which will be discussed in the next section.

Types of Syllogisms

To begin with, there are three major syllogistic formats: (1) the *conditional* (if A, then B), (2) the *disjunctive* (either A or B), and (3) the *categorical* (since A is a member of category X and B is a part of A, then B is also part of X). Each of these formats have a number of varieties or hybrids and can appear and operate in several forms. At the root of these hybrids, however, a basic form predominates and forms the skeletal and strategic structure of argument.

Conditional syllogism   The conditional syllogism has as its basic form "If A is true, then B is also true." This is the *major premise* of the syllogism, and it makes a statement about a relationship assumed to exist in the world (for example, "if you add water to Kool-Aid, you will get a refreshing cool drink"). Now we might argue about the truth of these relational statements, but we assume that if proven "true" they will accurately describe a situation in the world. The next stage or step in the conditional strategy is to present data that relate to or make a statement about some part of the major premise—or, tactically speaking, to present evidence. The following sentence is an example of a *minor premise:* "A is known to be true by all world experts." When put together with the relational major premise, a *conclusion* (in this case, that B is also true) can

troversy, 2d ed. (Boston: Allyn and Bacon, 1968), pp. 173–184, 194; Wayne C. Minnick, *The Art of Persuasion,* 2d ed. (Boston: Houghton Mifflin Co., 1968), pp. 136–140; and Henry Lee Ewbank and J. Jeffery Auer, *Discussion and Debate: Tools of a Democracy* (New York: F. S. Crofts, Co., 1946), p. 164.

be drawn. In the example cited, you could pour water into Kool-Aid powder or state that you had done so. Given these pieces of "truth," the persuadee and the persuader together draw the conclusion that a cool, refreshing drink is at hand.

In both of these cases, by affirming or stating the truth of the "if" part of the major premise (sometimes called the "antecedent"), we can then also affirm the "then" part of the statement (sometimes called the "consequent"). One of the combination rules for the conditional syllogism is the "affirm antecedent–affirm consequent" form. Another form is the "deny consequent–deny antecedent" variation (for example, there is no refreshing drink around, so obviously no one poured water into Kool-Aid powder). These are the only two "valid" combinations that can be made with the conditional form.

Remember, however, that many persuaders successfully use *invalid* combinations to achieve their goals. For example, one invalid form is affirming the consequent and thereby affirming the antecedent (that is, because B is true, then A must also be true—there is a refreshing drink available; therefore, someone must have added water to Kool-Aid powder). This form is invalid because a third and unseen factor may have caused the observed effect (for example, someone could have poured water into lemon concentrate). Yet advertisers often use this form as a strategy and argue that because one feels better the morning after eating cold tablets, then those tablets cured him. It is possible that the sleep, the hot toddy, or the shot given by the doctor had something to do with the cure. Likewise, with the other possible variation on the conditional syllogism—deny the antecedent and deny the consequent. The flaw here is like the flaw in the other invalid line of proof—there may very well be an interceding and outside third factor or combination of factors that may cause the consequent, since we have no rational reason to consider the antecedent as the one and only cause of the consequent. Nonetheless, this invalid form is often used by persuaders. But "truth" enters in.

For example, Hanes stockings for women are frequently sold through an if-then conditional syllogism. The pitch is that if you buy Hanes, then gentlemen will prefer you. It relies on a major premise stated by the persuader—gentlemen prefer Hanes—reinforced by a minor premise in the form of the visual that is usually placed with the slogan/major premise. This visual is an unusually attractive woman who is the center of male attention even though other attractive women are also on the scene. Our prize woman is wearing Hanes stockings so . . . . Of course, the advertiser hopes that you women will visualize yourselves as attractive and hence as sought after as the model in the ad. The problem here is not with the logic that is used or with the *validity* of the claim-linking system. The problem rather lies with the *truth* of the claim that gentlemen do prefer Hanes. So while a conditional syllogism may be perfectly valid in a logical sense, it may be largely untruthful. This is the trap that the persuadee needs to be alert to. Persuaders may use a logically valid syllogism to camouflage untrue premises. The persuadee who finds this strategy employed ought to search for other explanations and, in fact, will find that he is better able to engage in counterargument if he does look at syllogistic strategies in this way—searching for validity and truth and answering in accord with what he finds. The conditional syllogism is, as you have probably noticed, similar to the cause-and-effect linkage described earlier.

Disjunctive syllogism   The disjunctive syllogism has as its basic form "Either A is true or B is true." This sentence is the major premise of a disjunctive syllogism and is usually accompanied by some set of proof or evidence that suggests the probable presence of A or B, or the probable absence of A or B. The conclusion is then drawn on the basis of these probabilities.

A good example of the disjunctive or either-or syllogism at work in the world is the style of many of the "born-again" evangelists. They argue that "*either* you get converted in the same way as I did by coming up in front of the crowd and declaring your faith, *or* you can never be a true Christian—you must be born again." Of course the follow-up is that you will burn in hell if you are not converted. Taking this position is likely to lead to a number of problems. For example, not long ago on our campus a traveling evangelist made such a speech from the steps of the student union amid the jeers and heckling of about a hundred students. A girl jumped up and shouted at the preacher, "You are talking of the god of the New Testament—that was written by men. The god of the Old Testament never mentioned hell. My god is a god of love and my Bible was written by God not man." The speaker was confused and asked the girl what religion she was. He was baffled when she answered that she was Jewish. His either-or syllogism did not allow for a belief system that did not include a concept of hell and punishment. He would have had an equally tough time had someone jumped up and said, "The Bible says that you aren't supposed to let your right hand know what your left hand is doing. So aren't you being like the Pharisees who were braggarts about their faith and deserved condemnation?" Here the either-or syllogism would be unable to deal with a third alternative to "*either* declare faith openly *or* face damnation"; this alternative would be to declare faith privately.

So the problem with the either-or syllogism is that few things in the world are as clear-cut as that. Even in such a concrete area as life or death there is no easy answer to the "*either* you are alive *or* you are dead" riddle. Strict either-or logic cannot take other belief systems or three, four, or even more alternatives in a situation. The persuadee needs to examine persuasion framed in the either-or mode. The task ought to be to search for other alternatives or differing belief systems under which the disjunctive model would not work.

Categorical syllogism The categorical syllogism is a *spatial* kind of reasoning. The persuader considers the world as divided into separate spaces or sets and subsets, to use modern math terms. That is, every phenomenon is either a part of a larger kind or class of phenomena or the genus of some smaller set of species of phenomena. Thus, the major and minor premises in this form can be expressed in the sentence "All of A is included in category B." For example, a letter to the editor of *Playboy* magazine addressed itself to the debate about abortion. The writer stated: "I keep hearing about right-to-life groups. I presume these are the people working to abolish the death penalty."[9] The letter was a facetious jibe at the groups working to prevent legalization of abortion—groups like SOUL (Save Our Unwanted Lives), the Catholic Church, and others. These groups, at least in the letter writer's mind, were also likely to favor the conservative position of retaining capital punishment while promoting the equally conservative position of outlawing abortion. To the letter writer, there was an inconsistency in the two positions, best expressed in categorical terms: (1) Persons who want to retain capital punishment are not in the category of people who want to preserve human life; (2) persons who want to outlaw abortion are in the category of persons who want to preserve life; (3) therefore, persons who disavow abortion must also disavow capital punishment.

This kind of argument smacks of "guilt by association" or "you must be bad because you keep bad company." This kind of reasoning is often used in public persuasion dealing with political issues (for example, "since you look like a hippie, you must be a Commie because hippies tend to be Commies") as well as persuasion dealing with more mundane issues (for example, "join the Pepsi generation—and you will be going strong since members of the Pepsi generation all go strong"). Lewis Carroll used it even more cleverly in his descriptions of Alice in Wonderland—the pigeon tells Alice that she must be some kind of snake since she eats eggs and that is just what snakes do too.[10] All of these examples have the same characteristic flaw—because one possesses *some* characteristics of a group does not mean that he possesses *all* characteristics of the group.

Persuaders use and persuadees respond to the invalid "guilt by association" form of this strategy. The responsible persuadee must ask himself, when he finds the categorical syllogism operating as a skeletal structure in an argument, whether the categories are accurately represented. He must seek to discover whether the membership in one category necessarily implies full membership in another. (Because one is a member of the category of persons with long hair and beard, does this necessarily

---

9. *Playboy*, June 1972, p. 68.

10. Lewis Carroll, *Alice in Wonderland* (New York: Lancer Books, 1968), p. 58.

imply membership in the category of "left-wing Communist sympathizer"?) In this way, the categorical syllogism is like the congruency linkage described earlier.

Truth and Validity

As we can see from our brief investigation into syllogistic reasoning, there are some knotty problems here. First, true (empirically verifiable) statements can be linked logically or validly, but the same true statements can mislead the persuadee when they are joined in illogical or invalid ways. At the same time, untrue (empirically unverifiable) statements can be linked in logical and valid ways or in illogical and invalid ways. Furthermore, we seldom encounter clear-cut syllogisms in our everyday lives. Few persuaders, be they politicians, advertisers, peers, subordinates, or superiors, run around saying "If A then B" or "Either A is true or B is true but not both and at least one" or "All A's are B's and all C's are A's; therefore all C's are also B's." Instead, we find that persuaders arrange more extended pieces of persuasion, such as entire speeches or campaigns or complete advertisements, into syllogistic patterns. A classic example is the standard toothpaste, mouthwash, or deodorant advertisement saying that a person has bad luck on a date because he or she has forgotten to get shiny teeth, sweet breath, or dry underarms. We watch the product being used then immediately we see a church wedding scene. The syllogism is an "if-then" conditional one. (*If* you use Toothbrite toothpaste, *then* you will have a lover's mouth and get your desired love object. He brushed with Toothbrite. Conclusion?) Perhaps the best each persuadee can do is to outline, formally or informally, the general point of the persuasion and then to search for the relationships the persuader is attempting to "sell." Having discovered these, the persuadee can look for the traces of syllogistic reasoning in the arguments and relationships.

CONTENT PREMISES: THE TACTICAL LEVEL

As already noted, we seldom hear syllogisms formally stated and used by persuaders. Instead, they underlie larger pieces of persuasion. What do we typically hear in real-life situations? Typically, we hear statements of one of these categories or types:

1. Those that advise action or state conclusions

2. Those that present bits of evidence to support conclusions or courses of action

3. Those that explain why the evidence is related to courses of action or conclusions (The "linkages" described earlier are good examples.)

These three kinds of statements make up what we hear on the *tactical level* of persuasion—they are the stuff of which persuasion is made. A British philosopher and logician, Stephen Toulmin, has identified and labeled these three elements as the *data*, the *warrant*, and the *claim*. The assumption is that persuaders present data or evidence, which is linked by warrants or reasons, to claims or conclusions. The sample argument, as diagrammed in Figure 4-4, uses the Toulmin system.[11]

Your first response may be something like "Hey, that's not the whole story; there are other reasons for a bad job market—inflation, slowed government spending, and so on." On the tactical level, you do not have to search for underlying strategies. You are readily confronted with the real, immediate, and concrete elements of persuasion. You respond almost instinctively to them and have a sense for what ought to be said in response to the persuasive message. That is the point. We tend to respond to the smaller elements in persuasion rather quickly and automatically, but that is where the problem arises. Unless we, as persuadees, have first examined the strategy underlying the tactics, and unless we respond to the tactics we hear in more sophisticated ways, we are likely to come off as naive, argumentative, and sometimes stupid. You are proba-

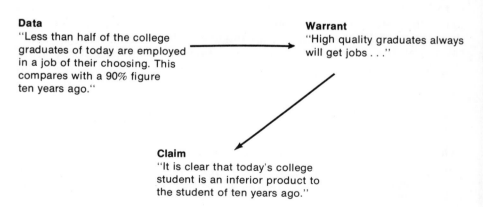

Data
"Less than half of the college graduates of today are employed in a job of their choosing. This compares with a 90% figure ten years ago."

Warrant
"High quality graduates always will get jobs . . ."

Claim
"It is clear that today's college student is an inferior product to the student of ten years ago."

Figure 4-4 *Toulmin System of Analysis: Sample Argument.*

11. Stephen Toulmin, *The Uses of Argument* (Cambridge: Cambridge University Press, 1969). See Chapter 3, "The Layout of Arguments," pp. 94–145.

bly all too familiar, for example, with those time-worn phrases parents use: "When you get a little real experience, then you'll see what I mean," or "Oh, all that baloney they teach you kids at college, it just isn't able to hold water," or "Well, that's just what you think."

Toulmin's system does afford us some opportunity to approach this tactical level of persuasion more specifically and systematically. So, let's look more closely at how the typical interpersonal attempt at persuasion flows or operates and then apply Toulmin's system to it.

Claim

Suppose that you want to persuade authority figures that they are over-looking important information that could affect decisions, which in turn affect you. Let's say that you want to persuade your teacher that he ought not give you an open-book midterm examination. You begin by raising your hand and saying something like "Why do we have to take an open-book test? Why not just have a take-home test? It's the same thing." What you have done, in Toulmin's terms, is make a *claim*—that take-home tests and open-book tests are essentially the same. You hope he will draw the conclusion that there is no need for a test in class, that another paper will serve the purpose. Let's assume that your teacher listens and seriously considers your claim. He then has three options. He may, if you have been persuasive enough, agree to accept your claim as it stands and permit you to write up a take-home exam instead of an open-book one. Another op-tion for him is to reject your claim out of hand; he might say, "Well, I run the class and I have scheduled the exam into the syllabus and have it made up already. We'll take the open-book test." His third option is to ask you to demonstrate further the reasonableness of your claim. He might say something like "Well, you may have something there and then again you may not. How do you know that these two kinds of tests are essen-tially the same kind of activity? What proof have you?"

Data

In Toulmin's terms, you are faced with a request for the *data* supporting your *claim*. Of the teacher's three responses, the first two typify im-mediate and spontaneous responses to persuasive tactics. The third re-sponse is closer to the critical and aware persuadee's response, at least on the content level of persuasion. Instead of making a snap *yes* or *no* judg-ment, the persuadee explores the issue further (in this case, the teacher decides to look into the comparison between two different types of examination) and suspends judgment. Unfortunately, most persuadees respond most of the time in the first two ways and not nearly often enough in the critical and reserved manner suggested by option three.

Warrant

Let us continue this interpersonal exchange. Suppose you have taken a course in tests and measurements and you have access to information about open-book and take-home methods. Your sources say that identical sets of subjects repeatedly scored essentially the same on take-home and open-book exams in an experiment conducted at several colleges. You tell this to your open-minded instructor, and he considers your evidence. Again, he has three options. He can accept your evidence as supporting your claim and agree to let your class have a take-home exam, or he may reject your data out of hand, saying something like 'Well, if they are the same, then I may as well give the open-book exam as I had originally planned," or he might again follow the third option (remember, he is a very open-minded instructor) and ask for more proof. In this case, however, he asks you to tell him *why* that evidence leads to the conclusion that you should have a take-home exam instead of the regularly scheduled test. In Toulmin's terms, he is asking for a *warrant* to link the *data* you have presented in support of your *claim*. The flow then goes from claim to data to the warrant, where the real philosophical elements in the issue are likely to arise.

Let us see what you will do next. Suppose you say in response to the instructor's request for a warrant:

> I assume that the most valuable asset we have as students and teachers is learning time together. Now the scheduled exam will take one entire class session and part of another in the critiquing process. We only have thirty class sessions together, and some of them are already eliminated by vacation days, convocations, and other matters. We can't afford not to have a take-home exam, since it is equivalent to the open-book test now scheduled.

That is pretty sound reasoning, and it seems to fit with your data and claim. The instructor may consider this sufficient evidence and agree to cancel his exam. He may want you to modify your request and agree to an open-book final exam if the midterm is a take-home, or he may be stubborn and refuse to reschedule or change his plans. In any case, he has the same three options—agree, disagree, or ask for more (in this case, for concessions in your request). If the issue is not as simple as this one, the persuadee may argue about the philosophical position inherent in the warrant. The interaction could then continue, but on issues central to the question and not on whether the experiments comparing take-home exams with open-book exams were carefully conducted. You would be discussing implication, not facts; and after all, facts are usually not very debatable.

Substantiating Elements

Toulmin's system has a number of secondary terms. For example, in the preceding case, the concession in the claim is called the *qualifier*. (Usually it is a simple qualifier—something like saying *"In most cases,"* or *"Probably* we don't have to take an open-book test," or *"It is likely* that open-book and take-home exams are parallel.") The point is that the term or concession qualifies or limits the claim; it allows for the possibility that this is not an "Either A or B" type of argument. The claim is *probably* acceptable and true, but there is the *possibility* that another factor may enter in and affect the final outcome. To continue our example, the qualifier to the claim would probably be something like "Open-book exams and take-home exams are *essentially* the same kind of test, *at least on the basis* of evidence now available."

Another minor term in Toulmin's system is the *reservation*, a statement attached to or related to the warrant. For instance, suppose, in the argument over examinations, it became clear that the instructor did not consider examination time to be an inferior learning activity but rather one that was just different from regular classroom activity. The warrant would then probably evolve into something like *"Unless there is reason to believe* that exams are a learning experience and not an evaluation experience, then class learning time between teacher and student is the most important asset which we have." Notice that the reservation states the conditions under which the assumptions and philosophical bases of the argument operate. This aspect of the reservation is often overlooked by persuaders and persuadees alike—they assume that both parties begin from the same point, from the same frame of reference. Only when we begin at the same point or when we make allowances (such as reservations) for these differences, can we really progress in any persuasive transaction. Coupled with the qualifier, the reservation allows for great flexibility in persuasion because both terms allow dialogue to occur; both provide the persuadee with the opportunity to object or agree to part but not all of the persuasion. As persuaders, we need to include these elements of flexibility in our persuasion. As persuadees, we need to request them of the persuaders who are attempting to get us to take action

Unfortunately, history is filled with examples in which legislation, for example, has been destructive because of the deletion of qualifiers or reservations. The lack of a reservation in the 1964 Tonkin Gulf resolution gave to the U.S. President unrestricted power to wage war, thereby eventually costing the United States thousands of lives in Vietnam. Earlier a gag rule in the U.S. Senate prevented the issue of slavery from being discussed for nearly ten years while various territories were being added to the country thereby necessitating continuous and informal negotiation and compromise. President Richard Nixon's interpretation of executive privilege as a concept without reservation ultimately brought the man to disgrace and political ruin. There is another danger also—the danger of having indefinite or vague qualifiers or reservations. For instance, the 1955 Supreme Court ruling on implementation of desegregation used the words "with all deliberate speed" to define the time frame in which to desegregate. As all of us know, this problem is still with us in the form of conflict over busing, racial quotas, and so forth. Clearly the phrase "all deliberate speed" had many meanings.

Advertisers are clever with the use of qualifiers (see Chapter 8). For example, the label on Cascade dishwasher detergent says that it will make your dishes "virtually spotless." Neat, isn't it? Not spotless, but *virtually* spotless, and who can say whether one spot or three spots or twelve spots qualifies as being *"virtually* spotless"? So the persuadee needs to be aware of two problems connected with qualifiers or reservations. One is absence of them, which can lock us in to one course of action or belief. The other problem is with the too-vague qualifier, which may allow persuaders to wiggle out of any commitment to product, action, person, or idea. It is far better to be specific about qualifiers, as was the energy-saving legislation of 1975 and 1976. This allowed for something of a "fudge factor" on gasoline mileage but set specific mileage performance for specific dates. Persuaders may still try to interpret the qualifiers to their advantage, but it is much more difficult when specificity and details are given. Persuadees need to think twice when confronted with lack of details and lack of specificity in persuasive claims. If advertisers say that their tires will stop faster, we need to ask such questions as "Faster than what?" and "Under what conditions?" For all we know, they may be comparing the tires with wagon wheels or doughnuts.

The final element in Toulmin's system for showing the tactics of argument is called the *support*, or sometimes the *backing*, for the warrant. Toulmin observed that many issues hang on this element—that it justifies acceptance of the warrant. Suppose the persuadee does not consider the warrant to be true or that he doubts some part of it. The persuader must then provide some kind of proof that would *support* or *back up* the reasoning expressed in his warrant. In a sense, there is a whole separate argument with a separate claim, data, and warrant going on when support is offered for a warrant. Essentially persuaders claim that the warrant is acceptable because of the support or backing offered. The backing is really data for this second claim. This same process of claim-data-warrant within claim-data-warrant can go further and often does—and creates the complexity surrounding most controversial and philosophical issues. (Figure 4-5 depicts a persuasive argument in these terms: (1) *claim* made by the persuader, (2) *data* provided by the source, and (3) emergence of the *warrant*.)

We can now see that the tactics of persuasion are not usually encapsulated into simple syllogisms. Instead of making statements like "If A

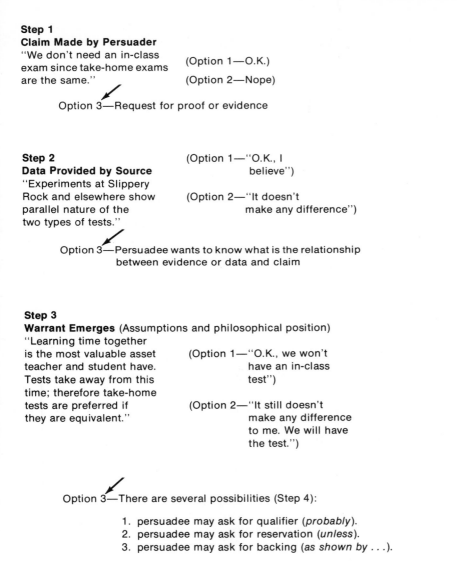

Step 1
Claim Made by Persuader
"We don't need an in-class
exam since take-home exams
are the same."

(Option 1—O.K.)

(Option 2—Nope)

Option 3—Request for proof or evidence

Step 2
Data Provided by Source
"Experiments at Slippery
Rock and elsewhere show
parallel nature of the
two types of tests."

(Option 1—"O.K., I
    believe")

(Option 2—"It doesn't
    make any difference")

Option 3—Persuadee wants to know what is the relationship
    between evidence or data and claim

Step 3
Warrant Emerges (Assumptions and philosophical position)
"Learning time together
is the most valuable asset
teacher and student have.
Tests take away from this
time; therefore take-home
tests are preferred if
they are equivalent."

(Option 1—"O.K., we won't
    have an in-class
    test")

(Option 2—"It still doesn't
    make any difference
    to me. We will have
    the test.")

Option 3—There are several possibilities (Step 4):

1. persuadee may ask for qualifier (*probably*).
2. persuadee may ask for reservation (*unless*).
3. persuadee may ask for backing (*as shown by . . .*).

Figure 4-5   *Toulmin System of Analysis: Steps in a Persuasive Argument.*

then B; A is true; therefore B is also true" or "Either A is true or B is true; B
is false; therefore A must be true," most persuaders make claims that
persuadees may (1) buy outright with no questions asked, (2) reject outright, or (3) ask for proof of. Persuaders then can provide data, which
again can be accepted, rejected, or questioned. If the persuadee continues

to request more, the persuader ultimately provides the warrant or reason for linking proof to request. Given enough time, three other elements may enter into the persuasive appeal:

1. The qualifier (which limits the force or universality of the claim or request)

2. The reservation (which states the conditions under which the warrant operates)

3. The backing (which supports or provides evidence to substantiate the validity of the warrant)

Some of you will be asking now how persuadees get their input noticed and considered. After all, there are thirty or more people in most classes, and not everyone will get a chance to participate; and the problem is compounded as time goes on and as the audience gets larger, as in political campaigns. Although that is true, you must also remember that in another sense persuadees *always* get input; they always are "heard" in a way. The persuader who knows anything about audiences will anticipate the kind of questions persuadees *might* ask if they had the opportunity. Furthermore, if not satisfied with the completeness of the argument offered by the persuader, the persuadee may decide not to follow the course of action suggested by the persuader and thus ask for more proof, reasoning, qualification, backing, or reservation. Finally, the function of the persuadee is to dissect the persuasion knowing *when* and *if* to be persuaded; it doesn't matter whether the persuaders are exposed to all of this analysis. They ought to catch on if fewer and fewer persons buy the product or vote or give rewards. What does matter is that persuadees are aware, critical, and fairly sophisticated and systematic as they are exposed to persuasion. Toulmin's system for analyzing the tactics of persuasion provides us with a simple but discriminating tool, which operates well with the kind of persuasion to which we are exposed every day.

For persuaders there are a few simple pieces of advice, if they intend to structure persuasion with Toulmin's system in mind. First, they must anticipate the audience's probable response. Second, they need to provide data if a claim is likely to be questioned. Many persuaders merely restate a claim if it is not accepted—a more appropriate course of action would be to provide the persuadee with good reasons (data) for following the advice of the claim. If they wish to bolster their persuasion, they need to demonstrate reasoning, or the warrant of the case. Finally, the probability of getting audience acceptance for the case will increase to the degree that it is less dogmatic and is well documented. Therefore, it is wise to qualify claims, taking any reservations in the warrant into account, and to provide substantial backing for the data.

Now that we have looked at how persuasion operates on this rule-governed or procedural or *content* level in strategic and tactical ways, let us consider what we do know about logical thought processes and the human responses to various kinds and amounts of evidence or proof.

EXPERIMENTAL EVIDENCE ON EVIDENCE

Since its inception, the field of speech communication has been interested in the nature of evidence—what it is, what types may occur, how much of it is necessary, who is most likely to be persuaded by certain types of evidence, and other similar issues. Aristotle, in his study of persuasion, observed persuasion and categorized the types of reasoning and evidence into what he called *topoi*, or topics or places where arguments of a rational nature could be found. The philosophers of the New Science during the Renaissance tried to establish scientific methods of proving things to be true or false.

In its simplest form, evidence can be thought of as an example in some form. It is in support of or gives credence to an argument or conclusion. If the evidence is statistical, then the support is the result of compiling numerous examples. If it is expert testimony, then the testimony is an example of the point being made. If the evidence is an analogy, it is also a kind of example. It is a narrative, which supports a premise or leads to a conclusion.

Researchers have tried various "scientific" means to test the impact of such things as evidence types, organization, and concreteness. A number of presumably typical persuadees (for example, several hundred college freshmen) are given varying degrees or types of persuasion and evidence (for example, emotional versus logical evidence, good delivery of evidence versus poor delivery of the same evidence). Following this treatment, the subjects' attitudes are measured, using an attitude measure. Then the results are compared with pretreatment scores on identical or similar measures, and the difference between scores is compared, by statistical methods, to determine the effects of the varying degrees or types of evidence characteristics.

Unfortunately, the overall results of the numerous studies have not shed much light on the questions that were bothering the ancients (for example, what kinds of evidence persuade best? what amount of evidence is enough? when should you use what kind of evidence?). Rather, the results are often contradictory or inconclusive. Richard Gregg observed that the overall results of these studies were disheartening when he noted that "the audience reaction to an argument may have little or nothing to do with whether the argument includes fully documented evidence, relevant or irrelevant evidence, weak or strong evidence or any evidence at all."[12] Yet we do know that people ask for evidence when in doubt. In spite of the pessimism suggested by Gregg, we do know *some* things about evidence, as a result of about a quarter of a century of behavioral study:

1. Evidence increases persuasive effects if the persuader is unknown or has low to moderate credibility.[13]

2. There seems to be little difference in the persuasive effects generated from emotional as opposed to logical evidence.[14]

3. Usually some evidence is better than no evidence.[15]

4. "Reluctant" evidence (that given by someone against himself or his own interests) is no more effective than biased or unbiased objective evidence.[16]

5. Good delivery can enhance the potency of evidence (but perhaps only when the source is unknown or has low credibility, so that the delivery makes him and his evidence more believable and therefore more persuasive).[17]

6. Evidence can make persuasive changes more permanent.[18]

7. Evidence is most effective when the persuadee has not heard it before.[19]

---

12.   Richard B. Gregg, "Some Hypotheses for the Study of Psychology of Evidence," as quoted in James C. McCroskey, "A Summary of Experimental Research on the Effects of Evidence in Persuasive Communication," *Quarterly Journal of Speech*, Vol. 55 (April 1969), p. 167.

13.   See the discussion on evidence by James C. McCroskey, cited in Footnote 20; and Gerald R. Miller and John Baseheart, "Source Trustworthiness, Opinionated Statements, and Response to Persuasive Communication," *Speech Monographs*, Vol. 36 (March 1969), pp. 1–7.

14.   See McCroskey, cited in Footnote 20; Cronkhite, *Persuasion: Speech and Behavioral Change*, cited above (Footnote 7); and Cronkhite, "The Relation of Scholastic Aptitude to Logical Argument and Emotional Appeal," cited above (Footnote 7).

15.   See the McCroskey summary cited below (Footnote 20); and Robert S. Cathcart, "An Experimental Study of the Relative Effectiveness of Selected Means of Handling Evidence in Speeches of Advocacy," doctoral dissertation, Northwestern University, 1953.

16.   William E. Arnold and James C. McCroskey, "The Credibility of Reluctant Testimony," *Central States Speech Journal*, Vol. 18 (May 1967), pp. 97–103.

17.   James C. McCroskey and R. Samuel Mehrley, "The Effects of Disorganization and Nonfluency on Attitude Change and Source Credibility," *Speech Monographs*, Vol. 36 (March 1969), pp. 13–21.

18.   See the McCroskey summary cited above (Footnote 12).

19.   See the McCroskey summary cited below (Footnote 20); and Karl W. E. Anatol and Jerry E. Mandel, "Strategies of Resistance to Persuasion: New Subject Matter for the Teacher of Speech Communication," *Central States Speech Journal*, Vol. 23 (Spring 1972), pp. 11–17.

8. The method of transmitting the evidence (live, on tape, and the like) seems to have no effect on evidence potency.[20]

9. People are likely to believe evidence that agrees with their own position more than evidence that does not.[21]

10. Highly dogmatic persons differ from persons who are not so dogmatic, in that the highly dogmatic are more affected by evidence.[22]

For the most part, these findings are not surprising or unpredictable. Many of them seem to be common-sense conclusions, and that fact has prompted many researchers to attempt to investigate the effects of evidence from a different perspective—that is, by observing persuasion as it operates in the "real world." After observing a number of both successful and unsuccessful persuasive efforts, the researchers draw some conclusions based on the general patterns observed. By now, you will have concluded that this is the admonition repeated in almost every chapter of this book—observe, search for a pattern, try to draw some conclusions about the persuader and the persuasion on the basis of these patterns, and then and only then respond to the persuasion confronting you.

Several patterns seem to emerge from the discussion in this chapter and from the assumptions underlying Chapter 2. First, *evidence is probably most effective when it encourages audience participation.* Earlier we noted that, in using emotionally oriented evidence, persuaders are most effective if they can present audiences with a dramatic scene or setting and can then ask the audience to emphathize with the character acting within that setting. By participating with their imaginations, members of the audience co-create the proof. They incorporate the proof into their own frames of reference—the persuasion thus achieved is more permanent and potent. In using intellectually oriented evidence, effective persuaders present claims and perhaps data to support them. They hope that warrants will be provided by the audience, but even if listeners do not supply the linkage that is needed and instead question the persuaders' conclusions, they are still participating in their own persuasion when they begin to play the game (that is, co-create a proof with the persuaders).

Consider the following extracts from an article in an admittedly white racist publication:

20. James C. McCroskey, *Studies of the Effects of Evidence in Persuasive Communication*, Report SCRL, 4–67, Speech Communication Research Laboratory, Michigan State University, 1967.

21. Victor D. Wall, Jr., "Evidential Attitudes and Attitude Change," *Western Speech*, Vol. 36 (Spring 1972), pp. 115–123.

22. Gary Cronkhite and Emily Goetz, "Dogmatism, Persuasibility, and Attitude," *Journal of Communication*, Vol. 21 (December 1971), pp. 342–352.

Leftist forces have long waged a relentless battle to have the death penalty abolished. Jack Greenberg . . . is representing negro Lucius Jackson, Jr. . . . He was sentenced for raping a White doctor's wife . . . What the Jew lawyers . . . have failed to tell the court . . . is the fact that blacks commit over 80 percent of all forcible rapes in this country. Remember that negroes are only 13 percent of the population, therefore their crime rate is far out of proportion to their numerical percentage in this country . . . the negro constitutes by far the most dangerous criminal element in America. Over half of all black males are expected to be involved in some crime during their lifetime.

There is no way to rehabilitate this entire race of people . . . We want to save White people from further murder, rape and plunder . . . Let's bring back peace, prosperity, safety, low taxes and all the improvements resulting from the elimination of slum ghettos and violent crime will be reduced by an astounding 85 %.[23]

The publication then repeatedly appealed for help in promoting a "Back to Africa" movement to deport all blacks as soon as possible. For a moment, try to avoid having an emotional response to the quotation. Instead look at it as a piece of persuasion, which attempts to use both kinds of evidence discussed in this chapter. There is a clear-cut attempt to appeal to the emotions and biases inherent in the audience. At the same time, there is an attempt to appeal to the audience in intellectual ways (for example, the citing of statistics and giving examples). In all likelihood, most nonsubscribers reading this newspaper article would not be persuaded by it.

Yet it demonstrates some of the things which we have been talking about. The article creates a dramatic scene with great potential for action. It includes data in support of claims and even draws the conclusion in some cases (for example, "therefore their crime rate is far out of proportion to their numerical percentage in this country"). Why does it fail as persuasion? Examine it more closely. The situation drawn by the persuasion is dramatic, but it does not allow participation or empathy (except perhaps on behalf of the Negro defendant in the death penalty case). The audience is not invited into the drama—it is not asked to use its imagination. The same thing occurs with the intellectually oriented parts of the message. This passage is a good instance of not allowing the auditor to participate in his own persuasion. The conclusion that black crime rates are higher than black population ratios is one that is easily drawn from the

---

23.   From an article entitled "Black Rape of White Women Grows," *The Thunderbolt*, February 1972, p. 2. The publication is published irregularly by the National States Rights Party, Marietta, Georgia.

80 percent to 13 percent figures, but the author insists on drawing the conclusion for you. The probable response to this kind of paternalistic persuasion is to question the conclusion that is drawn. Persuadees want to get in on the action. Since there are no openings here, they find one on the opposite side of the case. They start asking questions about the data given (for example, "Isn't crime caused by environmental factors like poor home life?") They look for faulty relationships or linkages. They wonder how lower taxes fit in with deporting people—it seems like an expensive plan at best. Sooner or later they reject the whole argument. It is doubtful that this particular passage could be doctored up to be persuasive in any meaningful sense; probably it is so extreme that it rules that possibility out. However, if the persuader had not tried so hard to lead persuadees through the message, drawing conclusions for them and so forth, chances for success would have been better. We are never invited to join the drama the persuader is presenting—he makes the picture too complete.

A second characteristic that seems to help, in using evidence for "logical" or content-oriented persuasion, is to highlight the evidence in one of two ways—either as part of a narrative or by use of some form of analogy. The earliest form of human ritual and entertainment was the *narrative* as it was used in dances, tales, and myths. It is not surprising that we remember the stories the minister told during the sermon while being unable to recall the point of the sermon itself. The narrative is a potent carrier of proof. We tend to remember narratives easily because we can participate with parts of the narrative or characters in it.

Closely related to the narrative is another form for highlighting proof or evidence—the *analogy*. The narrative uses the passage of time to organize evidence (that is, the beginning, middle, and end of a story takes place across time). The analogy uses space to organize proof. It is an attempt to show persuaders how the evidence is spatially like some other object, event, or place. For example, a persuader might try to convince us that present rates of fuel consumption will soon lead to severe shortages. An analogy can present proofs or evidence. We might say that our growing fuel-consumption rate is like air being pumped into a balloon. As the air or consumption increases, so does the pressure against the sides of the balloon. As long as the air is continually being forced into the balloon, there is the danger of bursting the balloon. The only way to save the balloon is to stop putting more air into it and to begin to release some of the pressure slowly by letting some of the "air" out. Here the size of the increasing consumption rates is analogous to the size of the increasing balloon. Space is what is visualized by the persuadee. This example would be much more effective than dry, dull statistics that trace percentages of increase in terms of millions of barrels of oil imported from year to year. The message is much more impactful in its analogic form.

The *example* is similar to the narrative, in that it is meant to provide a dramatic sample of whatever we are talking about. Hopefully, the persuadee will imagine and interact with the example. For instance, we might try to prove the value of cable-TV franchises by saying that one benefit is that people do their grocery shopping by tuning in the market and ordering their purchases electronically. The audience sees itself as acting through or in the example.

Sign argument observes certain symptoms, which usually indicate other things. For example, you might tell your parents that they are too conservative as shown by their unwillingness to get a faster car or by their doubts about college morals. You argue from symptoms here—the symptoms you cite are signs of conservativism. In a sense, this argument is a kind of analogy, since it provides perspective or a frame of reference for the audience—it correlates two perspectives.

Statistics are usually just large examples or generalizations drawn out from many examples. It is important to make them meaningful and clear for the audience. For instance, it would be better to observe that there are twice as many chances of being born seriously sick if one is the child of a poverty-stricken family than to point out that there are 1,567,900 children born with serious defects to poverty-stricken families and only 780,700 to average-income families. If we see evidence in perspective—in terms of something else—we are more likely to accept it and be persuaded by it.

A REVIEW AND CONCLUSION

Content premises do not necessarily rely as much on the internal states of each individual persuader as do process premises. Instead, they rely more on universally agreed upon norms or rules, in contrast to individualized processing of bits of information.

Evidence tends to be either dramatistically oriented or intellectually oriented. Users of dramatistically oriented evidence may lead persuadees to a "logical" conclusion, drawn from a content premise, by creating a dramatic scene for the audience and then by inviting the audience to join in the drama. Persuadees thus "prove" the validity of the premise to themselves. Users of intellectually oriented evidence, on the other hand, may lead their persuadees to "logical" conclusions by presenting them with a set of data in support of a certain claim or content premise. The persuadees provide the connective between this data and claim in the form of a warrant.

Both types of evidence rely upon a kind of self-persuasion on the part of the persuadee. The persuadee ought to participate in some way in his own persuasion, whether the evidence is intellectual or dramatistic—that is the basic principle. Some of the most fascinating research done in persuasion has focused on self-persuasion. Much of this research is based on Festinger's theory of dissonance, and studies usually ask persuadees to state arguments that are contrary to their own beliefs or that are counter-attitudinal (for example, why a dull experiment was interesting, why strange foods taste good, or why they might accept some group or idea that is counter to their beliefs). Having engaged in this kind of participation, the respondees tend to change their beliefs in accord with the false or counterattitudinal message they advocated. Though this issue has been plagued with problems in research measurement and design, the findings have been fairly consistent—when we engage in self-persuasion, even if it runs counter to our own beliefs, the effect of the participation is powerful.

From a strategic point of view, the traditional syllogism usually forms the skeletal structure of an overall argument or content premise. Within this overall structure, the tactics or particular arguments or premises are represented by claims supported by data and hopefully linked by audiences through warrants.

Finally, of the types of evidence available to the persuader, several seem more important than others. First, probably, are those that support the three major linkages: cause-and-effect, symptoms, and congruency. Also, evidence that provides perspective for the audience is probably more effective than evidence that does not. We have focused on two particularly effective methods of providing this perspective—the use of the analogy, which provides a comparative perspective, and the use of the narrative, which has the same ability to provide a perspective within a dramatic frame of reference. Both are also "artistic," in the sense that neither merely presents information; both depict evidence in dramatic or pictorial formats.

To sum it up, we are most effectively persuaded by our own experiences—real or imaginary. Successful persuaders will try to shape content premises, their linkages, claims, data, and warrants in terms of the audience's experience. If they can invite audiences to participate in the drawing of conclusions or with the drama of the proof, they will share in their own persuasion, thus being affected by it.

Questions for Further Thought

1. What are the three types of linkages? Give examples of each from news advertisements, political speeches, or some other source of persuasion.

2. Define proof. What constitutes adequate proof for you? Does it change from issue to issue? If so, in what ways?

3. Review some of the magazine commentary concerning a particular issue and attempt to identify the pieces of data which are offered. What kinds of evidence are they? Are they dramatic? If so, in what

ways? If not, are they persuasive and why or why not? What is the underlying syllogistic structure inherent in the discussions of the issue?

4. Read a contemporary discussion of some ideological issue. Try to identify the claims put forth. What kind of evidence is used to support them? Do the warrants for linking data and claim appear in the book? Are there qualifiers or reservations? Where is the argument most persuasive and why?

5. Identify several forms of proof in the source used for question 4.

6. Identify various forms of proof (for example, intellectually oriented or emotionally oriented, analogical, dramatic) in an issue being debated on the editorial pages of your daily newspaper.

7. What is the difference between intellectually oriented evidence and emotionally oriented evidence? Give examples and explain how they differ.

8. Give examples of the following: (a) comparison and contrast, (b) example, (c) sign argument, (d) statistics.

9. Give examples from your own experience of (a) opinion, (b) attitudes, (c) beliefs, and (d) values that affect *behavior*. Give examples that do not affect behavior. Why is there a difference?

Experiences in Persuasion

1. Read the "Letters to the Editor" section of a popular magazine (for example, *Playboy, Jet, Time*). A group of letters will usually refer to an article included in the magazine's earlier issues. Go back to this earlier article and see what prompted the letter to the editor. What kind of persuasion and evidence seems to have prompted the letter writer to go to the work of writing to the editor? Was he emotionally or intellectually stimulated? Was his response based on intellectually or emotionally oriented evidence? If you were to answer the letter, how would you go about doing it? Try to compose an answer utilizing the same kind of persuasion or evidence used by the author of the letter, by the author of the article, and by the author of a competing letter if there is one.

2. Tape-record a discussion on a TV talk program involving persons who are not entertainment personalities but who are associated with an issue. Trace the argument over the issue utilizing the Toulmin system of analysis. Retrace it using syllogistic analysis. What happened? How could it have changed? What kind of position and line of reasoning do you suppose would be used by the participants on other

issues—such as using quotas for hiring minorities or busing school children to achieve racial balance?

3. Involve yourself in a discussion with your parents, friends, or students in your dormitory over some emotional issue (for example, giving birth control pills at the health clinic on campus, trial marriages). As you discuss the issue, try to identify the path of the discussion. Does it go from claim to data to warrant? If not, try to make it do so by asking for clear articulation of claims; ask for evidence or data; question the philosophical basis on which these two are related; and see if the resulting discussion leads to the addition of qualifiers or reservations to the discussion.

4. Rewrite a piece of intellectually oriented persuasion so that it makes the same requests but is emotionally oriented. Now rewrite an emotionally oriented piece of persuasion to make it intellectually oriented. Identify the rational or reasonable elements in both pieces of persuasion. After rewriting the two, be prepared to argue for the relative effectiveness of one version over another.

5. Make a collection of advertisements in magazines and newspapers that are good examples of

    a. persuasion designed to change attitudes

    b. persuasion designed to change behaviors

    c. persuasion that operates from the three content linkages discussed in this chapter

    d. persuasion that uses dramatistically oriented evidence or proof

    e. persuasion that uses intellectually oriented evidence or proof

    f. persuasion that uses the various kinds of evidence discussed toward the end of the chapter (for example, example, sign argument, analogy, narrative)

Cultural Premises
in Persuasion 5

CULTURAL AND SOCIETAL
PRESSURE

CULTURAL IMAGES AND MYTHS

Wisdom of the Rustic

Possibility of Success

Coming of the Messiah

Presence of Conspiracy

Values of Challenge

PRESENCE OF AN AMERICAN
VALUE SYSTEM

USE OF NONVERBAL MESSAGES
AND CUES

Use of Artifacts

Use of Space

Use of Touch

Other Nonverbal Message Carriers

Using Nonverbal Behavior

A REVIEW AND CONCLUSION

Questions for Further Thought

Experiences in Persuasion

Each culture seeks to train its members in its beliefs, modes of behaviors, folkways, and norms. This training builds a set of premises in each member of that society and culture. These are much like the premises discussed in Chapters 3 and 4. They are understood by the audience, appealed to by persuaders, and reacted to by receivers. The only difference between cultural premises and process and content premises is that we are only faintly aware of the results of that training. This persuasion occurs at such a low level of awareness that we often react subconsciously to it. Consider the following instance of cultural patterning:

> Suppose that you are a member of an Eskimo-Indian tribe called "People of the Deer," whose sole food supply is caribou. You kill enough animals in the spring to last the tribe until the fall, when again the animals migrate south following the food supply. The tribal custom is to kill and preserve these deer in a period of a week or two. The tribes are perhaps 100 persons strong. Suppose that we have just finished our fall hunt. We discover that we face a severe winter without having killed enough caribou to feed the tribe until the spring migration. Death is certain without sufficient supplies of meat and fat. Imagine that you are part of a tribal meeting called to consider the matter. What would you do in this situation?

In several persuasion classes, students brainstormed for solutions to this problem and came up with these suggestions in this approximate order:

1. "Let's follow the deer and kill enough."

2. "Let's seek an alternate food supply—we can eat berries or fish or birds."

3. "Let's send a band of the tribe to get help."

4. "Let's ration food to make it last longer."

5. "Let's use all the parts of the deer—skin, horns, everything—in order to increase the supply."

6. "Let's send some of the people away to another place where food is more plentiful and thus decrease demand."

7. "Let's kill some of our tribe in order to decrease demand."

8. "Let's kill the most useless—the old first, and the very young next."

9. "Let's resort to cannibalism along with the killing."

The most practical solutions emerged first and then more desperate ideas until someone suggested cannibalism. The actual People of the Deer do nothing—they eat the food at their regular rates, knowing full well that they will not live through the winter. Then they sit and wait for death. The tribe simply does not enter into the problem-solving frame of mind typical of Western culture. They accept a problem and do nothing, while we try to find solutions for any problem even though it may be insoluble. We are trained to *do something*. In our culture, persuaders succeed if they outline a problem and suggest solutions. In other cultures, the same tactic would not meet with success.

The classic example mentioned earlier is the Music Man, Professor Harold Hill. You will remember he came to River City, Iowa, to sell band instruments. He created a need for these instruments by creating a problem for the townspeople—trouble. By the time he was through, the people of River City were not about to sit still as the People of the Deer might. They wanted action. Their need for action was met by buying band instruments. A cultural premise formed the basis for Hill's appeal.

In order to see how these premises relate to persuasion in general, let us look first at how we get them (cultural training and pressure). Then we look at three kinds of culture premises: (1) cultural images or myths, (2) an American value system, and (3) nonverbal premises. Bear in mind that a *value is an idea* of the "good" or the desirable that people use as a standard for judging means or to motivate others. Examples of values are honesty, justice, beauty, efficiency, safety, and progress. Because our value system is a major source of persuasive leverage, you may want to see how persuaders link proposals and arguments to our values.

CULTURAL AND SOCIETAL PRESSURE

I am sure that everyone has heard stories about the children of various Indian tribes. They never cried because it was essential not to frighten off game. Anyone who has been around a newborn infant must doubt these stories. Children cry when they are lonely, hungry, or for exercise. How, then, did Indians train their children not to cry out?

During the first hour of life, whenever a Sioux baby cried, its mother clapped her hands over the child's mouth and nose. The hand was removed only if the child stopped crying or began to smother. If this was done within the first hour of life, the infant never again cried out loud. Of course, as the child grew a pattern was seen over and over again. Parents and the elders spoke of the power of silence. They valued quiet and stealth in stalking game. The Indian brave was tested and proved his courage by experiencing pain and not crying out. The most significant test was the Sun Dance, outlawed for 50 years. Here a leather thong was sewn into the shoulder flesh of a brave. The brave would be tied to a totem pole at the center of a tribal circle. The test was to dance away from the pole until the pain of the thong forced him to fall (usually after several days of dancing). The fall usually tore out the thong from the shoulder. The brave was then a full-fledged warrior. Later he could do the Sun-Gazer's Dance. This involved dancing while staring directly into the sun. Sitting Bull is supposed to have done this for three days, after which he had a vision of the future massacre of Custer and his soldiers at the Little Big Horn.[1] Thus the pattern introduced at birth was seen at work throughout life.

Each of us goes through such cultural training seeing values demonstrated, and as a result we adopt the values. They become rules for governing ourselves as we interact. We do not even notice that they are there. We respond instinctively to them. This training underlies each of the three kinds of premises we are going to study. It lurks beneath our surface thoughts and acts. Sophisticated persuaders appeal to these premises directly and cleverly. They can appeal to cultural and societal premises because they believe in them themselves and hope that their audiences do also.

---

1.   For a good discussion of the trials by pain used by Indians, read *Black Elk Speaks* by John Neihardt (Lincoln: University of Nebraska Press, 1961). The Sioux's use of smothering to prevent crying is discussed in *These Were the Sioux* by Maria Santos (New York: Dell Publishing Co., 1961), p. 19.

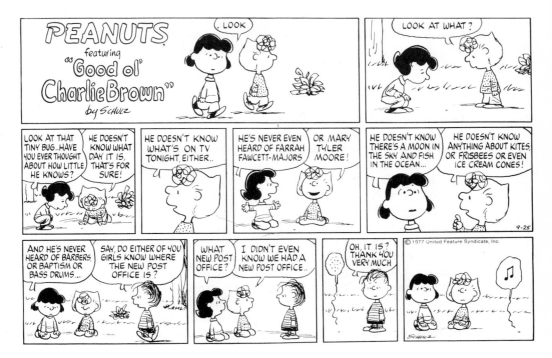

Figure 5-1 *Peanuts. Notice the many references to aspects of American culture. These could become ingrained enough to become kinds of cultural premises to which persuaders can appeal (for example, "Want to be loved? Want to be all-American like Farrah Fawcett-Majors? Join a Chicago Health Club today!"). (© 1977 United Feature Syndicate, Inc.)*

CULTURAL IMAGES AND MYTHS

Every culture has its own myths and heroes who do things valued by that culture. For example, early Greek society developed a series of myths surrounding the sin of pride. Eventually the myths became institutionalized in such Greek dramas as *Oedipus Rex.*

Parts of the myths related to physical acts, like trying to control one's own destiny, which were discouraged. Greeks placed a high value on avoiding prideful action. They elected leaders who were humble. They valued humility. We have similar beliefs. You probably know that the overproud student is less likely to be elected to office or chosen as team captain than the more humble person. We view the antics of a pompous person with disfavor. We ridicule needless pride.

What are some of the cultural myths or legends or images underlying American culture and society and how do persuaders use them? Are these images capable of being changed? If so, how? Are they being changed at present and if so, how? Stereotypes and proverbs are good indicators of cultural myths. Let us consider a few of these cultural myths.

Wisdom of the Rustic

One of the legends in American literature with great persuasive impact is the clever rustic. No matter how devious the opposition, the simple wisdom of the backwoods wins out. Numerous folk tales rely on this image. The Daniel Boone tales, the stories about the inventiveness of Paul Bunyan, and many Lincoln stories rely on the rustic image. We have faith in humble persons when we look for leaders. The small-town boy is chosen team captain. We believe in humble beginnings and we believe that difficulty teaches even the most uneducated of us to be wise in a wordly way.

Persuaders often use the image, portraying themselves as rustics who have wisdom. There are obvious examples—Abraham Lincoln, George Wallace, Charles Ingalls of "Little House on the Prairie." Advertisements focus on clever rustics or comparable figures (for example, Mrs. Olson of Folger's coffee fame or Josephine, the plumber). In these images are several cultural values: a faith in common sense; a belief in instinct (think of maxims like "trust your initial judgment"); and a reliance on physical and mental prowess.

At the same time that we seem to value the simple, common-sense rustic, we have a set of norms that devalues the intellectual or the educated. Alexis de Toqueville, in his book *Democracy in America* written in the 1830s, observed the same distrust:

> The nearer the people are drawn to the common level of an equal and similar condition, the less prone does each man become to place implicit faith in a certain man or a certain class of men [intellectuals]. But his readiness to believe the multitude increases, and opinion is more than ever mistress of the world. Not only is common opinion the only guide which private judgement retains . . . it possesses a power infinitely beyond what it has elsewhere.[2]

Richard Hofstadter also wrote about this anti-intellectualism in several places.[3] Persuaders often use the reverse side of our value in the wisdom of the rustic. The intellectual is often the brunt of jokes. Advertisers often have the rustic win out over the smart guy. Politicians frequently emphasize their humble roots.

---

2.   Alexis de Toqueville, *Democracy in America* (New York: Mentor Books, 1965), p. 148.

3.   Richard Hofstadter, *Anti-Intellectualism in American Life* (New York: Alfred A. Knopf, 1963).

Possibility of Success

The Horatio Alger myth is based on several novels written by Alger in the nineteenth century. They always told of a young man who through hard work, sincerity, honesty, and a faith in the future was able to make good. He might even rise to the top and own his own company, have a beautiful wife, live a fine life, and be able to do good for others. The myth has appeal and was believed by immigrants, the poor, and the downtrodden. They passed it on to their children, admonishing them to work hard and achieve success. One of the slogans on college campuses today is "Get a degree, get a job, and get ahead." That slogan is part of the Alger myth, which parents reinforce over and over, as the Indian tribal elders reinforced the value of silence.

In a sense, this myth—the possibility of success—links up with the wisdom of the rustic myth. If you follow the advice of the common man and use common sense, with sincerity and hard work, you will be a success. It has the values of hard work, sincerity, honesty, and law and order. Some persons claim that the myth was established to enslave the common man and to keep him on a treadmill. If you think that you have a chance to achieve success, you will not risk questioning authority figures. Instead, you will submit to them and try to gain power for yourself. Again, this myth was observed by Toqueville:

> No Americans are devoid of a yearning desire to rise; . . . All are constantly seeking to acquire property, power, and reputation. . . . What chiefly diverts the men of democracies from lofty ambition is not the scantiness of their fortunes, but the vehemence of the exertions they daily make to improve them. . . . The same observation is applicable to the sons of such men: they are born . . . their parents were humble; they have grown up amidst feelings and notions which they cannot afterwards easily get rid of; and it may be presumed that they will inherit the propensities of their father, as well as his wealth.[4]

You probably can see your parents and your relatives in this description. If Toqueville was right, you may see yourself also. You are ready for persuasion aimed at the possibility of success. If you follow the myth—work hard for your grades or job or pay, and if you have the faith and stamina, you will succeed. This myth was used by Richard Nixon in his 1972 campaign and by Jimmy Carter in 1976. It will probably be used by one candidate or the other in many elections to come. As a persuadee, you should expect to hear appeals for the myth. Persuaders will offer success

---

4. Toqueville, pp. 156–158.

as just around the corner, if only you will follow them and not the false prophets. They will offer the "big break" and the chance to have a better life for you and your children. Whether it is a speed-reading course, a body builder, or a weight watchers' club, the carrot is always the same—try and you will succeed.

Coming of the Messiah

Americans expect to be saved from disaster by great prophets or saviors. We mentioned this in Chapter 2 as one of the metaphors often used by persuaders. Let us investigate the values of this image.

First, what does the myth claim? Well, there are times so difficult, confusing and chaotic, that escape seems impossible. For the unemployed during the Great Depression, it was the total lack of job opportunities and the prospect of more of the same. For the 1950s, it was the increasing Russian domination. For America in the late 1960s, there were two problems: (1) a serious breakdown of traditional values and lifestyles, seen in civil riots, the use of drugs, common-law marriages, and communes, and (2) the seeming inability of public opinion to deter the war policy of the Johnson and Nixon administrations. In the 1970s, the problems centered around energy, inflation, and the ability of the country to live up to its promises of security for the elderly, health care for the masses, and equal opportunity for all.

The first element of the messianic myth is a problem perceived as insoluble. The second element in this myth is a person believed to have answers and solutions. In the 1930s he was a patrician with a common touch who combined great vision tempered by adversity—Franklin D. Roosevelt. There were others who sold the same qualities—Huey P. Long of Louisiana, Floyd B. Olson of Minnesota, and Father Charles E. Coughlin, for example. In the 1950s there were would-be prophet-messiahs. Senator Joseph McCarthy charged that the State Department was riddled with traitors. All of them claimed to have the insight and wisdom to be the savior of the country. Unlike the 1930s, the 1950s must not have demanded as much, for we chose a reluctant war hero—Dwight Eisenhower—and a witty intellectual—Adlai Stevenson—as major candidates. In the 1960s, other messiahs emerged to solve the insoluble—George Wallace, Eugene McCarthy, Robert Kennedy, and George McGovern. Again the situation was evidently not bad enough to warrant the election of any of these saviors. In the 1970s, the messiahs were technology and clever amateur inventions to create new fuel sources. One fellow invented an engine for cars or trucks that would run off the methane gas emitted from chicken manure! Interestingly, while we believe that all problems can be solved in the twinkling of an eye once the savior, good fairy godmother, or hero arrives on the scene, we are also leery of zealots.

What values does this myth have? First, it holds that there is no problem too great if the right man is given the proper chance to solve it. This intense optimism, which many persons from other countries have difficulty believing is genuine, is at the core. Another value in this myth is that there are superhumans or godlike figures who come to the fore in tough times. We talked, in another place, about TV saviors—Mrs. Olson and her coffee, Wonderwoman, and the Bionic Man. The myth may set idealism and technology against one another. Though the myth does not place a higher value on technology, the fact that the technocrat has so often been chosen in times calling for a messiah suggests that one of our values or God terms is technology.

Presence of Conspiracy

Another culture premise is the belief that big problems don't have simple causes. Richard Hofstadter calls the belief the paranoid style. This is a belief that when problems appear great, the only reasonable explanation for them is that a powerful group has conspired to cause them.[5] This conspiracy argument has recurred throughout our history in the form of alleged Papist conspiracies, Masonic conspiracies, and Populist conspiracies, among many others. Franklin D. Roosevelt used the argument in connection with the Great Depression: money interests and the great banking houses had caused the depression and should be "thrown out of the temple." McGovern claimed that a conspiracy was behind the bugging of the Watergate headquarters in 1972. Later Nixon, trying to deny Watergate charges, accused elements in the CIA of being behind the plot. At one point in the scandal he said that a "sinister force" was against him. The energy crisis is sometimes blamed on a conspiracy among oil producers and distributors. We can expect to see conspiracy theories from time to time in the future as well.

Though this myth does not really carry values of our culture, it does trace a pattern of response. If you hear a conspiracy argument (whether there actually is one or not), chances are the persons using the pattern hold these views:

1. They have something of value to lose. They are in possession of some kind of power or property.

2. They see themselves in danger of losing some or all of this power or property or as already having lost some of it.

---

5.   For a more complete discussion of the conspiracy argument, see *The Paranoid Style in American Politics and Other Essays* by Richard Hofstadter (New York: Vintage Books, 1967).

3. They see themselves as helpless to prevent loss.

It is easy to see how these beliefs could link up with the messiah. The messiah can defeat the evil conspirators and thus save the culture. Here lies one of the dangers of the conspiracy argument—it invites mass hysteria and charismatic leaders.[6] In times of trouble and confusion, we may see the rise of mass movements following leaders who are believed to be heroes or saviors.

Value of Challenge

Associated with the messiah or savior myth is another myth or image—the value of challenge. The myth is fairly simple and may parallel tribal tests of strength and character. The myth suggests there is a kind of wisdom gained only through great challenge and testing. There is a rite of passage or initiation, which gives one power, character, and knowledge.

You are probably now going through such a test in college. People say that going to college is a test of endurance more than a training ground for a specific job. College graduation shows that you can meet a challenge and handle it, that you have matured, that you have learned how to learn. Employers hire college graduates and then train them for a job after college. Boot camp offers another example of belief in the value of overcoming difficulty and in meeting challenges.

The more dramatic the challenge, of course, the more persuasive is the myth, and the appeals to it become more potent. Good examples of past uses of this myth are Hitler's references to his imprisonment as a test, the reminders of Roosevelt's testing when he was crippled with polio, and Robert Kennedy's references to his brother's assassination, and the challenges to American ingenuity and stick-togetherness.

The rite of passage or the meeting of a challenge underscores several values that persuaders use as appeals in our culture. First, it suggests that there is something good about suffering—you learn from it and grow emotionally as a result of it. Persuaders say that though the going might be rough, the lessons learned along the way are worth it. Remember your parents telling you how good it was for you to suffer through trigonometry or Latin? Second, the myth suggests that there are certain signs of maturity. One is the ability to behave with character when under duress. Finally, the myth suggests that greatness needs to be tempered under fire. No one who ever was great became so without suffering and lots of scars from the hurly-burly of battle. The battleground might be

---

6.   For a good discussion of the degree to which persons will follow charismatic leaders, see Eric Hoffer, *The True Believer* (New York: Harper & Row, 1951).

politics, athletics, or the grueling hours of training for artistic successes. All of the suffering prepares the person for greatness tinged with a humble nature. Try to identify the places in your life where the challenge has been brought up to motivate you or others around you.

PRESENCE OF AN AMERICAN VALUE SYSTEM

The myths we have just examined are actually fantasy forms of deep and enduring values that most Americans have. They are expressed in myths in order to simplify them. This makes them seem less lofty—more down-to-earth and ordinary. For example, we have a belief or value in this country that all persons are to be treated equally and that in the eyes of God they *are* equal. This value has been debated for more than two centuries through such issues as slavery, women's suffrage, civil rights, desegregation, and affirmative action programs. The value is acted out or dramatized in the possibility of success myth. We see the myth acted out in TV commercials. A middle-aged wife says, "We've worked hard for what we have and now we are going to take care of ourselves, too—we use Geritol." The film *Rocky* depicted a man rising to a championship boxing match through hard work. Many politicians say they have come up the hard way.

One of the early speech-communication studies that explored values was conducted by Edward Steel and W. Charles Redding.[7] They looked at the communication of several political campaigns and tried to extract core and secondary values. These were the core values observed by Steele and Redding:

> *Puritan and pioneer morality,* or the willingness to cast the world into categories of foul and fair, good and evil, and so forth. Though we tend to think of this value as outdated, it has merely been reworded. The advocates and foes of present marijuana laws and of legal abortion both call on moral values such as just/unjust, right/wrong, and moral/immoral to make their cases.

> *Value of the individual,* or the ranking of the rights and welfare of the individual above those of government and as important in other ways. This value seems to persist. All politicians claim to be interested in the individual. Cosmetics are made especially for you. We praise the house

7.   Edward D. Steele and W. Charles Redding, "The American Value System: Premises for Persuasion," *Western Speech*, Vol. 26 (Spring 1962), pp. 83–91.

decorating scheme that expresses individuality. Burger King lets you "have it your way."

Achievement and success, or the accumulation of power, status, wealth, and property. There was a short period during the 1960s and 1970s when young Americans seemed to reject this value. They joined communes, would not dress for job interviews, and so forth. Those persons are now often the classic models of success-minded organization types. Literally millions of dollars are spent every year on self-help products or courses designed to make success more possible for you. All these appeals rely on the value we place on achievement and success.

Change and progress, or the belief that society develops in positive ways measured by progress. Though this value is probably the one most often questioned today (Westinghouse does not claim that "Progress Is Our Most Important Product" any more, and environmentalists want to know the cost of progress), it still has a good deal of persuasive potency. Recall the frequency of maxims suggesting "You can never stand still; if you do, you fall behind." Again, even the most vehement ecologists still want change and merely define progress as the movement away from technological change and toward change and progress in lifestyle. Most auto advertisements suggest the value of change and progress.

Ethical equality, or the view that all persons are equal in a spiritual sense and ought to be in a realm of opportunity. Though the "equal in the eyes of God" aspect of this value has changed since the 1950s, the opportunity element remains potent. HEW's Affirmative Action proposal and the Equal Rights Amendment to the Constitution witness the power of this value. Most revival movements appeal to this value.

Effort and optimism, or the belief that hard work and striving will ultimately lead to success. This value is clearly incorporated in several of the myths discussed above—the value of challenge and the possibility of success, for example. Retirement programs are ballyhooed with this value.

Efficiency, practicality, and pragmatism, or the value placed on solution-oriented as opposed to ideologically oriented thinking. A key question often asked of any piece of legislation is "Will it work?" This value extends to other parts of our lives, too. We want to know if a microwave oven is energy efficient, if it is practical or handy. We want to know if the new diesel engine will save money and run longer and cleaner. We want to know if our schooling will lead to a job. In other words, we value what is quick, workable, and practical.

Even though these values were cataloged nearly thirty years ago, they still have a great deal of relevance. This, if nothing else, suggests their

Get Rich Quick!!

$$$$ Success
Can Be Yours Today!!

Hundreds of people have made their fortunes acting as our agents in distributing the miracle Weed-Abolish treatment for lawns.

For a minimal investment you can have
★ That home you've dreamed of
★ That vacation trip
★ Those moments of pleasure
★ And much, much more

Send now for FREE information to

Weed-Abolish Inc.
P.O. Box 122
Finlayson, MN

SEND   TODAY!!

Figure 5-2   *Ads like this can be found in almost every magazine. They play on our need for achievement and success.*

basic quality. The fact that political position has less to do with the strength of these values than the method of enacting them seems to underscore the probability that these are core values for Americans. Our culture has been effective in instilling a set of values in all, or very nearly all, of its members—radicals, moderates, and reactionaries all believe in the same things, but just operationalize them differently. The power of a social system or culture to train its members is immense, even though the members do not often realize this as they react to the dictates deeply ingrained in them.

Does this mean that values remain essentially static and cannot be changed? Not necessarily. It only means that values are so deeply ingrained in a culture that its members often forget how strong their pressures are.

USE OF NONVERBAL MESSAGES AND CUES

A final kind of cultural or societal predisposition for persuasion relates to symbolic behavior that is not spoken or articulated. The whole field of nonverbal communication is relatively new and the research is extremely broad—far too broad to be adequately covered in part of one chapter. To limit our consideration here, we will not consider those nonverbal signal systems that seem to be biologically oriented (for example, the fact that humans are right- and left-nostriled as they are right- and left-handed and that you use your dominant nostril to "sniff out" a new acquaintance for the olfactory cues he gives off—fear, hate, love, lust, or joy odors). Instead, we will just look briefly at the kinds of nonverbal signals that seem to be culturally related—that differ from culture to culture and that can increase or destroy persuasive potential. We will look at the use of artifacts or objects, the use of space, and the use of touch.

Use of Artifacts

We are probably not so far removed from animals, but there are some differences. Though birds feather their nests with bits of string, straw, hair, and wood, they do it for purely functional reasons—to keep their nests intact and cozy. We humans feather our nests not only for those reasons but also for highly symbolic reasons. The best way of discovering how this happens is to look at your work area in your dorm room or at the work area of your roommate or spouse. It is not only arranged so that work can get done, but people feather their nests with objects—artifacts—that symbolize them. Arrangement is also symbolic (certain types of persons have messy desks, while others have extremely neat desks, with each pencil sharpened and papers stacked in neat piles). Our culture has taught us to react in certain ways to the artifacts of others and how they are used. These patterns of responses form premises for persuasion.

A common type of artifactual cosmetology is revealed in the objects surrounding a persuader in a message situation (for example, in a public speech situation the banners, the bunting, the use of flags, the insignias)—all contributing to the ultimate success of the persuasive attempt. Another type of artifact is clothing. What people wear sends signals about what they are like (think of the differences between casual sports clothes and a tuxedo), what they believe (for example, a priest's collar or an army officer's uniform), or with whom they associate (for example, the hippie will probably not associate with too many go-getting young IBM executives). Thus, persuaders symbolize themselves through plumage.

Another type of artifact is exemplified in the personal objects surrounding a persuader. Consider how you feel when you go into a doctor's office with diplomas on the wall—no art, no colorful posters, or any other kind of decoration—just diplomas. What cultural signal do you receive about the type of person the doctor is likely to be? Compare that with the feeling you have as you enter a college professor's office with posters or abstract art on the walls. The artifacts symbolize the kind of persuasion you will be likely to hear—in one case, professional, concrete, and probably prescriptive and, in the other, abstract.

Large objects, like furniture, can also give off signals. We can expect a certain kind of communication to occur when we are told to sit down at a table and the persuader sits on the opposite side of the table. Persuaders who put a lectern between themselves and the audience will probably engage in a certain kind of communication—probably very formal. If they step out from behind the lectern or walk around while talking, they may well be more informal. Types of furniture can also symbolize certain characteristics. What kinds of persuasion and what kinds of persons would you associate with French Provincial furniture? What kind of persuasion is likely to occur in a room with industrial metal furniture? What kind in a Danish Modern room? Or Early American?

Use of Space

The way people structure the space around them is also a factor in communication that seems particularly related to cultural training. We can, if we wish, signal to our fellow communicators that we feel superior and that formal communication is called for. We can suggest that informal communication is called for; or we can suggest that intimate and extremely frank communication is called for. Edward T. Hall notes four general distances used by persuaders in American culture:[8]

Public distance, or distances we often find in public speaking situations where speakers are 15 to 25 or more feet from their audiences.

---

8.   Edward T. Hall, *The Silent Language* (Garden City: Doubleday & Co., 1959), *The Hidden Dimension* (Garden City: Doubleday & Co., 1966), and "Proxemics—A Study of Man's Spatial Relationships" in *Man's Image in Medicine and Anthropology* (International Universities Press, 1963) all provide further insights to the use of space.

Figure 5-3   *This glasses manufacturer (persuader) uses the communicative function of artifacts to show the reader of a woman's magazine (persuadee) how she*

The Fairfield Design Group introduces GROUP 1, a new line of eyewear for you!

Bridge Type

Bridge types like noses differ. GROUP 1 eyeframes are available with either saddle or keyhole bridges, so that the bridge of your frame fits the bridge of your nose.

Facial Contour

Fairfield's GROUP 1 collection comes in six different subtly brilliant styles, each with two bridge sizes and two eye sizes, designed to complement the shape of your face.

Individual Coloring

GROUP 1 comes in a wide variety of colors carefully chosen to harmonize with your individual hair, eye and facial color.

Depth and Width of Eyeframe

Fairfield's Design Group has created perfectly proportioned eyewear that subtly enhances the size and beauty of your eyes.

Eye Positioning

No two pairs of beautiful eyes are set alike. The Fairfield Design Group has considered the variables of both the eyes' horizontal plane and pupillary distance in producing frames that can be precisely fitted to your eyes.

The Fairfield Design Group has dedicated over a quarter century to creating just one thing. Superb, award-winning eyewear, worn worldwide.

Introducing GROUP 1. The result of their total knowledge of both the construction of eyewear and the structural subtleties of the individual face.

Your local eyecare specialist can help you select a hand crafted, hand polished and carefully inspected GROUP 1 frame. A frame designed for you.

GROUP 1 BY FAIRFIELD

A NEW LINE OF EYEWEAR FOR YOU!

may be sending an unintended message. What is it? Would it be persuasive or not? (Courtesy Fairfield Optical Company, Inc.)

Informal persuasion probably will not work in these circumstances. Persuaders who try to be informal in a formal situation will probably meet with little success.

Social or formal distance, or the distances used in formal but nonpublic situations like interviews or committee reports. The persuader in these situations, though formal in style, need not be oratorical. Formal distance runs about 7 to 12 feet between persuader and persuadee. You would never become chummy in this kind of situation (regardless of whether you were persuader or persuadee), yet you would not deliver a "speech" either.

Personal or informal distance, or the distance used when two colleagues or friends are discussing a matter of mutual concern. A good example might be when you and your roommate are discussing this class or a problem you both share. In these situations, communication is less structured than in the formal situation; persuadee and persuader are both more relaxed and interact often with one another, bringing up and questioning evidence or asking for clarification. Informal distance, in our culture, is about 3½ to 4 feet—the eye-to-eye distance, if you sit at the corner of a teacher's desk, as opposed to the formal distance created when you sit across the desk.

Intimate distance, or the distance people use when they mutter or lovingly whisper messages they do not want others to overhear. Persuasion may or may not occur in these instances; usually the message is one that will not be questioned by the receiver—he or she will nod in agreement, follow the suggestion given, or respond to the question asked. When two communicators are in this kind of close relation to one another, their aims are similar, in all probability. The distance ranges from 6 to 18 inches.

When distances are used to encourage or discourage a certain kind of persuasion or when a persuader oversteps the boundaries "agreed upon" by the persuadee, results can often be startling. For example, during the 1972 presidential campaign, George McGovern, after being heckled during a speech, walked up to one of his hecklers and when he was in intimate distance said to him "kiss my ass" and walked away. The message—an intimate and certainly not a persuasive one—was overheard by some members of the press and then written up in the evening newspapers and related over the television news—a public kind of exposure. The response did not help the candidate's image.

In studies of communication flow and its relation to ease of conversation, leadership emergence, and a number of other variables, researchers discovered that the most used communication channels at a conference table (see Figure 5-4) were those across the corners of the table (or informal distance), the next most often used channel was directly across the

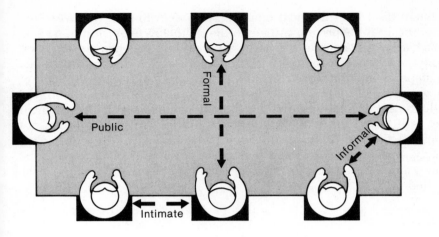

Figure 5-4 *Communication Channels at a Conference Table.*

table (or about the distance we have called formal distance), the third was down the length of the conference table (or about what we have called public distance), and the least used was between persons sitting next to one another (or about what we have called intimate distance). In conferences, we feel fairly comfortable to converse, to discuss, to persuade in informal ways; we do not often engage in intimate conversation and thus avoid speaking with those next to us. Most persons form few intimate relationships and probably feel uneasy responding *as if* in intimate relation with another person. Think of what you do in the front seat of an auto when there are three passengers or at a banquet table when you must talk to the person next to you. You probably move away from that person's face or you speak to a spot in midair—perhaps the windshield of the car or a centerpiece on the banquet table. You rarely allow yourself to communicate in intimate distance unless you are on an intimate basis with a person.

If you want to encourage communication flow, try to arrange informal spaces for persons to use; if you want to discourage communication, arrange intimate spaces for persons to use. Be alert to the persuader who is adept at using space this way and to the persuader who seems to have misjudged his relationship with a listener. In either case, the use of space indicates something about the persuader.

In *The Making of the President: 1960,* Theodore H. White tells an interesting anecdote about the use of space in describing the 1960 election-eve activities at the Kennedy compound in Hyannisport. Throughout the early evening hours, the "Irish Mafia" and aides who had helped John F. Kennedy in the campaign sat watching television election returns while they ate popcorn and drank beer and wine. Later in the evening it became apparent that the final results would be close and not decisive until at least the next morning. JFK went to bed. He awoke the next morning in his private cottage to the radio and television news that Illinois had gone Democratic, thereby assuring him the adequate electoral majority—he was the President-elect. He dressed and went out to the front steps of the cottage where his friends and aides waited. None of them seemed willing to enter a 10- or 15-foot circle of space around the President-elect until he gestured for them to come forward. They seemed to feel as if their former informal or even intimate relationship was not now called for, and they would have to be invited by President-elect Kennedy. Many persuadees and persuaders are not as perceptive as the Kennedy aides—they assume intimacy or informality when other patterns are called for.

Use of Touch

One of the strange inconsistencies in American culture is the way we regard physical touch between human beings. One often sees the heads of state in various European countries hugging and kissing one another when they meet after trips. Can you imagine what the press would do with a televised and photographed incident in which our President and Vice-President hugged and kissed after the President had returned from a trip abroad? In spite of new freedoms granted to homosexuals, public opinion would probably not be in favor of physical suggestions of homosexuality between public officials, even if there were no doubt in anyone's mind about the relationship. At the same time we have no strange feelings when the wives of the President and Vice-President hug and kiss. Touch is perfectly acceptable between two men on a football field or between two grade-school chums or between a man and a woman. Certainly touch is one of the most important systems of communication with infants—the sureness of a mother's or father's touch can calm and soothe an infant in distress.

Generally, in Western culture touch between men is limited to shaking hands or backslapping. Persuaders who are too "touchy" with persons around them (for example, with fellow candidates for office, with other persons on interview shows, or with other members of the board of directors) are likely to offend not only the person touched but also the persons observing the touch. Credibility can be drastically undermined if persuaders misread a relationship and respond inappropriately with touch.

Examples of misread physical touches abound in the literature of politics and social relations. Robert F. Kennedy is supposed to have been extremely touchable as a candidate, often in a day of campaigning losing several pairs of cufflinks and ending the day with clothing torn and hands and shoulders bruised by the "press of the flesh." At the same time he hated being touched in a formal situation such as a dinner or reception. I once worked with a group of firemen in a communication training program. For this group, the only acceptable touch from another male was the handshake or backslap. I wanted them to understand the importance of touch as a communicative device. A fireman must sometimes calm frantic men, women, and children to get them out of a burning building. They resisted rehearsing any kinds of touches. Not until we played a game in which one of the men was trapped and ordered to break out of a circle formed by the others linking arms and waists did the group begin to accept the idea of touching one another. The game gave them a culturally acceptable way to hold one another's arms and waists. Once past this initial barrier, we could talk about how touch could be used to calm people in crisis situations. The laying on of hands used in some religions is sometimes given credit for conversions when it is possible that touch is persuasive enough to prompt people to come forward and convert.

Other Nonverbal Message Carriers

There are other carriers of meaning that do not use words and that are peculiar to our culture or various parts of our culture. Duration of words, for example, is often a cue to the end of a sermon in black congregations. The preacher will say, "And for all of this we can thank Jeeeeeessssuuusss!" emphasizing the last word not only by increasing volume but by stretching it out. In other cultures this emphasis would seem out of place. This characteristic of the Negro church service was picked up by the Civil Rights Movement. Martin Luther King, Jr., in his last speech before he was assassinated during the Memphis garbage workers' strike, finished his speech urging workers to a final rally and march. He said, "Mine eeeeyyyyyeeeeessss have seen the glory of the coming of the Lord," stretching the word "eyes" out as a signal to his audience that he was finishing and that they ought to join in with "amen" and "right on." Eye contact or the lack of it can signal important messages in our culture. We say people should be able to look us straight in the eye if they aren't lying. If they happen to have artifical eyes or visual handicaps that do not allow direct eye contact with both eyes, we are uneasy. President Nixon was often accused of having shifty eyes and of avoiding direct eye contact with reporters or the television camera during the unfolding of the Watergate scandal. We sometimes speak of a person's having lively eyes and associate this attribute with high spirits, a good sense of humor, and ambition. The raised eyebrow asks a question or expresses doubt. The rate of eyeblinks one has is associated with one's level of conscious awareness of the world. Packard reports a research study which found that the eye-blink rate in supermarkets slowed down to a near hypnotic state for some shoppers. A person who is very tense will blink about once a second compared to the normal rate of 25 to 30 times a minute. Packard's shoppers dropped to an average of 14 blinks a minute.[9]

Other facial movements can have cultural messages. A researcher named Ray Birdwhistell has cataloged facial movements that carry meaning. He can describe literally hundreds of combinations of mouth, eye, cheek, and brow movements that carry meanings common to most persons in our culture. The furrowed brow, for example, usually signals concern, worry, or anxiety. Couple this with a high degree of lip tension and perhaps a repeated wetting of the lips and a pretty consistent message comes across. Birdwhistell even claims to be able to tell what part of the country one comes from by looking at facial position while speaking. New Englanders, for example, keep the upper lip pulled in and pressed tightly against the teeth—the grandpa who sells Pepperidge Farm bread is a good example. Of course, his regional accent reinforces his regional facial expression.

Smell may also have a message-carrying quality. We all recognize the power of the smells of fine food being cooked. This may or may not be intentionally persuasive, but a real estate agent I know often suggests that persons who want to sell their homes should keep two or three loaves of raised bread ready to pop into the oven just before bringing a potential buyer in to look at the house. The homey smell seems to have a persuasive quality. Certainly the use of deodorants, perfumes, after-shave lotions, and powders are meant to be persuasive. Slogans like "Want him to be more of a man? Try being more of a woman. Use Luvasmell perfume" exemplify the power of smell. Some recent research suggests that we have a dominant nostril just as we have a dominant hand if we are right- or left-handed. We turn the dominant nostril slightly into any situation that we are encountering for the first time. Our language suggests the power of smell—"It doesn't smell right to me," "Something is rotten in Denmark," and so forth. The persuader and persuadee need to become alert to the power of this nonverbal device.

Using Nonverbal Behavior

Again, we need to emphasize that nonverbal behavior—like the other cultural predispositions for persuasion—occurs at a very low level of awareness, almost instinctively or automatically without our being aware of it. Nonetheless, we respond to nonverbal uses of objects, space, touch, and other symbolic cues like facial expression; we feel at ease with what has happened or with what we observe if the observed actions are consis-

---

9.   Vance Packard, *The Hidden Persuaders* (New York: Pocket Books, 1964). See Chapter 16.

tent with what our culture has taught us and if they seem sincere. We began this discussion of nonverbal cues in persuasion by saying that though man may not be far from animals, he engages in the symbolic use of artifacts, touches, and space when he attempts to persuade. The same notion applies as we receive messages—we trust our nonverbal reactions because of what we believe these unspoken messages symbolize about the persuader. We do not look at the use of touch or clothing as happenstance; we see it as intentional, even if only at a low level of awareness. There is "leakage" in nonverbal cues—though we may try to pretend or to fake nonverbal signals, we are unable to prevent our true motives from seeping through. The perceptive and sensitive persuadee will be on the alert for these cues.

Obviously, the use of artifacts, space, and touch are not the only nonverbal dimensions with persuasive impact. In evaluating persuasion, you should also consider the roles and meanings of such nonverbal cues as tone of voice, directness of eye contact, facial expressions, and gestures. In a persuasive situation, what meanings may be attached to silence on the persuader's part?

A REVIEW AND CONCLUSION

As you have probably felt by this time, the world of the persuadee in an information age is not an easy one. There are so many things to be aware of—the persuader's self-revelation using language and stylistic choices, the internal or process premises operating within each of us, the interactive rules for content premises, as we have called them, and now we have glimpsed societal and cultural predispositions for persuasion—which may also act as premises in persuasive arguments. Persuaders, either because they have studied and analyzed our cultural predispositions or because they instinctively appeal to these trends, rely on the societal training and shaping of belief and action in the persons they are trying to reach. On at least three separate levels, this training has an effect on each of us—in the cultural myths or images we respond to, in the sets of values we consciously articulate, and in the nonverbal cues we respond to (uses of artifacts, space, and touch, to mention a few).

Questions for Further Thought

1. What are the three types of culturally or socially inculcated predispositions for persuasion? Give examples of each from your own experience.

2. How does culture or society train its members? Give examples from your own experience.

3. You are in school for a reason: What is it? How did you become motivated to come to college? Why? Is this related to any particular myth or image repeated to you? What were the elements in it? (For example, as the child of immigrant parents, I was repeatedly told that though "they" could take away your house and job, "they" could never take away an education—it spelled success in America.)

4. How do you rank the core values mentioned in Chapter 5? How do you operationalize them (that is, put them into practice)? Are there other values in your own value system not mentioned by Steele and Redding? What are they? Are they restatements of the core values? If so, how? If not, how do they differ?

5. How do you use space in the classroom? How far does the teacher in your favorite class stand from the members of the class? In your worst class? In classes in which you were most successful when it comes to grades, what kind of distance was used most often (for example, social, intimate)? Which are you most familiar with or most at ease with? How do you use space when you interact with persons where you live (observe your behavior at mealtime, in conversations, and the like)?

6. How much do you touch others? Try to increase the number of touches you use and observe the responses of others. Does the increase cause a different effect? If so, how?

7. What are the artifacts you surround yourself with? What do they mean to you? (Some students have reported that the first thing they do after unpacking for dormitory living is to purchase "conversation pieces" or artifacts that symbolize themselves.) What about your roommate? What artifacts does he or she use? Do they symbolize him or her? What about your family members?

Experiences in Persuasion

1. In a group of four or five, observe a television talk show without the sound being turned on. Concentrate on one participant and his nonverbal gestures and movements. Report on the nonverbal interaction between guests and host and between other guests. (This exercise is particularly revealing if the show is a controversial one in which emotional behavior is exhibited.)

2. Observe the entertainment page of a newspaper from a town or city other than your own. What kinds of values might you predict for the

inhabitants of that city based on your observations? Justify your conclusions.

3. Rearrange the personal artifacts and space of your roommate or a family member. Observe and record his or her reactions. Interview the offended person after your experiment and see which objects mean most to him or her. Find out why. Report on your findings.

4. Interview foreign students on campus. Try to find out what their culture inculcates through the use of myths or images, and through values. How does their nonverbal system differ from ours?

The Persuasive
Campaign or Movement 6

Most changes in attitude, behavior, belief, or action are not the result of a single message. If this were the case, persuasion would be hopeless. It would imply that people are so fickle that they bounce from pro to con minute by minute. It would be useless to try to persuade them, for at any time another persuader could happen along, deliver a single message, and undo all. People do not sway from pro to con and back again on the slim basis of single messages. They reflect at length before acting. Of course, all of you can think of instances in which you were persuaded by a single message—in an instant, so to speak. Perhaps you decided to date a certain person as the result of a single visit with him or her. A particular teacher was able to open a whole new perspective to you in a single lecture. Most of the time, these instances are not really the result of the single incident you recall. Rather, you were ready for the message that changed you. You were exposed to many pieces of data, and the combined effect was your change of mind. You were the recipient of a series of messages that could be called a campaign. The series led to your decision, not the single message. Most persuasion occurs as the result of many message inputs, as the result of a campaign or movement and not a single speech. This chapter focuses on the campaign. We look at how it works, how it develops, and how we can listen to and evaluate the campaigns and movements that occur around us.

ASPECTS OF CAMPAIGNS AND MOVEMENTS

In considering persuasive campaigns, we need to look at why campaigns and movements differ from other methods of persuasion. These elements that we shall consider are common to all campaigns. Generally, they can be seen as two types. The first type includes the functional aspects of campaigns. The second comprises the formal aspects. The functional aspects are those strategic and broad elements that shape the thrust and direction of the movement or campaign. There are seven of them. Although there are a variety of formal elements in campaigns or movements, we are concerned here with only one—the system of communication used by movements or campaigns.

Functional Aspects

A campaign is not just a series of messages, all dealing with the same issue. Nor is it a debate over an issue. What makes the campaign different? One of the differences is that campaigns and movements are developmental in nature. They move from stage to stage. They have a beginning, a middle, and an end, so to speak. Also, if they are to succeed, campaigns must create a sense of the dramatic in the mind's eye of their audiences. Movements or campaigns need to depict their cause as one of historic magnitude. Then they need to invite others to join and share in the great cause in some real or symbolic way. Campaigns also need to communicate so that audiences align themselves or identify themselves with the person, product, or idea being promoted. This is because all persuasion involves self-persuasion to some degree. The audience members have to become involved in their own persuasion. They must add something to the persuasive mix for change to really occur. Getting them to identify or align with the campaigner's goals or purposes is a step toward such participation or co-persuasion.

These two functional characteristics work well together, for the ideal developmental format is one that is also dramatic. Viewing a TV serial is like following movements or campaigns. Each of the daily dramas leads to the conclusion of the serial. Each episode adds to the overall result of the campaign or movement. Though the episodes can stand alone (each has its own beginning, middle, and end), they draw on one another. They rely on one another. They meld into one another until a collage is completed.

Formal Aspects

As already noted, a campaign or a movement is not just a collection of messages about the same topic. The thing that makes campaigns differ is the systematic flow of information through four basic steps. These four steps are like those of a computer system as it works. There is (1) programming, (2) information input and dispersal, (3) re-formation of the information, and (4) the end product of the newly arranged information—the representation to the audience of the campaign's central cause.

You may want to explore campaigns in much more depth than we will here, read accounts of campaigns, participate in one, or perhaps even plan and conduct one. Discover how you are persuaded by campaigns. In finding how we are affected and swayed by campaigns, we ought to be able to see trends we can use in our campaigns. We may feel a need to object to a college or university policy. A campaign can help elect a member of the student senate who will work to change minds and actions of people. A campaign can get parents' support for the purchase of a car or for the right to live your own lifestyle.

TYPES OF CAMPAIGNS

Three kinds of movements or campaigns predominate. They are the politically oriented campaign for office, the product-oriented advertising campaign, and the issue- or cause-oriented social movement or campaign. At first glance, you may think the first and last types are not really different. Political campaigns focus on people. They are campaigns with the goal of winning voters to believe that one candidate is more sincere, wise, or active than another. The issue-oriented movement or campaign gets audiences to support a certain course of action or to embrace a certain belief.[1] As such, the issue-oriented campaign does not rely on a single leader. Its leadership may shift. First one person leads and then another. No one person is the spokesman for the cause. We might distinguish between the three types of campaigns by saying that the first tries to convince people of the value of a man. The second tries to convince them of the value of a thing or object. The third tries to convince them of the value or goodness of an idea, a belief, or an ideology. "Person," "thing," and "idea" are the three key words. Many of the characteristics of person campaigns and idea campaigns relate to product campaigns, and vice versa.

The information discussed here can be used and thought of in connection with campaigns for particular offices in student government organizations or in groups like fraternities or perhaps in offices like that of the campus newspaper. It also relates to those campaigns promoting a certain philosophy. The campaign to keep legal abortions on the law books is one example; the counter campaign to outlaw abortion is another. Idea campaigns seem to come and go in cycles depending on the

---

1.   A good discussion of the differences between the issue and the image of candidates for political office and what that difference implies is available in "Political Myth: The Image and the Issue" by Dan F. Hahn and Ruth M. Gonchar, *Today's Speech*, Vol. 20 (Summer 1972), pp. 57–65. Hahn and Gonchar conclude that the image may well be the best indicator of a candidate's future behavior. Issues change and fade, they maintain, but image indicates a pattern of behavior independent of issues.

times. If things are bad and there is an exciting leader like Hitler, Franklin D. Roosevelt, or Dr. Martin Luther King, Jr., an idea campaign can develop. If either of these two elements—the man or the times—is missing, the idea campaign is not likely to flourish. The years of our involvement in Vietnam saw the many leaders come and go. As a result, there was no lasting change nor was any well-known leader associated with the anti-war movement. Perhaps in good times it is hard for even exciting leaders to make themselves heard. Reverend Jesse Jackson of Operation PUSH is a charismatic man. He was trained as a lieutenant to Martin Luther King, Jr., in the Southern Christian Leadership Conference (S.C.L.C.). He emerged on the scene when the issue of civil rights was not in vogue. As a result, he has never been able to get a true mass movement going as King did in the early 1960s. Nonetheless, it is useful to be aware of the tactics and strategies of idea campaigners.

The campaign to promote a product has been with us since the first snake-oil pitchman loaded his wagon and headed for the boondocks. The goal then and now was to flimflam the gullible yokels out on the frontier. He would usually come into town with much hoopla, leaflets, and ballyhoo. Often the next stage of the campaign was some form of entertainment—an Indian show, magic, music, or oratory and dramatics. Once a sizable crowd was gathered, the huckster would begin to sell the product, using on-the-spot demonstrations, testimonials, and so forth. Frequently, listeners sampled the product. Finally, the flimflam artist talked about his need to be moving on and suggested that they had better take advantage of his offer right then and there. It was their last chance to get a bottle of the Formula X elixir to cure warts, baldness, hot flashes, and anything else that might ail anyone. Things have not really changed that much, when you think about it. We turn on the television to watch the $6 Million Man. Steve Austin, a man "barely alive," is brought out to fight for justice by the miracle bionics in him. That is the hoopla and ballyhoo of the medicine show. Then we are entertained by the show, just as the snake-oil pitchman entertained the audience. At intervals during the entertainment we get the sales pitch. Most contemporary products promise almost as much as Formula X did. Platformate in Shell gasoline gives longer engine life, better mileage, less pollution, and a quieter running engine. Purina Puppy Chow not only "makes its own milky sauce" but provides the extra protein and iron needed to build strong muscles during puppy's important first year of life. It also helps build strong teeth and bones.

In spite of their differences, there are many similarities among these three kinds of campaigns. Many lie in the kinds of communication strategies that they use to sell their person, product, or idea. The persuadee who wants to be aware of the "snake-oil" that is being pushed, who wants to spot doublespeak, needs to be aware of these strategies. The next section looks at several such strategies, which we can see as we examine the mass-media culture we live in and its many campaigns.

Those discussed below are by no means all the communication strategies that could be cited but are only representative ones.[2]

DEVELOPMENTAL PATTERNS OF SUCCESSFUL CAMPAIGNS

One of the communication strategies that occurs in all three types of campaigns is that they are *developmental*. They do not run on the same level or pitch throughout. They do not repeatedly pound away on the same pieces of information. They do not always have the same strategy at various times in their existence. Instead, they grow and change and adapt to audience responses and as new issues emerge. You might think of it as a fishing expedition in which the strategists of the campaign try in various ways to get the attention of the audience. They use different methods or lures. If one method does not succeed after some use, they try another and perhaps another. As the mood of the audience develops, the mood of the message must also change. The whole thing must be planned so that each shift follows from what came before.

For instance, suppose you are hired to establish product X (say, a new kind of building material) in the public eye—to get across the idea that this is the greatest, most impressive development in construction since the steel beam. What would you do first? You would not blindly go about trying first this method and then that method. Instead, you would outline the major points you want to make about this new product. What kinds of persons would be buyers? What are their values and beliefs about construction? How to reach them? Now suppose, after your first advertising attempt, you discover that you failed. People are not buying the durability of the product. They are more impressed by its cost. You will have to shift your strategy. You would never have discovered the flaw between what you thought was important and what was the key factor if you had not first tried to focus on durability. The discovery will affect your next ads for the product. Campaign planners adapt to audience responses.

Five Stages of Development

Well, how do campaigns develop? There are several possible answers to this question, depending on the theory you begin with. In 1960, Theodore H. White believed that presidential campaigns developed by the careful

---

2. Some of the strategies arise out of communication research, others out of theory and research in other areas—history for example—but all of them have been verified in numerous campaigns. At Northern Illinois University, we have looked in depth at more than 600 different person, product, or idea campaigns. Not all of the strategies occur in each campaign but those listed seem most prevalent.

use of a mass media created "image" that could be elected. A campaign could be traced by looking at the candidate and his or her relation to the information media.[3] Four years later, in 1964, he saw the political campaign as the ongoing challenge to the daring of the voter.[4] Four years later still, White saw the political campaign as somehow linked to the ability to explain, step-by-step, the chaos and change surrounding the audience.[5] He had changed his perception again by 1972 and again by 1976. The power of money (1972) and the critical mistake (1976) seemed to best explain those campaigns.

The important thing to note is that most critics seem to agree that a campaign must demonstrate change, growth, or development. One theory comes from study of the development of emerging nations.[6] There are five steps in the development of a national image or character. They are identity, legitimacy, participation, penetration, and distribution. Each stage must occur before the next can develop and emerge.

Identity   For instance, suppose that Transylvania has just declared itself a nation. The first step is to characterize itself. It needs a mask that will show it to the rest of the world. The new nation must seek an identity. There are ways to do this. Transylvania may design a flag. It may develop hero myths. Or it may fight wars or have building projects.

A movement must do the same thing to show its identity. It needs some kind of handle or label by which it can be identified. The Black Power Movement developed such things as a flag, a salute, a handshake, a hairstyle, and a style of dress.

In 1974, a new football league called the World Football League (WFL) was established. It got identification by changing the rules. It permitted more players in the backfield than did the National Football League (NFL). The goalposts were moved to make field goals easy. Team names were not animals like bears or lions as in the NFL. Instead they were tied to the home cities of the teams—such as the Chicago Fire, the Shrevesport Steamers, and the Honolulu Suns. These plus the team songs

---

3.   See Theodore H. White's *The Making of the President: 1960* (New York: Atheneum Publishers, 1961). This volume was the first to deal comprehensively with the candidates in a presidential election. It won the Pulitzer Prize in 1961.

4.   See Theodore H. White's *The Making of the President: 1964* (New York: Atheneum Publishers, 1965).

5.   See Theodore H. White's *The Making of the President: 1968* (New York: Atheneum Publishers, 1969).

6.   Leonard Binder, et al., *Crisis and Sequence in Political Development* (Princeton, N.J.: Princeton University Press, 1971), especially Chapter 1. I wish to thank William Semlak for calling this source to my attention; Mr. Semlak utilized the suggestions offered by the volume to analyze the campaign of George McGovern for the Democratic nomination in 1972 in a paper for a seminar in Movements and Campaigns offered at the University of Minnesota in the summer of 1972. Professor Bernard L. Brock, who taught the seminar, was kind enough to let me join it while I was a visiting professor there in 1972.

and colors were all identification devices. The league and the teams all achieved this first step in the development of campaigns. Later, as we shall see, they failed; but, in this first stage, there was a high degree of success for the WFL and its teams.

Candidates for political office also need to get identification and use many of the same tactics. They choose color codes—Jimmy Carter, for instance, was known as the green-and-white candidate during the 1976 primaries and maintained that combination after he had won nomination. Most politicians think that red, white, and blue are the only colors that can be combined, but other combinations have been used in campaigns at all levels of government. The candidate also usually chooses a slogan. The slogan "He Has the Guts to Do What's Right" was used to help reelect a Republican from a very conservative part of Illinois even after he had voted to impeach Richard Nixon. The slogans are tied to the logo or emblem of the campaign—an American eagle in flight, the ecology symbol, or some other trademark. Politicians usually have theme songs or campaign songs that are used to identify them to voters and supporters. Products have jingles that do the same thing.

So the identification stage is an important one for all types of campaigns, and all three types seem to use similar tactics to get identified in the minds of the target audience.

Legitimacy The second of the five related stages is to establish a base of legitimacy. Transylvania may seek alliances, entrance to the United Nations, and so forth. All of these give the country a legitimacy or a kind of credibility. This signals that Transylvania is not a fly-by-night operation. It is a force to be reckoned with. Legitimacy is another way of saying that the movement or campaign has power. For the product, a certain amount

Figure 6-1 Many devices are used to gain product, person, or idea identification in campaigns. Logos, like the one above, are one kind of device. Why is the winged foot of Mercury used? What does it communicate? Why put it between the word "Good" and the word "Year"? Answers to those questions help explain how product image or identification develops. (Courtesy The Goodyear Tire and Rubber Company.)

of sales may be the key. Volkswagen became a "legitimate" threat by selling half a million vehicles a year. The U.S. auto industry began to design its own compacts. The Black Power Movement of the late 1960s demonstrated that it had power by destruction in ghettos. Legitimacy of the Student Power Movement was shown by the "occupation" or "liberation" of pieces of university property—classrooms, offices, files, flags, and deans. A political campaign shows legitimacy by being tied to power figures or centers. The candidate usually is seen with important members of the party leadership. Candidates may also choose to demonstrate how power works. They have rallies. The student hoping to live in an off-campus apartment gets legitimacy or power through a summer job that will cover the costs or by joining ranks with several fellow students to share costs. The student running for fraternity president establishes legitimacy when fellow group members begin to support him.

In a sense, incumbents in any election have already shown power, they are already established and do not need to show legitimacy. Challengers have a tougher time. They must first defeat all other contenders for the nomination. They must also demonstrate legitimacy during the campaign itself. John Kennedy did not accomplish this until the famed Great Debates with Richard Nixon were televised. Carter did it by winning primaries outside of the South.

Products have to show legitimacy, too. The patent medicine show demonstrated that some of the claims made for the product were at least partly true. The pitchman showed that baldness had apparently been cured or had someone give a testimonial about the product. Today's products frequently use similar tactics to establish legitimacy. Football players use the product, so it should be durable—or at least compatible with a strong he-man image. Beautiful women use the perfume so it must enhance feminine sex appeal. Sometimes before our very eyes we see how Top Job cleans a filthy wall with just one simple wipe of a sponge. This stage of a campaign is crucial for it leads to the third and highly involving stage, the participation stage. In participating, scores or hundreds of persons get in on the action by working, voting, or buying.

Participation   The third stage is like the second stage. This stage involves more and more people in the campaign in real or symbolic ways. People are invited to join. They may be asked to fly the flag or to join the army or to open their houses to tourists. They may be asked to share in some project like a five-year plan.

The distributors and users of products participate in the use and profit of the product. Coupon offers are made to product users. They buy and use the product and get money or gifts. In some instances, stores are paid to allow some of their space to be used for special displays of certain soaps, wines, and so forth. The dealer may get a cut rate for pushing a certain product. Similarly, a movement may urge participation in real or symbolic ways. Women stopped doing housework in a one-day strike. The slogan of the women's day strike was "Don't iron while the strike is hot!" In other situations, people may be asked to wear arm bands or badges, to yell slogans at rallies, or to put signs around their houses or on their automobile bumpers. During World War II, it was hard to get bread sliced at bakeries. The reason was to conserve electricity for the war effort. The power thus saved was never really devoted to the war effort, but participation in this way on the part of the average citizen increased commitment to the war. The same sorts of stories are told about saving tinfoil, lard, and tin cans. A person running for student body president may ask persons to participate in his campaign by canvassing dormitory floors or student groups. For a Campus Crusade for Christ rally many students were asked to distribute leaflets and urge others to attend. This kind of activity gets persons involved in the campaign or movement. It guarantees further active support. Persons who put bumper stickers on their cars will vote for the name on the sticker most of the time. Movements ask supporters to do something, even if it is only symbolic. They can march, hold a vigil, or salute. The effects of this are to increase commitment to the cause. It activates the kind of self-persuasion discussed in Chapter 3.

Political workers are asked to wear compaign buttons, use campaign pencils, nail files, or matchbooks. All these are designed to give support to the candidate and more importantly to get people involved. I once offered to purchase all ten barbecue tickets in the book, if only I did not have to go to the rally—or approach others to get them to buy tickets. The offer was refused, and the explanation was that that would do no good. No one was making money on the rally. It was a break-even affair—its purpose was to get persons involved. The purpose of this stage is twofold. First, it gets people involved and committed to the cause. Second, it shows the legitimacy of the campaign or movement.

Penetration   Stage four—the penetration stage—is the most difficult to explain. Think of it this way: Suppose that you have been totally unaware of some movement—say, consumerism—then you are exposed to it. You probably first hear about the movement after the first three stages have already taken place. You are part of the mass of people who will never engage in the movement. You will never be the person who brings consumer charges against the manufacturer of a product. You will never organize a boycott of an inferior or dangerous product. Instead, you merely get the messages of the movement. Nonetheless, the movement needs your silent support. Without it the persons involved will remain a minority. This minority status, shared by all movements and campaigns, must lead to large-scale support among the people. Various terms have been coined for this stage, such as "the grass roots," "a ground swell of support," and "the silent majority." The fourth stage of a movement or campaign builds a general public attitude toward the movement—preferably favorable, of course. People reflect this attitude in some way. They respond on a poll, recognize the name of a product, are aware of the issues, or perhaps agree with the goals of a candidate. In a sense, this stage is getting through to a good-sized part of the market. For a movie like *Star Wars*, an all-time top-ten moneymaker, this stage means getting old duffers like me to it for my once-a-month movie.

Though these steps seem distinct and clear, they often merge and flow from one to another. The steps flow in a logical way from one to another, but there are times when stages may so merge as to become indistinguishable. This may occur in very rapid sequence. Every campaign aims at the penetration stage. The real point at which penetration occurs is when the movement or campaign has succeeded and has power. tion, it has no real penetration. Until a product reaches the kind of threshold that Volkswagen reached in the 1950s, it has not penetrated. Candidates for public office may become identified as certain kinds of Candidates for public office may become identified as a certain kinds of characters and may even demonstrate legitimacy by having large rallies or winning primaries. They may identify with power personages or power organizations. They may also get wide participation, with hundreds of volunteers. However, until significant numbers of the large mass of voters support such candidates, effective penetration has not yet occurred.

A movement may go through the same initial stages of getting an identification and a kind of legitimacy or power, coupled with highly active participation on the part of some of its followers. Until a large part of the masses support it or until the movement gets the change in the status quo that it desires, it too fails to complete the penetration stage.

In different circumstances, a majority of persons in the United States probably supported the changes started by President Franklin D. Roosevelt in the 1930s. Though he did not really overthrow the status quo, he did achieve a ground swell of public support for significant changes. He achieved penetration. This stage may also be reached in the campaign for an off-campus apartment when your parents begin to offer less and less resistance to the idea and when they begin to identify reasons of their own for allowing you to live outside the dorm (it's cheaper, handier, and so forth). Some products establish a penetration stage rapidly. For example, Tide, the washing product, was the first detergent to come on the market in the 1950s. The difference between Tide and soap products was so obvious that it quickly became the top-selling wash product, thus establishing penetration in a short time. The same thing occurred with the first cold-water washday product—All. It penetrated the market quite fast. Soon we were using the words "cold-water washday" when talking about other similar products. Those words originated with All and became names of a class of products. Similar things occurred with products like Jell-o, Kleenex, and Hershey's which have such great market penetration that their names are frequently used to stand for all gelatin desserts, nose tissue, and chocolate bars.

Most product penetration is not so dramatic. In the toothpaste market, for example, Crest and Gleem had great penetration throughout the 1960s due to their tooth decay claims and fluoride. There was another segment of the market. Soon a product named Macleans came out. It promised whiter and sexier teeth. It made little or no claim about being able to prevent decay but soon had high sales and thus penetrated at least the whiteness/sexiness market segment. Other manufacturers realized this penetration and responded by putting out their own whiteness/sexiness toothpastes—Pearl Drops, Ultra Brite and others. However, Crest and Gleem still capture three quarters of the market, the rest being split among the brightness/whiteness and house brands. The World Football League thrived through the first half of its first season and then more or less disintegrated. The novelties had worn off. The teams and league never achieved penetration.

Distribution　In the fifth and final stage of development—distribution— the campaign or movement becomes institutionalized. Having achieved the control they sought, the leaders of the campaign or movement must now live up to their promises in some way. They must signal to the people that change is going to occur. The likely moves are the designation of subgroups of the campaign staff or of the movement's leadership to positions of power with tasks to complete. These tasks fit with the promises made in the campaign and with the goals of the movement. This stage does not always occur in the object-oriented campaign involving products that are being sold. However, such things as rebates, money-back coupons, and incentives to store owners are kinds of distribution that we see in product campaigns. In an emerging nation, the new government begins land reform, court reform, changes in the social structure, and other changes to show that power is now being divided and shared with the people, the faithful, the party, or the movement leaders.

Unfortunately, this stage is rarely instituted except in symbolic ways. The end of the Civil War in 1865 did not result in a change in the status of most Negroes in the South. Black Codes were instituted, and reconstruction officials neglected to institute much meaningful change in the daily lives of most former slaves. Following the overthrow of the Batista regime in Cuba by Fidel Castro, little land redistribution actually took place. The distribution stage, so it seems, often contains within itself the seeds of its own destruction. By setting itself up into bureaus, it is open to the same kinds of criticism leveled at the old order. Perhaps that is why most people are cynical about political party platforms and why many people say, "It doesn't make any difference who gets in; politicians are all crooks anyway."

The first of the functional aspects of campaigns and movements, then, is that they are developmental in nature. They go through stages, each of which is logically related to the others. Usually these stages flow in order, but at times they may meld into one another. The first four stages must occur for a campaign or movement to be complete.

As you observe campaigns for public office or movements to change social thought, you ought to be able to identify their stages. The real difference between campaigns and movements is that while the political campaign focuses on the image of a person, the movement develops acceptance of an ideology or lifestyle. The advertiser develops acceptance and use of an object. All three follow the stages of identification, legitimacy, participation, penetration, and distribution. Many campaigns and movements never reach full bloom; typically they die out at the participation or penetration stage. Social and political movements, upon reaching this stage, usually distribute the power and privilege wrested from the opposition only superficially. Thus, as a movement or campaign develops, it sets for itself not only its next stage of development but ultimately the raw material for a countermovement or countercampaign. This development aspect of campaigns is particularly suited for the second functional characteristic of campaigns—their reliance upon the dramatic metaphor.

Invitation to the Drama

We have already talked in several places about dramatic impulse in human beings. We see the world and identify its forces in ordered ways. The most common form of ordering is the dramatic episode. It is interesting to observe in our own lives how often we tend to structure the world in episodes. We see meals as having a "plot line." They start with prayers. Certain foods like salads are followed by other courses in a neat, orderly progression to an after-dinner liqueur with coffee. We see our workdays as divided into episodes: first-hour class, opening-the-mail time, lunch at the dorm, and others. We see our weeks ordered the same way. Wednesday is called humpday, since it is the halfway point. We see those around us as actors in the drama. Our parents may be villains and our friends may be heroes and heroines. Others around us are engaging in applepolishing to get on the good side of the teacher or the boss. Our fellow workers are classic stereotypes—the gossip, the bitter old-timer, the good-natured fellow, the footloose-and-fancy-free jokester, and so on.

This impulse for the drama is deep and powerful. It is one of the universals that link movements and campaigns. In fact, unless a movement or campaign can create a drama or pseudoevent, it has little chance of getting the support of the people it needs. The success of a movement or campaign depends upon its ability to create in the minds of its audience the sense of a momentous event or series of events. They must be lived out or else the whole world and all people involved will suffer. Given such a drama, the movement or campaign succeeds to the degree that it can also invite the audience to participate in the drama in real or symbolic ways.

Let us look at the dramatic impulse. What is it that creates a sense of drama? How are dramatic elements used by persuaders? How do they occur? What effects do they have?

The first thing we need is a setting or *scene*, to use Burke's terms (see Chapter 2), with dramatic potential. For instance, someone's backyard may have dramatic possibilities, but they are limited. A posh New York nightclub or an impressive apartment or perhaps a deserted junkyard all obviously have dramatic possibilities much broader than the backyard scene.

Given a dramatic scene, we now need the second element— *characters*. To keep it simple, let's limit ours to the good guys and their helpers and the bad guys and their helpers. We need to see our dramatic scene filled with opposing forces that are going to do battle. So in a political campaign it may be the politicians of compassion and understanding versus the politicians of special interests. In many washday products it is the good character—Mr. Clean—versus the baddies of dirt and grime. Television commercials for STP motor oil have played this bad guys/good guys theme out in a familiar drama. A poor distressed auto engine is shown surrounded by four villains—dirt, heat, cold, and rust dressed as attacking Indians. They are spotted by four cans of STP coming over the brow of a hill dressed as cavalry. A bugler sounds the charge, and the cavalry gallop down onto the plateau and chase off the nasty villains to win the gratitude of the coy engine, which is now safe. In an idea campaign, the forces of good and evil may be personified or they may be hooked to certain groups. For example, a factory safety campaign may focus attention on the evil represented by the bored worker who becomes careless and causes accidents. The campaign to end pollution of the Fox River may see its villains in the boardroom of U.S. Steel. In any case, a drama necessitates opposing forces—of good and evil, of wisdom and folly, of youth and age, or the like. Going back to the stylistic attributes of persuasion in Chapter 2, we find that Weaver's notion of God terms and Devil terms relates here. The persuader creates the dramatic mood he desires by choosing hierarchies or families of terms that delineate the good guys and the bad guys in his drama.

The third element of the dramatic characteristic that is common to movements and campaigns is a *plot*. Most movement or campaign plots are also simple. The weak are exploited, and a hero arises in their midst to lead them to liberty. Another variation may be the one in which members of a group are being enslaved or exploited. Through some event or other means, they become aware of their grievances and then try to overthrow the bad guys. The Women's Liberation Movement uses both of these plot lines, with men being the exploiters and women needing to take aggressive action to avoid slavery. Sometimes the villains are institutions that cleverly hide the slavery. Banks, for example, do not allow women to lift the heavy bags of coins at the tellers' windows at the end of a working day. There was a time when management argued that anyone who could not do the whole job really could not become a bank officer so few women, until recently, even moved up to executive positions. "Once conscious of the trick, you can fight it, so get consciousness" can be a theme of a campaign using the second variation. We could cite numerous examples of dramatic plots, but generally they are subplots of three or four major lines of action:

1. The overcoming of odds by a group or under the leadership of a hero (Franklin D. Roosevelt, the nomination of George McGovern, or the legal conviction of an industrial polluter)

2. The quest for a goal or to avoid a pitfall (the Horatio Alger myth)

3. The establishment of long-needed change by a group or through a leader (civil rights, women's liberation, the change in grading procedure)

4. The purgation of symbolic sin in our midst, or the removal of an evil man, situation, or the like (movements for the consumer or for ecological issues)[7]

If one has the raw materials of the drama at hand in the setting or situation, in the characters, and in the plot, the task of the persuader is then to utilize the raw material in such a way as to invite the potential supporter of the movement or campaign to enter into the dramatic setting, to do battle with or to lend support to the characters of the drama, and to act out a part of the plot line. In this way, the participation stage mentioned earlier is fulfilled. Supporters of the movement or campaign feel that they share in the victory. Their actions result in ego rewards as they see payoff in election returns or as they see some authority figure lose his temper because of wisecracks, comments, or chanting. In other words, the supporters' actions become part of the whole theme of the movement or campaign. They engage in the drama as in a work of art.

Many movements must fight off competing dramas, and their own dramas never really take hold. At other times, leaders of the movement or campaign do not invite participation. They prefer to dwell on ideology or

7.   See Kenneth Burke's *The Rhetoric of Religion* (Boston: Beacon Press, 1961). "The Epilogue in Heaven" is especially instructive on this point. For three political plot lines, see Murray Edelman, *Politics as Symbolic Action* (Chicago: Markham Publishing Co., 1971), pp. 77–79; see also Edelman, *The Symbolic Uses of Politics* (Urbana: University of Illinois Press, 1967).

on praise for themselves. The mudslinging campaign, though interesting for its conflict aspects (everyone likes to watch a fight), is a risky kind of campaign to run. There is a high risk that it will backfire. The audience may oppose the persuader who calls names or tries to set up a dramatic "fight" for persuasive purposes. At the same time that mudslingers besmirch the adversary, they seem to be praising themselves. Both arguments are called the *ad hominem*—to the personality or about the person. Audiences suspect people who attack others and then praise themselves. The whole tactic reeks of self-interest and a big ego. In everyday terms, the audience feels that "you don't fight in a gutter without getting dirty."

Some dramas fail to be fully played out in the audience's minds because the campaigners choose to dwell on issues of philosophy. People want to see ideas acted out. They do not want to be preached to. For example, the American Indian Movement (AIM), failed at first by preaching its ideas. It succeeded later by acting out demands when AIM members captured the entire Pine Ridge Indian Reservation in South Dakota. The setting had the drama needed. It was not far from the site of Custer's last stand. It included the site of the massacre of Indian women and children at Wounded Knee, South Dakota. There were two types of villains—the Bureau of Indian Affairs and persons from the government who would not deliver on various demands. The Indians were easy to depict as underdogs. There were various subplots that could be played out as well—such as the ruin of the Indians when they went to the cities, and cheating whites who tricked the Indians by giving them firewater.

A second characteristic of movements and campaigns, then, is their tendency to succeed when they focus on the dramatic—when they act out their ideology instead of preaching it. When action invites the audience to the drama in real or symbolic ways, the movement becomes vital and attractive. It succeeds to the degree that it is able to avoid overstatement and being preachy and to the degree that it can present historic dramas. Hitler invited the German people to join him in finding Germany's "place in the sun." Martin Luther King, Jr., invited others to join in his "dream."

When a movement gathers speed and power and begins to have effect, the receiver can hear other dramatic invitations. Though many persuasive campaigns do not focus on high drama so obviously, they do nonetheless rely on dramatic raw material. The student trying to get a trip to Europe subsidized may outline the dramatic dangers of staying home during a boring summer, or he may highlight the dramatic potential of exposing oneself to other cultures and languages and of possible advantages that might accrue from exposure (for example, he may be able to write columns for his home-town newspaper, or he may get a better job later because of the experience). Many product campaigns rely on dramatic input also—many commercials are, in fact, mini-dramas. For example, a girl rushes out of a restaurant crying because her boyfriend has told her that she has horrid-smelling breath. Her friend produces a bottle of Breathsweet and saves the day. The final scene is at the next party where the two lovers gently nuzzle one another. The story is a minor adaptation of the overcoming of great odds, a plot line already noted.

There are, then, *functional* aspects of campaigns and movements that shape and direct their course. They are the strategic moves campaign leaders make to attract support. Though there may be many of these functional aspects, two of them—already discussed—are of interest here. They provide us with a means for examining movements or campaigns. They are the developmental nature of the campaign or movement and the need for a dramatic invitation to be extended to the audience. These two aspects work well together, for the developmental flow of movements and campaigns seems well suited for dramas. At the same time, there are formal aspects of campaigns and movements. We will consider only one: the use of communication in systematic ways.

Power of a Communication System

Campaigns seem to succeed to the degree that they communicate systematically.[8] We are not saying that movements succeed by communication as such, but that they succeed when communication is systematic. Let us look into this aspect more deeply.

What is a communication system? Begin with what happens in a computer and think about the flow of information from input to output. The computer is a system with great power. It communicates with itself and with its users or audience. The planner establishes a path or program for the flow of communication in the machine. The programs tell the machine to "think" in a certain way—to accept and process data in certain steps. The next step is to introduce data as input, which begins to flow through the program. Next comes the processing of the data—the computing and coupling of the many small bits into a complete picture. At this stage, data may be stored in a memory core, to be held till needed, or bits of data may be sent to some other part of the machine, for example, to the printout mechanism. The data are dispersed in a variety of ways. Once the data have been sent to parts of the system, they are considered and combined in new ways. The data are "discussed" by the machine and the program. In a final step, the data are abstracted and sent out of the system in the form of a printout. The printout does not contain each of the

8.   I wish to thank Professor Ernest G. Bormann of the University of Minnesota and the students in his 1972 summer seminar, "The 1972 Presidential Campaign as a Communication System," at the University of Minnesota, for many ideas discussed in this section.

data bits. It does not contain the program of the machine. Nor does it contain the combinations of data. It simply contains a new product based on all of the forms of information but separate from them.

The system in a campaign or movement is like this. At the early stages, planners of the campaign or movement establish the routines by which data will be combined and considered. For instance, in a political campaign the candidate's staff and advance men establish the ways in which messages will be presented to the public (radio, TV, papers, and the like). They set up speaking tours and arrange for proper publicity. They prepare pamphlets; they arrange for rallies, press conferences, and news releases; and they coordinate the candidate's activities. In other words, the staff teams with the candidate, acts to program the campaign.[9] The same thing occurs in a product campaign when an agency staff is charged with selling a certain product. They, too, program media, style, and the timing of messages.

Even in smaller campaigns, we can see a system at work. For example, one of the ways to conduct a campaign to get a date with a certain person is to let a friend of the person know of your hopes. This data input is thus programmed. Taken with the dropped hint, the meeting of the date, and the offer of assistance on a class project, all act to move the data through the system. Of course, success will be measured by what goes on in the potential date's mind. This same process can occur when one wants to convince a teacher to change the date of an exam. Several persons can come to the teacher at different times, with varied reasons for changing the date—there is to be an assembly that day, the debate squad will be out of town, there are a lot of exams planned for that day, and so forth. There is a program to get data into the system.

In idea campaigns the organization is much looser, and as a result the systematic aspect of the campaign is not so clear-cut. The supporters of the factory safety campaign are not likely to get much direct payoff, and so they are not so committed as advertisers or politicians. The resources available to the safety campaign or the United Fund campaign are usually limited. Their budgets are small, and they have to rely on volunteer labor and free publicity. In short, the programming aspect of idea campaigns is loose.

Given a program, data now can be distributed—the local offices of Citizens for Senator Fogbound can begin passing out leaflets, meeting voters, running TV and radio spots. Most of the local campaign headquarters for a presidential candidate do not know what the candidate's stands on issues are, and they are limited without this information. In the disper-

---

9.   For a good discussion of the details of this situation in political campaigns, see Dan Nimmo's *The Political Persuaders* (Englewood Cliffs, N.J.: Prentice-Hall, 1970).

sal stage, however, this is made available. The same thing occurs in product campaigns. The local grocer does not know the details about a certain soap that is being introduced on the market. The manufacturer provides displays, posters, coupon advertisements, and TV spots to disperse these data to buyers. In the movement, the plan is not so strict, but still pieces of data flow into the system and are sent to sectors of it. A group in one of my classes decided to try to get student support to pass a local school-bond issue. A key element in the campaign planning of the group was how to disperse data. They used many means to get data spread throughout the student body (door-to-door visiting, sing-along meetings, access to the local cable TV station, and broadcast of a TV "documentary" on the condition of schools). As noted earlier, the informal persuasive campaign for a date or for delay of an exam also disperses data through many channels.

One of the key elements in the dispersion process is the use of media. This applies to movements, campaigns for political office, and product campaigns. The mass media are channels for the flow of data from program through dispersal centers and to the public. As far back as 1896, the power to control these channels became important in presidential politics. In 1896, large numbers of business interests poured in support for the faltering campaign of William McKinley. The interests feared that William Jennings Bryan would take the country off the gold standard if elected. The money was used to purchase newspaper space. In the 1930s, with the advent of radio and the widespread use of cars, men like Huey Long were able to disperse information using handbills, posters, newspapers, and the radio. In fact, because of his media skill in 1936, Long was a threat to the two major parties. He planned to run for the presidency on a third-party ticket. George Wallace in the 1968 and 1972 campaigns used the media with great skill. Persons in favor of his candidacy had to *pay* for the campaign messages they displayed (buttons, bumper stickers, posters, and so forth). Many persons were shocked at this, but by that time people were beginning to be glad to pay to promote a product if the product name was printed on a T-shirt or hat. The dispersal of campaign messages had become pop art, and with them we spoofed our world of ad gimmicks.

In the 1950s, only about 10 percent of American households had TV sets—there were 4.2 million sets. By 1967, 95 percent of American households had them (there were 54.9 million sets and 58.2 million households). Furthermore, these sets were being used from three to six hours a day.[10] Clearly, since Americans spend from a sixth to a third of their waking hours receiving TV messages, this machine has to be the key channel for message dispersal. Although we will deal with the power of

---

10.   As quoted in *The Image Candidates* by Eugene Wyckoff (New York: Macmillan Co., 1968), pp. 12–13.

media and especially of TV later, suffice it to say here that, in the dispersal stage, TV is a potent channel. Various movements, persons, and groups try to attract the attention of TV cameras, which testifies to the power of the medium. This power explains the tactics and strategy behind the use of violence, bizarre events, costumes, and other attention-getting devices (the staging of fights, the burning of flags, the use of nudity).

In campaigns or movements, programmers have least control over the third stage—or when data are "discussed" and recombined. In a computer, recalling information—putting it together in new patterns—is highly controlled. In a campaign, however, the data are combined with other information, past history, and other factors in the audience. Computers do not have this kind of problem. In campaigns, data are considered and combined, but not before they have been compared with many parts in a persuadee's image of the world.[11] Clearly, the campaign or movement planners cannot control the audience's image of the world. All they can do is hope that by exposing the audience to the same or similar pieces of data a number of times, members of the audience will fit all or part of the message into their image of the world. Of course, the information becomes more or less central in the minds of voters or buyers, depending on the data they are exposed to, what their own self-interest happens to be, and such uncontrollable factors as personal problems like a traffic ticket or a fight with a spouse. In movements, the philosophical view of life held by audience members plays a part. For instance, some women oppose the Women's Liberation Movement because they view women's role as subservient. Others oppose it because they may feel that the movement threatens their femininity. In political campaigns, elements other than the candidate himself may sway voters. Some persons voted against Thomas Dewey in 1948 because he had a mustache. In 1968, Eugene McCarthy got good audience reactions by appearing on the same stage as Paul Newman. In 1972, George McGovern's wife probably won as much support for him as he did.[12]

One example of how this image-building process occurs was the campaign for the United States Senate in 1964 in Oklahoma. The G.O.P. candidate was Bud Wilkinson, the former Oklahoma football coach and a person thought to be a shoo-in if only for his coaching record. The Demo-

---

11.   For an excellent discussion of how one's image of the world is built, see Kenneth Boulding's *The Image* (Ann Arbor: University of Michigan Press, 1961).

12.   For the most part, candidates' wives have been relegated to the status of objects in presidential campaigns—they accept bouquets of flowers, thank mayors for keys to cities, and look pretty. This trend may be changing, however. See, for example, Martha Thomson Barclay's "Distaff Campaigning in the 1964 and 1968 Presidential Elections," *Central States Speech Journal*, Vol. 21 (Summer 1970), pp. 117–122. In 1972, the McGovern staff decided to produce the *first* five-minute television spot almost entirely about the candidate's wife.

cratic candidate, Fred Harris, faced by his opponent's huge lead in the polls, wanted to know what Oklahomans had as the image of a senator. Harris won, but needed to know who the gubernatorial candidate would be in 1966. His staff asked a sample of Oklahoma voters whom they would rather have as their governor: Ben Cartwright of *Bonanza* fame, Perry Mason, Gomer Pyle, or James Bond—each of whom roughly matched one of the contenders. The runaway winner was Ben Cartwright—the robust, self-assured, and sincere Pa of the Ponderosa. A candidate resembling Lorne Green began to project a Ben Cartwright image in many ways and won. Though he later lost the general election, the image data were used by Harris's staff to plan the campaign.[13] The same kind of image making occurred in the campaign of 1960, when John Kennedy built an image that whittled a 16 percent lead by Richard Nixon to a ½ percent victory for Kennedy.

At any rate, in the final stage the re-formation of data takes place in the audience's mind. There it is re-formed with other input—none of which is *exactly* what the planners had in mind.

---

13.   Private correspondence with Ross Cummings, Oklahoma City, the advertising agent for Senator Harris. The letter is reproduced below:

Thank you for your letter of March 12. For the most part, Bill Carmack's recollection is accurate.

Having served as the advertising agency for Fred Harris' successful campaign in 1964 to fill the unexpired term left by Bob Kerr's death, we were very interested in trying to determine who the Democratic nominee for governor was likely to be in 1966, when Fred would have to run again for a full six-year term.

Most polls conducted by politicians are done on a name basis. They select a number of likely names, attempt to rate them in various degrees of public awareness and acceptance, and match them against each other.

As though advertising did not exist.

We had just helped our candidate prevail over two former governors (one an incumbent Senator) and the greatest popular hero in Oklahoma since Will Rogers. Polls taken 60 and 90 days before election day had shown Fred as an unknown and an ignominious third in a field of three seeking the Democratic nomination.

We knew that images can be affected during a campaign, but only during a campaign does the public become sufficiently interested to let an emerging public figure gain massive acceptance. So how can you measure something like this before a campaign starts?

We were not attempting a serious study of issues, since candidates most often join each other in embracing identical issue positions. We only wanted to know what sort of *identity* the people of Oklahoma might prefer for governor.

We had seen "young men's years," when the public swept out the old guard politicians, and other years when established businessmen with mild messages had the greatest appeal.

We first considered a questionnaire describing candidates by personal traits, but discarded that as too wordy and awkward. We then decided to use identities everyone would know—and this led us to the use of TV and movie characters.

We used James Bond, Perry Mason, Ben Cartwright, Andy Griffith, and Gomer Pyle . . . . Our known political contenders fit these characters loosely . . . .

Well, Ben Cartwright won handily, garnering some 60% of the votes, and pointing toward a tendency on the part of the voters to favor an older candidate. Andy Griffith did poorly even in "Little Dixie," indicating a pull-back from an unrelieved rural image. James Bond ran last, indicat-

While the re-forming occurs parts of it are seen in two kinds of images of the campaign or of the movement's cause. The first is that held by the audience members. The second is that held by the planner. These images are a shadow of what was fed into the system but only that—a silhouette that resembles but is not the original. At this step, the "computer print-out" is not neatly squirted out by a print-gun but it emerges in unclear and abstract terms. At the end of a campaign, we know more about the product, but we do not know all; and we are certainly in error about some of the things we believe. For instance, Richard Nixon was often thought to be "tricky" due to his image at the end of campaigns early in his career. This image was probably in part true, but the "new Nixon" image of 1968 and 1972 was of a master technician. That image was later broken by Watergate. The end product, then, consists of an image about a candidate, product, or cause. Part of the image is true, part of it is part-true, and part of it is false. All three parts yield the final image and also change the initial image the campaign planners were trying to build. After a campaign, even the planning staff sees the candidate differently. They see him in their original image of him, in the experiences they have had with him, and in the image the public holds.

The same thing happens to causes or issues in movements. At the end of the movement for women's suffrage, for example, woman's role was different from the early view of that role. To start with, the suffragettes fought for the right to vote. At the end of their campaign, they saw the need to carry women's rights further—jobs, birth control, and so forth. In this sense, a movement is never really over because the fourth communication step—representation—is just that. It presents the cause or issue in a new light.

---

ing dissatisfaction with handsome young playboy types. Perry Mason was second, but far enough behind Ben Cartwright to indicate that rugged, partriarchal directness was a more desirable characteristic than urbane, articulate competence.

We decided the likely winner in the Democratic primary was probably Preston Moore. Although he still had touches of Perry Mason about him, he fit fairly well with the Ben Cartwright character. We speculated that Raymond Gary's rural image would hold him back under circumstances indicated by the survey. David Hall, the urbane young Tulsa county prosecutor, did not seem to be favored by the results, but a strong possibility for public acceptance if he would avoid being too "country" would be Clem McSpadden, a glib senate leader and linear relative of Will Rogers.

We picked Moore to win the primary and he did. However, in his campaign he failed to show the frontier wisdom of the head of the Cartwrights, and in the fall he was defeated by a Tulsa oilman who never developed a real image of his own, Dewey Bartlett. This candidate, defeated for reelection as governor but beating Ed Edmondson in 1972 by characterizing him as a liberal, is a protest candidate whose victories grow from public dissatisfaction with his opponents. I don't believe our polling method could have picked him up on the radar screen.

...I would not seek to palm myself off as a political witch doctor but as a professional communicator.

On second thought, there are some unbelievable fees in being a witch doctor.

At the end of a campaign, such as to have a date with a certain person, you may be disappointed with the outcome, not because you never got the date but because the prize changed as a result of the campaign. We all know what it means to work to attain a goal and then find that it was not what we thought it to be. A good example might be what sometimes happens to persons who have their hearts set on certain jobs. They go through job interviews. They write letters to the employer. They follow up by telephone. They may seek ways to get further input into the decision-making process. They send recommendations from prestigious persons. They pick up hints from persons who already work for the company, and soon, after struggling to land the job, they may discover that their image of the company has changed. It may be much better than they had thought it was because they had to fight so hard to get the job. On the other hand, it may be less than they imagined because the campaign may have been frustrating or for other reasons.

Other Communication Characteristics of Campaigns

There are several other characteristics of campaigns that relate to how they communicate—what messages they send overtly and what messages they send less openly. In many cases this second kind of data is much more potent in persuading than that which is clear and easy to observe. Take a product like prunes, for example. What can we say about prunes on a real, sense-data level? They are black in color; they are kind of gooshy and sticky; they don't smell too bad; and they taste pretty good. That is the *reality* of a prune. However, in the buyer's mind there is another set of information. Crabby old-maid teachers are called prunes. Scout leaders always made you eat prunes at breakfast when you were on a field trip. When you get stewed prunes, one is always split open and is leaking. People are always making jokes about prunes and their laxative quality. One of Dick Tracy's villains was a guy called "Pruneface" who was ugly and wrinkly. Those are the subconscious dimensions of prunes. Both sets of data—the real prune and the *symbolic* prune—have persuasive potential, but buyers usually do not sense the reality inputs as they purchase. That is, they do not usually touch, taste, feel, smell, or look at prunes, though they might try to recall what prunes feel, smell, taste, or look like. They do, however, go into their storehouse of symbolic data and use those data in making a decision. That is probably why the National Prune Institute has gone to so much trouble to build a new image for prunes using humor ("These prunes aren't for me. They're for a friend").

So the symbolic messages that are sent in a campaign are processed at a very low level of awareness. They may be the key message factors in a campaign because voters, buyers, and believers rely on these more than on reality-based data. Part of Jimmy Carter's appeal in 1976 was tied to his choice of colors for his campaign message—green and white. Green has all sorts of symbolic meaning—life, lushness, fertility, safety, cleanliness, and so forth. Most voters did not consciously process those meanings, but the color surely had effect. Let us briefly look at some of these kinds of campaign factors. Most of them work on the storehouse of potent symbolic meanings which we carry with us and which can be prompted by a clever campaign. Most of them relate to some communication theory which operates in many places. Only the way in which the theory is put to work has changed when it is used in a campaign.

First characteristic   *Successful campaigns usually communicate a sense of credibility about their product, person, or idea.* We follow the advice of those in whom we have faith—those whom we feel we can believe. I have never bought Imperial margarine because I cannot believe that it will make me a king in my own family. Yet some people believe the TV spot in which Mr. Average Guy gets a crown for biting a muffin with some Imperial margarine on it. The campaign has plucked some source of symbolic data in many people. These data may not make sense to you or me, but they do to Imperial buyers. Credibility relates to a number of factors, but prime among them are *dynamism, trustworthiness,* and *expertise or competence.* Perhaps the Imperial folks have sent a message of simple trust in their character Mr. Average Guy.

In other instances, persuaders build credibility by dramatizing that their product, candidate, or idea is dynamic. The man and the bear ads for Hamm's beer develop a macho character who is well liked by everyone. He is fearless even in the presence of an 800-pound grizzly bear. He flies

WINTHROP   **by Dick Cavalli**

Figure 6-2   *Winthrop is not responding to reality-based information. The symbolic associations we have with the product or words (here, "Rumpelstilskin") overshadow reality and often result in ludicrous association (for example, Imperial margarine will plop a crown on your head). (Reprinted by permission of NEA.)*

the bush country, canoes, rides trail horses, and walks miles in the wilderness. He is dynamic. If he drinks Hamm's, it must be pretty good stuff. You can be like him if you join the big beer (bear) drinking brotherhood of Hamm's. Those ads communicate credibility far better than the Hamm's ads that feature a cartoon bear that stumbles and bumbles around the land of sky blue waters. Some candidates communicate credibility by showing how expert they are on some issue—farming, defense, or whatever. Others develop credibility by referring to their trustworthiness. "I'll never tell a lie" was Carter's key tactic. Others simply act dynamic. They are athletic, rugged, attractive, and articulate. The end result of all these tactics is to make the persuadee believe and follow the advice of the persuader. The source is credible.

Second Characteristic *Successful campaigns hook their messages into the prevailing climate of opinion.* Times change. That is a cliché that passes for folk wisdom, and it is accurate. In 1976, Americans probably elected a politician who said he would not lie because we were soured by the lying of the previous administrations. It was *in the times* to look to an outsider who did not have ties to cronies. This use of messages that fit the times is characteristic of campaigns for products as well. In 1968 the world was filled with revolt over the war, racism, pollution, and so forth. It was a time of revolt—moral precepts were broken left and right. Beards sprouted on young men's chins. Many young women went braless. Four-letter words became acceptable in casual talk and class lectures—and even in some sermons. There were full-scale and mini-riots in the streets, on campuses, and in corporate boardrooms during stockholder meetings. Some products hooked their message into this prevailing climate of opinion by suggesting that you could revolt by buying the Uncola, joining the Dodge Rebellion, or taking up a new lifestyle with Dr. Pepper or Pepsi. Again, the times were fit for that kind of appeal. As times changed, Uncola had to show you that you could "See the Light" and later that you could "Undo it." Dodge's rebellion lasted only a few years. Then "Mean Mary Jean" took over and featured physical fitness and Dodge. By 1977, M.M.J. was through and you could be "car-napped" by Dodge Magnum. Idea campaigns, more than others, rely on timing to fit their campaign goals to the prevailing climate of opinion. The civil rights campaigns of the 1950s and early 1960s gave way to Black Power, which in turn gave way among blacks to a much lower profile and a focus on economic equality. The times changed; so the movement had to change its appeals. As a persuadee, you will want to see if your feeling for the mood of the times matches up with what persuaders appeal to in their campaign messages. What does this politican seem to think the mood is? What does that advertiser think? Do the current idea campaigns fit the times—the Equal Rights Amendment? racial quotas, pro or con? other campaigns?

Third Characteristic *Successful campaigns seem to aim their messages at opinion leaders.* Studies done in the late 1940s, which were aimed at discovering how farmers adopted new farm methods (contour plowing or crop rotation), found an interesting thing. Most farmers did not respond to direct appeals from the Department of Agriculture. Instead they seemed to adopt the new methods only after a highly respected farmer or an opinion leader did. This pattern was labeled the *two-step flow* theory of communication.[14] We are most persuaded when an opinion leader does something in response to what a persuader says. Later studies demonstrated that this flow had many layers or levels and the two-step notion was elaborated to a *multi-step flow* of information. The Successful Farmers followed the lead of the Super Farmers. They were leaders in turn to the Good Farmers, who were opinion leaders to the OK Farmers. Even OK Farmers were opinion leaders to the Dumb Farmers. Of course there were some Zero Farmers who never adopted the new methods. They know that corn planted in the ground grows and can be harvested but that was about as complex as they could get. Crop rotation didn't fit into their scheme of things.

In other campaigns, this targeting of opinion leaders also occurs. The politician will have TV spots of him listening to well-known and respected farmers, shop foremen, union leaders, leaders of veteran's groups, and others. Products are shown being used by persons who would be opinion leaders to us if we knew them—daring mothers who are scientific researchers recommend Tang. Parachutists who sky dive drink Blatz. Famous persons do not have problems getting credit if they have an American Express card, and so on. Ideological movements also rely on the use of opinion leaders to prompt action. Famous movie stars are asked to support the drive against muscular dystrophy. The names of well-known supporters of the United Fund are printed in the ad appealing for donations. The American Indian Movement had supporters from Hollywood—Steve McQueen, Marlon Brando, and others.

Fourth Characteristic *Successful campaigns make the ordinary seem unusual; the banal becomes unique.* A recent TV ad depicts an ordinary housewife fixing dinner for hubby. She is busy at work on the salad, and it is a pretty humdrum salad until . . . Chef's Delight! As she opens the foil package, a symphony begins to play. The lights dim as the camera cuts to an elegantly set table. By candlelight, hubby pours the vintage wine from a white linen towel. In the final shot, he romantically eyes humdrum housewife, who now is a knockout. All human effort—cooking, voting,

---

14.   An early reference to this phenomenon is found in P. E. Lazarsfeld, B. Bevelson, and H. Gaudet, *The People's Choice* (New York: Columbia University Press, 1948), which identified two-step flow in the 1940 presidential election. Later elaboration to a multi-step flow can be seen in J. N. Rosenau, *Public Opinion and Foreign Policy* (New York: Random House, 1961).

working, learning, and so forth—has some humdrum aspects. The clever persuader takes these boring events or routines and makes them unique. The banal things in life are dressed up to become really special, and this shift draws our attention in potent ways. We enjoy the out-of-the-way, the special, the unique things in life. The clever persuader tries to tie the product, candidate, or idea into such unique or special events or moments. Hundreds of times each day on TV, ads like the one for the salad seasoning make many mundane things unique, such as washing clothes, brushing teeth, making coffee, mowing your lawn, or driving your car. Politicians make themselves unique through their actions. In our town, one rode a horse along the route of a proposed freeway to "visit" with the angry farmers whose land was to be used. Others might note that they have children who are handicapped. Some make themselves unique by dressing in costumes such as a western-style shirt, cowboy boots and a stetson.

Fifth Characteristic *Successful campaigns have messages that make persuadees feel* OK. Thomas Harris, in his book *I'm* OK—*You're* OK, noted that all humans want to feel OK, but that most of us do not.[15] This relates to the many years during childhood when we were not able to do the things needed to support ourselves. For instance, we were too little to drive or cook. This feeling of NOT OK is deeply recorded in our minds like a kind of tape recording, says Harris. It forces us to find ways to feel loved, competent, witty, well liked, and so forth. The campaign offers rewards for taking action that will make you feel OK. These rewards make us feel OK in lots of ways. The woman who fears that her husband is losing interest is advised "Want Him to Be More of a Man? Try Being More of a Woman. Use Emeraude Tonight." The reward for using the perfume is shown in a photo of a very handsome male model nuzzling a very lovely female model who has just applied Emeraude. So you can be made to feel more OK about your sexual role by using certain products.

You can feel more OK if you follow certain ideologies. Mirabel Morgan in her book *The Total Woman* tells women that they will be more sexy and will get their way with their husbands if they do certain things. She suggests that a wife might try meeting her husband at the door wearing only some Saranwrap—if he does not notice her then, she must be NOT OK. We can also be made to feel OK about our work roles or social roles. The working mother who feels guilty is assured, by the makers of Tang, that even a woman marine biologist gives her children Tang to make sure the kids get off to a healthy start on the day. Dad is advised that he will

---

15.   Thomas A. Harris, *I'm* OK—*You're* OK: A Practical Guide to Transactional Analysis (New York: Harper & Row, 1967).

move up to more and more OK positions in the company if he reads the *Wall Street Journal.* Parents are told that they will be more OK if they read *P.E.T.* (Parent Effectiveness Training). Finally our national role is OK or NOT OK, depending on whether the persuader is in office or a challenger. In the 1976 campaign, Gerald Ford said that he was "Feeling Good About America," while Jimmy Carter thought that things were not so OK and that we needed "Leadership—For a Change." So the goal of linking a reward or OKness to a persuader's advice is likely to aid in the success of a campaign. Persuadees need to observe when and how they are being made to feel NOT OK or when their NOT OK state serves as an internal premise for the persuader.

Sixth Characteristic   *Successful campaigns usually rely on information, experiences, or memories that are already inside persuadees rather than trying to "teach" the audience to follow advice.* In his book *The Responsive Chord,* Tony Schwartz advises trying to make your message ring true with or resonate with feelings that the audience has.[16] In the campaigns of 1972 and 1976, he served as an advisor to the McGovern and Carter campaigns. He often gave advice that showed the resonance approach. For example, he advised buying TV time during *Monday Night Football* in 1972 in which to challenge Nixon. Football viewers are primed for a fight in reaction to the game. They have seen and heard smashing blocks, battering tackles, helmet slaps, bump-and-runs, and so forth. Plugging into this set of experiences, on the Monday night before election day, can be very useful. The persuader does not try to approach the audience in order to get data across or to "teach" listeners about issues. Instead the resonance theory approaches audiences in order to see what can be gotten out of them. A good way to sell a drain cleaner is to show someone sticking hands into a stopped-up sink full of greasy water that is filled with food bits, coffee grounds, and the like. Most persons have had to do that at least once in their lives and so already have the feeling imbedded in their experiential storehouse. Then someone pours in some Liquid Plumber, and we watch the sink drain out as the faucet pours out clean fresh water to wash away the grime. This is another great clean feeling that those of us who have had to unclog sinks can relate to. In this ad, the persuader gets the meaning *out of* the viewer. Contrast that with the commercial that explains how traps in sinks get clogged with grease and hair. The ad then shows a cutaway of such a trap and goes on to explain that the grease can be cut by either an acid or an alkalyde. Since acids can damage plumbing, he suggests that we use Drano, an alkalyde base, to

---

16.   Tony Schwartz, *The Responsive Chord* (New York: Anchor Press/Doubleday, 1973).

dissolve the grease and unclog the sink. The ad then shows that happening. This ad is busy trying to *get something into* the viewer.

In a sense, there is no persuasion that does not involve self-persuasion. We must agree to be persuaded and then find good reasons for doing so. The most careful readers of a Chevy ad will be recent Chevy buyers. The sixth pattern of successful campaigns, as well as Schwartz's theory, shows the power of this kind of self-persuasion.

A REVIEW AND CONCLUSION

You will notice other communication patterns that seem to be associated with the successful campaign—things like timing, choice of theme music or score, and clever uses of colors in print and TV ads. Noting them is the most useful thing that you can do, even if you don't verify them through some high-falutin' scientific system. You will be tuning your persuadee's ear to the kind of doublespeak that will be spewed out at us all in campaigns seeking new buyers, new voters, or new joiners.

We have seen here the process of stages that most campaigns seem to go through. We have looked at how a system is needed to direct the flow of messages in a campaign. We have also looked at several communication patterns that go hand-in-hand with successful campaigns.

Questions for Further Thought

1. Define each of the developmental terms and identify examples of the first three stages in some magazine or newspaper.

2. What stage of the campaign or movement is represented when we vote for or against a particular candidate or proposition? Why?

3. We have been told more and more lately that increased trade between our country and others (for example, Russia, China, and Cuba) is a valuable thing to do. Since there is a feeling against this trend, it must be changed through a persuasive campaign. If you were trying to change the average American, what would you do for identification? What would you do for establishing legitimacy of the movement to reestablish ties? How would you get audience participation? How have our government officials done these three things? Rate their success or failure and try to determine why they succeeded or failed and at what stage.

4. As we are exposed to more and more TV series like *All in the Family*, we are probably being exposed to an informal and vague campaign.

Nonetheless, these programs do change ideas and beliefs. At what stage is Archie Bunker as a persuasive symbol at the present time? Is he clearly identifiable? How would you justify your answer? Does the program have legitimacy? Justify your answer. Has it achieved any sort of audience participation? How? Has the point of the program penetrated? What is the point (persuasively speaking) of *All in the Family* and shows like it?

5. Identify a movement of recent times (for example, the consumer movement or the E.R.A. movement). Trace its development. Where was it most dramatic? How was this achieved? How effective was or is the movement in communicating its messages? Explain.

6. What elements of the drama are successful in capturing audience attention? Look at your local newspaper as well as at national news events and nationwide ads. Who are the heroes of the dramas? Who are the villains? Are there common plot lines? values? settings? and so forth.

7. Give examples in which you identify the six patterns of successful campaigns. How do they differ from campaign to campaign? Are some better with one kind of campaign than others (for example, the person, thing, or idea categories)? Why or why not? Create a campaign message that tries to use some or all of the patterns.

Experiences in Persuasion

1. Trace the history of some recent movement (for example, the Women's Liberation Movement or the anti-abortion campaign). Use your library resources, and if the movement is still going on, establish a clipping file to gather coverage of the movement in newspapers. You may wish to collect radio and TV spots of the movement or campaign by contacting TV or radio stations and by recording off the air. Once you feel that you have enough material to give you a good idea of what the movement or campaign is like, begin to search for a pattern. Ask if there is a drama. Is there a plot? Are there characters, villains, heroes, settings? Are there favorite metaphors (see Chapter 2 for help in identifying metaphors)? Ask if the campaign or movement follows the stages outlined in Chapter 5. If so, at what stage is the campaign or movement? What has it done at various stages? In short, do a complete analysis of the campaign or movement.

2. Research a movement of past history (for example, the suffrage movement or the Populist movement). Use all materials available to you from libraries, interviews, and other sources. Then do the same kind of detailed analysis outlined in project 1. Look at historical

novels focusing on the same movement (for example, *T.R.* by Noel B. Gerson, which deals with Teddy Roosevelt as a populist). How does the dramatized version compare with the historical facts you gather?

3. Join a campaign or movement on campus. Keep a communication diary of the experiences you have while you are a member of the movement or campaign staff. Look for dramatic and developmental aspects of the campaign. Try to identify metaphors, plots, and so forth. Report on your findings.

4. Read the reports of various campaigns (for example, any of Theodore H. White's *Making of the President* books on presidential campaigns). Do the kind of analysis already outlined. Ask what stages the campaign or movement is in or has passed through. Where did the movement or campaign appear strong and most persuasive? Why? What was done to exploit this? When was it weakest? Why? How was this used?

5. Research one of the questions raised about persuasion in this chapter. For example, you might want to look at other sources on the use of TV and its powerful impact or on the usefulness of metaphor—how to identify it and how to interpret metaphors, or the importance of the dramatic format in modern society. Reanalyze the campaigns or movements sketched out in Chapter 5.

6. Research the journals in speech and other disciplines to see what has been done concerning political, advertising, and ideological campaigns or movements. Look for the common assumptions used by the researchers. Are there trends in the ways the researchers describe campaign strategy? Report on your findings.

7. As a class, try to develop a mini-campaign on your own campus. Set your strategy to develop in stages. Build in a feedback method to see whether you are being successful. Try various methods suggested here. (*Note:* In the author's course, several groups have run members of their group for office—alderman, student senate, and even a delegate to the Democratic nominating convention in 1972. They have also tried to persuade administration and student associations of the need for bicycle paths, no-profit bookstores, and other projects.)

Becoming
a Persuader 7

O ur overall focus in the first six chapters was on the training of receiver skills, that is, how to learn to do some careful study of doublespeak in the mass-media world in which we live. Since the first edition of the book, however, students and teachers who used it asked for some attention to learning how to persuade. We all have to do this. It is essential for us to persuade others. For the salesman it is an everyday problem, as it is for most teachers. For all of us, there are times when we will have to persuade a given audience, even if it is only one person. Parents have to persuade children to follow advice. Husbands persuade wives and vice versa. As they get older, children need to persuade parents to allow them freedoms. We will all probably have to persuade some complaint manager at a department store to let us return some piece of merchandise. Some of us will be asked to make persuasive presentations to larger groups—the ad department may need to persuade the marketing staff to use more print media and less TV time. The computer programmers will need to persuade the sales staff that a new system will work. The Y.M.C.A. director will want to persuade his board of directors to raise money to build indoor tennis courts, and so on. Our attempts to persuade do not have the drama of the political campaign nor are they so well financed as those of the ad campaign, but they will be as important to us. You become a persuader through three stages or steps: (1) knowing your audience; (2) shaping your message; and (3) sending your message. Throughout the first six chapters of this book, you train yourself to "discover the available means of persuasion" that are being used on you. These means can also be used by you. Try to think of a formal kind of presentation you might have to make someday (though what we discover can apply to the interpersonal and informal context as well). Perhaps it will be the persuasive proposal made in a sales department meeting or the speech in favor of a certain motion at a student association meeting or the attempt to sell fraternity brothers or sorority sisters on some new way to build the float for the homecoming parade. This possible attempt to persuade can serve as your model of the three stages in persuasive message building.

KNOWING YOUR AUDIENCE

Of course it is common sense to say that you have to know your audience before you can expect to persuade them. However, the problem is "How do I get to know my audience?" There are lots of ways to do this. Some of the things which we have already looked at address this problem. We listen to persuaders' language use—their key terms—to understand what they are trying to do in their persuasion. We also listen so that we can persuade them should the need arise. So you can get to know your persuadees by listening to them. Recall what kinds of things they have said in informal talks, in letters or other memos they send out, and in their attempts to persuade others. Chapter 2 is useful for tuning oneself as persuadee and as persuader. Then you can see what process, content, or culture appeals they make when they persuade. We all assume that if it would persuade us, it will persuade others. Take me, for example. I am persuaded by examples and stories. When I try to persuade others, I load the message with examples and stories or jokes. A clever persuader who listens to me can spot my weakness. This persuader can get to me through the story or narrative.

FRANK AND ERNEST   **by Bob Thaves**

Figure 7-1 *Frank knows his audience's preference for certain kinds of words. (Reprinted by permission of NEA.)*

Demographics as a Means of Audience Analysis

One way persuaders in advertising and in marketing analyze their audiences is through the use of *demographics*. This involves dividing up an audience by factors that are easy to measure; age, sex, religion, and income averages would be examples. You might ask how persuaders get these data. Sometimes it is very easy. If you are going to give a speech to the women's group of the Goodview Golf Club, you already know some of it. The group will probably be made up of women, over 30, whose family income is in the upper middle class, and who are married. They probably have children, and are probably not Catholic or Jewish but are likely to be Protestant. That much would be very helpful if you were trying to convince these women that they should support the bond issue for a new hospital or to begin to conserve energy. Because of their "overall/average" nature, they will be for good health care or in favor of keeping the nation energy independent. Furthermore, most members of the group will have above-average IQ, so you can use certain kinds of proof that might not appeal to other groups.

In the case of the Goodview Country Club group, the demographic information was easy to find, even if we were just guessing at some of it. What about groups that are not so well known? What should you do then if you hope to know your audience? What are the steps you should go through?

Significant Factors?

The first step is to locate things that will be important to know about them, given your topic. Clearly average age will be very good to know if your topic is "Tax Planning for Retirement." It will not be if your topic is "Scrap Reduction." Sex will be a key factor if your topic is "Support E.R.A." but not so important if it is "Improving Our Company Image." Average income is central if you are trying to persuade someone to install expensive solar-heat devices. It will matter little if all you are asking is to use caulking and weather stripping to conserve heat. So your first task is to determine which of the demographic items will be one that will matter for topic, time of presentation, and so forth. Let us suppose you have been asked to speak to an alumni group. Your purpose is to convince the alumni to support the building of new handball courts on campus. Which of the following will be factors you will want to explore about your audience:

1. *Average Age?*   Will it matter if they are all over fifty or if they are all under thirty-five? Probably.

2. *Income?*   Will it matter if they are well-to-do or just struggling along? Probably not so much, since it is the group's money that will be used and not personal income. However, handball is a sport that is

costly. Most persons have to rent a court. It will be good to tell about the value of handball for off-season times for members of the baseball team. The moves in handball are similar to those needed in fielding a baseball. You can sell your idea on more than one level here.

3. _Sex?_   Are your alumni likely to be male or female and does that matter? Say that 90 percent are male; and that will matter since they are aware of the need for regular exercise. They know that a good exercise program is best when started in the college years.

4. _Religion?_   Are Jews, Catholics, or Protestants more likely to favor handball? This factor is one you can ignore for the most part.

5. _Family Size?_   Will it matter if your audience members have zero, two, or five children? Again, probably not.

6. _Political Party?_   Will it matter if they are Republican or Democrat? No, but if you had reason to believe they were Socialists, that might make a difference.

Of course there are other factors that you would like to explore, but the key thing is to determine which factors are most central to your topic. If your audience is from the Chicago area and they went to a public university, don't tell any Polish jokes. Chicago has more Poles than Warsaw, and many of them go to public colleges. They will be in your audience in large numbers. If you are dealing with a Minnesota alumni group you would not have this problem, but you might have others—don't knock Swedes or Danes.

Once you know the key demographic factors for your group/topic/ context, the next stage is to explore them. The president of the alumni group will be able to tell you about some of these. Member lists will show you where they tend to live. That can cue you to income and age. Their past actions can be useful in finding out if they prefer certain projects. If they have turned down past requests from students, you need to know why. If they have not funded athletic requests, you need to explore that too. Sometimes, just talking to one or two typical members of a group before you begin to persuade can be helpful. I once was asked to speak to a group of hairdressers. I expected to see the chairs filled with dainty men and heavily made-up women. The group was mainly made up of middle-aged black women from Chicago who ran beauty shops out of their homes. I learned to ask ahead about my audience after that! Knowing the make-up of your target is valuable as a first step in becoming a persuader.

Determining Audience Needs

We have already touched on this topic in Chapters 3, 4, and 5 when we looked at the kinds of premises that people hold. Some are emotional, some are logical, and some are cultural. Looking at the motives likely to persuade our target audiences will have to be guesswork. We are not like advertisers who have techniques for doing such targeting. They can get at the kinds of deep needs many persons have (for example, Packard's hidden needs, which are discussed in Chapter 3). Advertisers can test out certain ads by showing them to people and then interviewing in depth. The Leo Burnett agency used this method and found out that the Jolly Green Giant had better stand still in ads. People said they were afraid for the valley dwellers when ads showed the giant moving. Burnett invented the Sprout to allow for movement in the ads. Sprout is a *baby* giant and so will not squash anyone if he walks around.

End-needs analysis is a technique using a series of cartoon balloons. People are asked to fill in a balloon to complete a statement like "I use Sta-Pruf on my husband's shirt and that is good because. . . ." The answer written down is carbon-copied to the next page where it becomes the new response. For example, suppose Mrs. Homemaker completes the first statement by saying "that is good because his shirts look crisp and white." "His shirts look crisp and white and that is good because. . . " becomes the next statement to be completed. The interviewed person completes as many such chained answers as he or she can. The result is an *end-need* around which an ad can be built. Let us suppose Mrs. Homemaker ends up saying in her *final* answer "and that is good because my mother will love me." The ad-exec can then build a message around a mother visiting her daughter on laundry day and oohing and aahing over the crispy white shirts. Mama says that they will help Ralphy get a promotion at the office, which will make the whole family proud.

Although we cannot usually get into such complex anaylsis, we can rely on the work that has been done by others—usually ad agencies. You can identify audience needs that are being appealed to in TV commercials today. One type that seems to sell well are cures for a general feeling of incompetence. Many ads give people a way to feel more competent. Mrs. Olson uses Folger's coffee to make more competent wives. Ford uses family tradition through four generations of a family who have all owned Ford trucks. Grandpa, at age 92, has given the whole family confidence in choosing trucks since he owned one of the first Fords, and it is still running. Many men apparently can become irresistible lovers if they shave with "Great Balls of Comfort" before going out. How can these data be used when we try to persuade the alumni group? There are several ways. We could focus on this need for being self-confident and try to sell our handball courts on the basis that athletes are self-assured because they do *something* well. Now the alumni can let others feel the same way by opening up the handball option. Or we could talk about body image. We need to keep in good shape in order to be healthy in our minds—"and more than 50 percent of hospital beds are for persons who are having mental problems." All these appeals and many others hook into key needs in today's world, if we judge by present advertising strategy. So though we do not have the resources that marketeers have, we can borrow some of their ideas and focus on subconscious needs in people.

All audiences have some sets of shared experiences. Persons my age can tell you exactly where and when they first heard of the murder of John Kennedy. It is an experience that can be used by a persuader dealing with people born before 1955 or so. All parents know what it is like to fret over the first baby. During the hellish first two months, a baby goes through dozens of diapers a day, never seems to stop crying, and just is not very lovable, smiley, or clever. That two-month ordeal can be a prime source of examples if you are trying to convince parents to treat themselves to a night out, for instance. McDonald's did this for years with their slogan "You Deserve a Break Today!" People who have been to college share memories of the madness of registration for classes, making grades, dealing with stubborn profs, dorm food, and so forth. All these stored data can be building blocks when someone tries to persuade you to pay $399 to go to Florida over break.

So in the process of audience analysis we can also try to locate the key experiences that relate to our topic or goal. In this way, we will get a message out of the audience, in Schwartz's terms (see Chapter 6), instead of trying to get something across. The next time you need to persuade someone, try to list the experiences that he or she has likely had. Can some of these be tied into your message? If so, try to work them in; they will be key parts of your message.

Another factor in audience analysis is also suggested by Tony Schwartz. In his book The Responsive Chord, he favors messages that are built for the time and place, when and where they will be heard.[1] If you were an ad agent trying to send a message to people telling them to vote for someone and you knew that they would hear it on Labor Day weekend, how would you design the message? You would want to plug into the picnic mood, the out-of-doors, and the family fun that people are having on that weekend. You might have the candidate talk about conservation for us and for our children or about the need to make it easy for friends to be together. The same thing can be done as we get ready to persuade other persons—the alumni, the sales force, and the job interviewer. What is the likely mood for the alumni? They will be relaxed. They will remember old times. They might be bragging to former classmates. Take these things into account and design your message to do its task, using the good mood, nostalgia, and feel of success. Remind them of the good feeling of competing with classmates on the athletic field and how that feeling served them in later years. Remind them of the new people they met. Then tell them that there is a chance to make that kind of feeling available to more

---

1.   Tony Schwartz, The Responsive Chord, (Garden City, N.Y.: Anchor Press/Doubleday, 1973), pp. 40, 88–91, and 100–105.

students through the handball courts. Though you will be only guessing at the mood of your listeners in this stage, your guesses can be more than random-chance flings if you spend some time getting to know the audience. They will help you to shape your appeal.

SHAPING YOUR MESSAGE

Once we know something about our target group and how its members feel toward our topic, we can begin to shape the message, be it speech, interview, ad, or rally cry. There are many aspects to the shaping process. First, we need to organize the message in the most useful way. People recall things that are well organized better than things that are helter-skelter. Since we want the audience to remember our speech, clear organization can help us achieve our goals. Then we need to support our claim. In Chapter 4 (Content Premises), we said that each claim has a kind of minimum threshold of proof needed to convince people. So we need to select those items of proof or support that have the most effect. A third step in shaping the message is to judge our believability and what can be done to improve it. Finally, we need to consider what might be the best style to use. Are the listeners likely to respond to the pragmatic or to the unifying style (see Chapter 2)? Will they accept or reject figures of speech? Will they prefer a down-to-earth, "lay your cards on the table," straightforward style? Or are they more open to a less blunt approach? Once we have thought about all of these factors, we can shape the message and prepare to send it with a good chance of success. Let us explore each of the four factors in the shaping process in a little more depth.

Forms of Organization

There are a number of ways to organize messages so as to make sure they can persuade and are easy to remember. We will look at five such formats here—the topic format, the space format, the time-flow format, the stock issues format, and the format called the Motivated Sequence.

By topic   This format is most useful when the message that you want to convey seems to fit into several topics or issues. For example, let us suppose that you want to persuade a company to hire you for a job. You will have a chance to presuade during the talk you have with the company representative. Your message will not be a public speech, but it can still have organization. Since there are several reasons why you think that you would be a good person to hire, the topic format is the best. It allows you to group your reasons for being hired. It also allows you to present part of it—say, past work experience—during a single phase or exchange in the interview. Another—say your educational background—can come during another phase. Your résumé probably has grouped data by topic. Your presentation will reinforce what is there in the résumé. Your topics might be the two already noted plus your own interest in the firm, the good things you have heard about them, the pay, and location of the firm. They want to keep the persons they hire. Thus you can persuade on two levels using the topic format. First you give them good reasons to hire you. Then you lead them to believe you will stay. Your format might look like this:

Topic 1: Past Work

    Sold products as a youth

        Christmas Cards, driveway sealer, and others

    Sold in retail store in high school

        Clothes and florist (gift items and service)

    Sold ads for college paper

        Top seller three of nine months (8 others in sales)

        Dealt with major accounts (Dayton's, Minnesota Twins, and others)

        Dealt with major ad agents (layout, copywriting, logos)

    Sold film programs to students

        Student Center Board—ad director

        Film coordinator (ads, posters, etc.)

Topic 2: Education

    Majored in speech communication

        Courses in persuasion, interpersonal communication, and campaigns, among others (G.P.A. 3.7 in major)

    Minored in marketing/sales

        G.P.A. 2.9 in minor

    Other sales experience

    Paper

    Intern at ad agency

    Fraternity rush

Topic 3: Interest in Firm

    Sales is relied on for success of any firm

    Salespersons make higher salaries if successful

    Salespersons promoted faster

Topic 4: Interest in Foursquare Company

    Growing industry

Good salaries and fringe
Friend gave good recommendation
Located in a major city

You might not take the outline with you. You can keep it in mind and perhaps open the interview by saying, "I think there are four good reasons why you should add my skills to the Foursquare Company." The topic format here lets the interviewer recall you and your reasons when reviewing the day.

By space   This format is useful when you try to persuade others of the size of a problem or solution. It is like the analogy since it allows the persons to visualize the topic. They can recall its parts because they can see it in their mind's eye. Suppose you want to persuade local businesses to form an environmental agency for the town. You might tell them about the size of the problem. How much water pollution is in the county? How much air pollution? How much other pollution? What part is due to schools and what part to the town? How much is caused by visitors and industries? What is the effect of the new K-Mart store and the Ford plant likely to be? Each of these is a factor—a slice of the pie. A graph could present the amounts accounted for by city, campus, and so on. You might ask the businesses to think of the pollution as a map of the United States. The eastern states up to the Ohio River is the part of pollution due to townspeople. Up to the Mississippi River is due to the campus. Up to the Rockies is due to industries and visitors. The rest is from other sources (trains, buses, and cars). The picture changes when we look at nuclear pollution, though. Maine is the part due to townspeople, the campus, and others. All the other states are due to industry. Being able to see the problem helps you understand and recall it. The use of space is helpful when you want the audience to see differing dimensions.

By time frame   Sometimes we want to persuade people that it is time to take action. The goal is to make them aware that time has passed, and things have happened that need attention. The time frame format is most useful here. It traces an issue or problem across time. For example, suppose that you hope to persuade your parents to let you bum around Europe next summer. They have a whole set of biases against this idea. They are afraid you will be arrested by Communist secret police. They know you do not speak the languages of those countries. You need to persuade them that you and the world are different now. This is not the 1950s or 1960s. You could trace what has happened across the past fifteen years to you and to eastern Europe. You could trace your own growth as a travel veteran. Your first trip away from home was when you were eight and took the train to Duluth. Then you continue the time tracing, noting your walking trip across canoe country and your hitch-hike trip to the

West Coast. You can bring them up to date, reminding them of your bike trip through western Europe last year and Mexico before that. Time tracing could also be done for eastern Europe. More and more people tour eastern Europe. Now they have English lessons over state TV and radio. Almost everyone speaks English now. The time tracing lets them see that their early ideas were wrong. They need to change their view of the world. That change leads to your taking the trip.

Stock issues Sometimes we want to change a policy. Since the policy is in place and working, and since people are used to it, it will be hard to change. The stock-issues approach works best in this kind of situation. It has three steps—showing of a need for change, usually by citing symptoms of a problem and causes. A second step provides a new method or plan that can handle the problem. Finally, one offers data showing that the method will work, perhaps by noting where it has worked. Suppose that you want your college to change its late-add period. This makes it easier for people to join classes that are under way. Your speech to the add-drop committee might begin with statistics as to the number of late-adds at present, the number denied, and so on. This shows a need for change. There is "trouble in River City." You also show a cause of the problem—the stringent one-week deadline for adding a course. Your new plan is to extend the late-add time to two weeks, with teachers asked to provide newcomers with notes and an update.

The motivated sequence Another organizational pattern that resembles the stock-issues approach is the motivated sequence suggested by communication scholars Alan Monroe, Douglas Ehninger, and Bruce Gronbeck.[2] It has five parts and is often used by persuaders to get persuadees to attend to their message, to feel a need to follow the advice of the persuader, and most importantly to take action related to the advice. Thus the motivated sequence is a good pattern to use in sales, recruitment—say, for the armed forces or some organization—in politics where the action step is the vote, and in many other instances.

The first part or step in the motivated sequence is the *attention step*. No persuader can be successful if the audience is uninterested in the persuasion. So, capturing the attention of the audience is the first task for the persuader. There are hundreds of ways to do this. A persuader might begin the message with a startling statistic, for instance—"Over 70 percent of the heart attacks today are related to the kind of person you are—type A or type B. Today you can decide for yourself what kind you want to be."

2.   Alan H. Monroe, Douglas Ehninger, and Bruce Gronbeck, *Principles and Types of Speech, Communication*, 8th ed. Copyright © 1978 by Scott, Foresman and Company, pp. 142–163.

The persuader might use a joke or humorous anecdote. We often hear this on the after-dinner speech circuit and even in sermons. Another approach used by political persuaders is to make an important announcement in the first few moments of the message. The president announces settlement of a strike or a new peace initiative in the Middle East. A senator gives a "Golden Fleece" award for wasteful government spending. It is also used by advertisers who make startling announcements or offers to capture attention. You can "get the fourth bar of Lifebuoy Free!" announces the store label. Or an advertiser states that *Motor Trend* magazine has declared the Plymouth Horizon to be the "Car of the Year."

All these tactics and many others are useful in capturing the attention of the audience. Dramatic actions also draw attention; shooting off a pistol to start a speech on gun safety would complete the attention step. As you prepare to persuade, try to think of your audience as a group of bored and uninterested persons who need to have their attention drawn to your message. Then set about designing an attention-getting device.

The second part or step in the motivated sequence is the *need step*. The task here is to demonstrate to listeners that they have a specific unfulfilled need that can be met by listening to your advice. Again, there are many ways to demonstrate this need. The best ones usually flow from the attention step. For example, take the speaker on gun safety. Following the attention-getting step of shooting off the pistol, the persuader might say, "Three of the persons in this room are going to be shot with handguns in the next year. Two of the shootings will be because someone was not trained in gun safety. Each of us is in danger of falling victim to accidental shootings as the number and variety of handguns increases."

By trying to relate the attention step directly to the audience, the persuader begins to create a need in the audience. This need can be satisfied by following the persuader's advice. As persuader, you describe symptoms of a problem. Your receivers may be only dimly aware of the problem or they may not have known about it at all. Then you identify a cause for the problem and the symptoms. By doing this you begin to create a need in your receivers. The encyclopedia sales representative gets attention by offering to "place" a set of books in your home. This attention-getter is followed by showing you how much you need the books—libraries in schools are out of date and crowded and refuse to lend reference books; sometimes you need your information *now* and not when the library opens; or the set of books is increasing in price from week to week, and this alone is reason enough to buy the books today. With each argument, a need is created. Try to create needs in your audience—needs that can be met only by listening to you and your advice.

Steps three and four—*visualization* and *satisfaction*—are often interchangeable, depending on the persuasive purposes. For example, suppose you are trying to get people to protect their health by eating more fiber or roughage in their diet. You can get attention by noting the United States has the highest rates of cancer of the colon in the world. Then you can work to create a need by telling your receivers of their chances of getting cancer and other diseases of the intestinal tract. Then you can choose to offer either a dramatic visualization or a satisfaction step (like a plan in the words of the stock-issues approach) relative to the need that you have just created.

For instance, you can ask the receivers to picture themselves in coffins and to imagine what their loved ones will say at the funeral. Stop-smoking clinics often use that tactic; it causes the persuadees to visualize the need. Another approach is to describe a hypothetical case. "Joe first found out that he had colon cancer on his twenty-seventh birthday. He was told he had three years to live. But he didn't really live during those three years. He had painful colon radiation treatments. These involve . . ." The verbal picture of the need that you paint can make your point vividly.

In the alternative approach, the persuader offers the satisfaction of the need first, then visualizes it. Suppose I am selling new cars. I might get your attention by offering some special premium or opportunity to get you into the showroom. (In Chicago, one car dealer regularly has past Playmates of the Month from *Playboy* magazine as guests on weekends. They offer autographs and pinups. The traffic created this way leads to a need in the customer—to buy a new flashy, sexy-looking car.) In selling cars I would probably also offer a free road test. You begin to feel the need as you compare the smell, feel, and handling of the new model with the rattles of your old car. After your road test, I might try to visualize what your satisfaction might be like if you follow my advice. I might say "In that car, you'll be able to take that trip up to Lake Geneva and feel like you own the place. You'll be the hit of the tennis club, too. I'll bet your weekly sales level will rise just because of the image this GT will give you." Thus I visualize not the *need* as with cancer of the colon but the *satisfaction* of the need. Whichever approach you choose, be certain to get your receivers involved in picturing themselves either in trouble or well satisfied. Get them to visualize these things as vividly as possible. A professor I once had said that we got 80 percent of what we know about decisions we have to make through our eyes and our ears. Too often we forget to use the sense of sight in verbal persuasion.

Finally, the persuader who uses the motivated sequence or similar patterns must offer an *action* step. It is not enough to get attention by citing a statistic on colon cancer, then to create a need by vividly depicting the stages of the disease, then to offer a preventive—getting more roughage into the diet. These will not get action. The persuader needs to suggest some specific action step that is reasonable and that can be taken soon and easily. A good one in the colon cancer case might be eating whole wheat bread instead of white bread daily. This action step might be verified by citing statistics to show that as little as one slice will provide the daily minimum to prevent this disease. The action is specific, reasonable, easy, and effective. Given the attention, need, visualization, and satisfaction steps that preceded it, we can reasonable hope that the persuadees may follow our advice.

A common action step used by students in persuasive speeches is to suggest that class members write letters to their elected representatives. Though this is the single most effective thing people can do to affect legislation, few of them actually ever write. Even the staunchest supporters of the Equal Rights Amendment in my district of Illinois—advocates and officers of women's rights groups on campus and in the communication profession—had not contacted their legislative representatives at all before a crucial vote in 1978 in which the proposition was defeated by two votes. Perhaps this action step seemed to them too mundane or even useless. A persuader had to capture their attention—"Did you hear about the representatives in our district on E.R.A.?" Then the persuader had to create a need—"They are wavering on E.R.A., and I know you support E.R.A., don't you?" The satisfaction step followed in this case—"You can register your opinion in the short time remaining by using the telephone, you know. Why don't you?" This satisfaction was then visualized—"You can call their toll-free Springfield offices or their local offices and tell the person who answers why you support E.R.A. You might even get to talk to the representative yourself or his administrative aide. They are both easy to talk to and will really probe you for your reasons for supporting E.R.A. and that's the kind of opinion which needs to be fed in, don't you think?" The visualization will lead nowhere in many cases unless the persuader provides the easy outlet or action step—"Here is a slip of paper with the toll-free and local numbers of the two representatives in our district who are wavering on tomorrow's vote. Call them now and register your opinion."

Though some receivers, even those who claim to share the need you have sketched out, will opt out of this action step, more will choose to follow your advice on this telephone option than will write letters. It takes time to remember to pick up writing paper, envelopes, stamps, and so on. Then it takes effort to compose the letter, type it error free, and send it off. The form-letter response that usually results reinforces the commonly held notion that letters are usually filed in the wastebasket. Legislators can tell the difference. They discount the identical letters and postcards produced by organized campaigns, but they do pay attention to communications individually thought out by constituents.

In effective persuasion, it is essential to give the persuadees a realistic action step, whether it is signing the sales contract, phoning the representative, or boycotting the nonunion food market. Build such steps into your persuasive attempts at sales, recruitment, and so on, and you will find your percentage of success increasing dramatically.

Forms of Support

We want good reasons before we change. Even if we are sure the change is good, we need proof of it. We want what we called data in Chapter 4. There are many kinds of data or forms of support that a persuader can use.

Statistical evidence   Sometimes the most effective kind of support is statistical. For instance, car buyers are interested in gas mileage. They will be more persuaded by the Environmental Protection Agency (E.P.A.) figures than by all the reassurances from the sales staff that the car is a real gas saver. Statistics are most useful when they are simple and easy to understand. When persuaders decide to use statistics, they need to make them clear. They need to provide a reference point for the numbers. For example, the car salesperson needs to say that the 21.5-cubic-foot trunk on the Fairlane is twice what you will get in the more costly Volkswagen Rabbit. The comparison makes the cubic feet meaningful. When we decide to use this form of support, we need to make it clear and simple.

Narratives and anecdotes   We have noted the power of drama, stories, and jokes. The narrative makes examples come alive. It makes them easy to recall and relate to. The persuader who tells of a person who rose from rags to riches by using a success system will have more success than one who relies on statistics.

Testimony   We suspect persons who try to convince us of a certain idea if it is based only on their own feelings or brainstorms. That is why the testimony of another person is so useful. Even if the person testifying is unqualified (for example, Joe Namath endorses pantyhose), the testimonial still has impact. Of course, it is much better to have an expert witness as to the wisdom or folly of the idea, person, or product. Even better is testimony of a hostile or reluctant witness. This has impact because it runs counter to the self-interest of the witness to speak in favor of the product or idea. A recent ad features a top executive at American Express Company. He advises you to get yourself a Carte Blanche credit card. It is counter to his self-interest as head of Carte Blanche's biggest competitor to say such things. As a result the ad has double impact. Actually this strategy works to the advantage of both credit card firms. It will increase sales for both American Express and Carte Blanche.

Visual evidence   We have noted how useful it is for an audience to see or experience evidence. This is why visual aids are used in sales work. If you have ever walked into a department store where a salesperson was showing a veg-o-matic or a doughnut maker, you know of the power of visual data. You see the product at work, and seeing is believing! This was also the most powerful kind of data for the tribal medicine man who made sure to add visual proof to his magic—smoke powder, and so forth. Sometimes

I think my doctor does a lot of razzle-dazzle for the same reason—to persuade me that I am getting my money's worth. Though you may never be so dramatic in your persuasion, you can use visual aids like graphs, charts, or even cartoons to reinforce your ideas. A student in one of my classes used Snoopy drawings to highlight the points of his speech on safe driving habits. It was easy to recall and organize the data he gave us. We considered it in depth with Snoopy there to help.

Comparison and contrast   Sometimes it is hard to really see a problem in perspective. We see the issue from a single viewpoint and cannot really judge it accurately. So it is wise to provide something with which to compare or contrast the issue, product, or action. For example, we might point out that the new graphite body on all Fords is 1,250 pounds lighter that that of a comparable Chevy. It sounds like a lot but would not be much if each car weighed 50,000 pounds. However, if the source says that this is one third less we can get an idea of how important the reduction is. If the source extends the comparison saying that this will add 30 percent more to gas mileage and 15 percent more space in the passenger compartment and 50 percent more space in the trunk, the comparison makes it easy to favor Ford when we shop for a new car. Candidates often compare with their opponents' records their own records in Congress or their positions on a variety of issues—E.R.A., farm prices, and the like.

Analogy   We noted the analogy as a form of proof in Chapters 2 and 4. It is a useful but risky form of support to use. As a special kind of comparison, the analogy has two types—figurative and literal. The figurative type compares a familiar idea or object with an unfamiliar idea or object. For example, we might want to explain the value of zero-till planting to farmers. Our analogy for the values of planting without tilling the soil might be trout fishing. One tries not to disturb the surface of the water before putting the bait in. The literal analogy compares two nearly identical ideas or objects. Candidates might compare their accomplishments with those of their opponents. They might stress that both have been in office the same length of time, have been on the same number of committees, and so on. Yet Jones, he says, has a much better record than Smith.

Credibility

All the evidence in the world, organized perfectly and delivered well, will not persuade if listeners do not trust the speaker. This happens time after time in politics. Presidents will all suffer from a credibility gap. We see it in the world of sports when coaches and players come out of long meetings over salary or during trades. They *say* that everyone's happy, but we know better. You do not fight over your future and come away without any bad feelings. Surely, in many product appeals, credibility suffers. It is hard to believe that we can have an instant change in personality, social life, and sex appeal due to hair dye or after-shave lotion. We accept some of this "incredibility" as part of the game, but in matters such as persuading the boss to give us a promotion or parents to let us marry before graduation, credibility is a key factor. What makes some persons credible while others are not? How can we build our own credibility before and during persuasion? Let us look further at some answers to these questions.

Aristotle thought that a speaker's credibility is composed of a reputation as a person of good will, wisdom, and character. These are the reasons for being believed that speakers bring to speechmaking. During the speech they can improve on these with flair and vigor. They can shape the speech artistically in response to audience reactions. Current research shows three key factors that account for most of one's credibility. They are *trustworthiness* (good will and high character), *expertise* (wisdom and experience), and *dynamism* (an active, artful style and delivery). These are central in most speaker ratings. How do persuaders communicate trustworthiness, knowledge and experience, and dynamism? Further, how can these be used by sources such as advertisers when they cannot know what their listeners are thinking or doing while being persuaded?

Trust   We trust people for many reasons. We trust them because they have been trustworthy in the past. We trust them because they give off trustworthy cues—direct eye contact, a calm voice, and so forth. We trust them because we know it would not be in their self-interest to betray us. A good example of this might be airplane hijackers, who trust the passengers and crew not to gang up on them—to do so would endanger all their lives. Usually, it is the first two kinds of trust that we wish to communicate. We want to tell our employer that he can trust us because we have been constant in the past. We want to tell voters to support us because we have been faithful to campaign pledges in the past. Or we tell customers that they can trust antiseptic Listerine because it has been helping since Grandma's time. We also try to give off cues of trust. We look at our persuadees directly. We try to sound sincere, even if we are not (though this isn't always effective—our nonverbal messages "leak" and tell that we are lying). Persuaders who want to have a trust relationship with the audience need to remind them of the past record for trust. They need to refer to times when it would have been easy to break trust. Sometimes this can be worked into the persuasive speech or exchange early. For example, the worker tells the boss, "You'll recall the times I had to take charge of the cash receipts for the day. Sometimes we had over $20,000 in cash." The husband reminds his spouse that "there were lots of chances for some action on the side at work." The youth reminds the parent that "there was plenty to tempt me not to study at the dorm. There will be no more at the house I hope to pledge, I'm sure." We communicate our trust during the speech. We look at receiver eye-to-eye; we have relaxed posture; we speak with a sure voice. All help to develop credibility and trust.

Expertise   How do we know if someone is a true expert on a topic or job? Mostly we look for data from past success at a task. If a person was a good treasurer for the Luther League, he or she will probably be good for the student council. Sales representatives who did well in the Midwest should also do well in the larger and more complex East. A person who has had experience in many areas of the company—shipping, sales, and so on—is much more credible to workers than the person who has had experience only in one area of the company. So a persuader can refer to past experience. As in the job interview situation discussed earlier in this chapter, applicants can show that they are experts in sales and can refer to past successes. Sometimes we refer to our expertise during the persuasive presentation. At other times a letter, résumé, or even a verbal introduction can cover the topic. Some persons believe that you can make yourself look like an expert by giving off competence cues. John T. Molloy, clothing researcher, has written two books dealing with how one's clothes can give off messages that say, "I am competent and in charge." In fact, he even records typical success signals. A "uniform" for women who want to make it in the business world is the dark skirted suit and blouse but not a vested or three-piece outfit.[3] Molloy says that these items tell the world that the woman is a person who is headed for success while still being feminine. Student speeches are more successful when the student comes dressed *up* instead of *down*. Finally, you can signal expertness during a speech by being well prepared; by suggesting that you really know about the topic, issue, or case; and in question-and-answer sessions.

Dynamism   This factor is elusive and even mysterious. It is sometimes related to physical appearance. The taller candidate seems to win more often. Attractive persons hold attention better. This kind of dynamism is sometimes labeled charisma. It probably cannot be developed very much. Some cosmetic things can be done (for example, through clothes or the use of proper makeup and choice of color when on TV as in the Nixon-Kennedy debates of 1960). There are persons who are not large or attractive, but who have charisma. They take up a lot of psychic space when they enter a room or speak up. They have stage presence. These persons have done something to appear more dynamic, more central and important. They speak with authority. We can learn to project better or to speak with more volume. These will lend to our image. We can improve our image by associating with dynamic persons or by referring to them as friends. Politicians are often photographed with sports figures and thus "borrow" a dynamic image from them. Doing active things can signal

---

3.   John T. Molloy, "Dress For Success," *The Chicago Tribune*, October 30, 1977, section 5, pp. 1 and 4. See Molloy's two books *Dress For Success* and *The Woman's Dress For Success Book* (Chicago: Reardon and Walsh, 1977).

dynamism. Referring to one's athletic interests might be an example here. Again politicians work hard at getting pictured *doing* things. We like to follow men and women of action. Certain words can give off a sense of dynamism, and if they are used the image of the source is improved. McCulloch chain saws feature the word "power" in their ads and refer to things like "triggers" and "revving up" the machine. So, a statement with high-energy and powerful words can help develop a dynamic image for a speaker. This image along with trust and expertise can be of help in achieving persuasive goals. Persuadees want persuaders to be credible. They rely on the three dimensions of trust, skill, and dynamism to judge that credibility.

Stylizing Your Message

We covered style in Chapters 2, 3, and 4 from the *persuadee's* viewpoint. Let us now look at what a *persuader* can do to develop style. Most persons are affected by dramatic words and styles. They react to stories and to exciting words and phrases.

Rewriting messages is a good way to improve style. We often rehearse our words before saying them. Sometimes we do this silently. As you wait to get the floor during a meeting, you "practice" what you are going to say. During this rehearsal, we can edit and work on style. Would the word "smash" be better in talking about our goal of defeating the other sales staffs or would it be better to use "destroy" or some other word? Try out different options as you rehearse in silence.

Using a *narrative* as an introduction to a message can also improve style. We all listen to a story and can then be drawn along into the rest of the message.

Figures of speech are useful, given the right time and place. In a group of union men debating the new company offer on wages at the local bar-and-grill, flowery words would backfire, but a strike leader could successfully urge a vote of "no" on the new contract by using a figure of speech. He could say, for example, "Give them a message they can't ignore"—or a more earthy version of the same idea.

Finally, *nonverbal aspects of style* can be used by the persuader. We can dress persuasively. We can decorate the setting with an eye toward our goals. John T. Molloy also noted that the label a woman executive puts on her door signals her image. Mary L. Smith was more effective that Mrs. Mary L. Smith, which was better than either Ms. Mary L. Smith or last-place Miss Mary L. Smith.[4] A paneled office with leather-covered chairs and a filled pipe rack prepares a persuadee for a certain kind of message.

---

4.   Molloy, "Dress for Success."

That message is not expected in a ceramic-tiled office with metal desk and chairs. Albert Scheflen described the meaning attached to some thirty postures. For example, when persons want answers to their statements, they raise their heads slightly at the end of a statement.[5] Of course, we cannot rehearse and plan all these movements in detail, but paying some attention to them can add to our hoped-for effects.

In conclusion, the second stage for persuaders—shaping the message—has several dimensions that can effect the final outcome of a message. These include such things as organization, forms of support, using credibility, and, finally, stylizing a message to fit our needs. With a well-planned message, a persuader can focus on delivery. Here the advice is simple and straightforward.

DELIVERING YOUR MESSAGE

Usually we think of delivery as source matter. That is, it is something that only the source itself can affect. To some degree, this is true. However, there are at least two factors in the process—the channel and the audience—that can affect the message and that sources often overlook. The careful choice of channels used to send the message is often important. Would the ad be better on TV, radio, or billboards? Should we ask for the raise over the phone, in a letter, or in person? Receivers can also affect the final impact of the message. They get the message sent by the colorful package in the store, but they may be too relaxed by the soothing music piped in to buy the item. So we need to pay attention to all three elements in delivery. The source is clearly the one over which we have most control and that will have most impact.

Delivery—The Persuader

Among the things that a persuader can adjust before and during delivery are posture, eye contact, bodily movement and gesture, articulation and vocal quality. Other things that are under the speaker's control are the use of visual aids and other nonverbal signals.

Posture We have all seen persuaders who are so nervous about their speeches that they cannot stop pacing back and forth. When they do stop,

---

5. Albert E. Scheflen. "The Significance of Posture in Communication Systems," *Psychiatry*, Vol. 27 (1964), pp. 316–331.

they stand so ramrod stiff that it looks like they might freeze into statues. At the other extreme we have seen speakers who are so relaxed that they do not seem to care at all about their messages. They slouch lazily across a podium or they slide down into their chairs during a meeting. They rarely look up, and you wonder if they will nod off in the middle of a sentence. So, it is clear that posture can signal something if you are either too relaxed or too nervous. The ideal posture lies somewhere inbetween. The persuader should be alert and erect. The shoulders should not be tensed but should not be slouched either. There should be no visible signs of nervousness or tension. I wiggle my toes, but no one can see that. Overall, there should be a message of confidence. Try to observe persuaders in differing contexts—interviews, speeches, arguments, and so on. You will see that the effective ones avoid both the nervous and the "nearly asleep" extremes.

Eye contact   There is some truth to the folk wisdom that a person cannot lie to you and also look you straight in the eyes. It is true most of the time for most people. We are believed better if we get eye contact with our audience. We do not need to look at everyone, but we need to look at various areas in the audience. Politicians know this and use things like Teleprompters to enable them to read a speech and appear to be looking around at the same time. In a one-on-one context, you will want to have repeated eye contact with your persuadee. Again, politicians make sure to look directly into the TV camera and hence to have apparent eye contact with each viewer. In a meeting, you will want to have eye contact with many persons or maybe even everyone at the meeting. It is clear that eye contact can effect persuasion.

Body movement and gesture   We can move during a speech, if the movement is not likely to distract. We can likewise gesture during a speech, if we do not distract by doing so. During a meeting, we can gesture or pound the table for effect. In an interview, we might include such things as touch in our gestures. We can gesture with our faces as well, and facial expressions can have impact in all three contexts. Again, the rule is to be natural and to avoid the extremes, as with posture. Vigorous arm-waving by speakers distracts. Frozen and inanimate persons seem bored with it all and so lose effect. Persons whose faces are expressionless come across as dull. Those who have eternal smiles pasted on signal insincerity. For most persons, facial expressions happen naturally and without forethought. Those gestures are probably the most useful.

Articulation and vocal quality   Everyone has heard persons who have speech defects or who pronounce words or sounds incorrectly. What is the result of these kinds of errors? Mostly we focus on the error and not on the message. In other words, the mistake distracts us away from the message. Persuaders who succeed listen carefully to themselves and try to work on articulation. Listening to ourselves on tape pinpoints our own careless articulation and can help us to focus on our vocal quality. Another good idea is to transcribe your articulation from a tape. If you know the phonetic alphabet, your mistakes will become crystal clear. Vocal quality—nasal sounding, wheezy, breathy, or a voice pitched too high— can be improved by using some of these methods as well. If you are really interested in persuading others, you will spend some time working on your voice and your articulation.

Delivery—The Channel

In a campaign that I once studied, the candidate put much of his money into billboard space. I was surprised because I assumed that in a television age, the major cost would be TV. The reason for the apparent mistake relates to the factor of the communication channel. His district was a large one, stretching nearly half the length of the state. No single TV channel reached all of the district. To use TV would mean paying a triple load to get a single message across. However, everyone in the district drove. The district was large, and residents had to drive to do shopping, business, or farming. Thus the billboard was a channel that could touch nearly all the voters in the district. The candidate was careful to choose the key spots for his signs. For example, he did not want to buy space next to a billboard for his opponent or just before a shopping section along the road or by an x-rated theater. The best billboard channels were at stoplights; cars had to wait. A good spot was on the way out of most towns where drivers would see signs after the distractions of the downtown area.

The same kind of care ought to be taken when persuaders make up their minds to succeed in a conference, in an interview, or with larger audiences. Again Schwartz's notion of creating a task-oriented message comes into play. What is the best way to tell the boss that he is being undercut by his assistant? Perhaps dropping a hint might work best. Maybe using the grapevine through the departmental gossip would work. Or maybe going in and telling the boss outright would work best. You need to be as careful about choosing your channel as the politician is about choosing the spots for billboards. A good place to start is by listing all channels that you could use to send your message. The list will vary from task to task. Identifying the channels gets you thinking in the right direction. Then locate which channels you can control. Then try to psych out your persuadee in terms of which channel will be most useful in getting his attention. Finally, shape your messages to fit your channel and to hit your target. Clever use of channels can make the difference between success and failure.

A student who wanted to get a job in the mass-mail industry used a receiver approach. He had been in the business before and knew that mass mailers were impressed by paper quality. So he had his résumé printed on the best parchment paper. It cost $400 to print the résumé. He also knew that mailers like simple design and a lot of white space. He made the résumé open like a poster with only a phrase on each page so that the unfolded brochure simply and clearly stated his past job experience. He he was clever to leave the fact that he had been thrice decorated for gallantry in battle until last for full impact. Within two weeks of mailing 100 résumés, he had more than half a dozen job offers, several of them starting at better than $20,000 a year. His use of the right channel to the right people with the right message spelled success. Spend some time thinking about the effects of various channels on your message as you get ready to persuade.

Delivery—The Audience

It is not easy to get the audience to help you with your delivery, but when speakers are able to do this, the results are impressive. For example, speakers can get audiences to respond to questions. The speaker says, "Eighty-seven senators voted for the Medicaid bill"; the audience roars, "But not Senator X!" Members of the audience feel that they are a part of the speech—that they are delivering it, too. So the clever use of questions and active feedback can get persuadees involved. Though not so dramatic as before a large group, the question can also be useful in the informal meeting. The persuader might ask a direct question of the audience (for example, "What is the problem here? Bill? Bob?"). Or we might let the receivers "fill in" for us by beginning to list examples and then letting our listeners provide some of their own. We could say, "So there are a lot of ways to save heat, like weather stripping your doors and windows and by. . . ." The persuader can try to shape the situation to make the audience feel like being persuaded. In some situations, we can do this with lighting, music, setting, and so forth. A minister of the largest Lutheran congregation in the world had a control switch in the pulpit so he could bring up the lights during the bright spots of his sermon and dim them on the hell and damnation parts. At other times, we can use the introduction to get people in the mood. One speaker I know always gets the audience on their feet to get the blood going in the first minute or so. He says this increases his success ratio. W. Clement Stone, the originator of P.M.A. (Positive Mental Attitude) asks his audience to stand up and shout, "Yes, I can!" You can be creative in setting the mood for persuasion. Consider what would make your persuadees want to be convinced. Then try to get them involved in their own persuasion.

SOME COMMON PERSUASION TACTICS

If you think about the key focus of the chapters you have read so far, it is that the *strategy* of persuasion is to find out what the audience already believes. Then speakers need to take that common ground and build on it, tying their own goals into what the target group or person thinks. What follows are some *tactics* for doing this. Tactics are the working tools that put strategy into action. These tactics are by no means the only ones that you can use.[6] You can add to this list as you try new techniques of persuasion in your own life.

The Yes-Yes Technique

A common tactic used in sales and other persuasive appeals is the technique called yes-yes. The source attempts to get the target group or person to respond "yes" to some of the parts of the appeal, holding the key request until last. Having agreed to most parts of the appeal, the target person is somewhat tied into saying "yes" to the key and final request. For example, suppose that you were trying to sell a lawn service. The service provides yearly fertilization, raking, and weed-killing. You might ask the homeowner, "You would like to have a beautiful lawn, wouldn't you?" The answer is going to be "yes"; all homeowners want nice lawns. Then you ask, "And you'd like the weeds removed?" Another "yes" is likely. You might follow up with, "And wouldn't it be nice if these things could be effort-free, huh?" A "yes" answer is likely again. Now that the homeowner has accepted all your points in favor of the service, it is nearly impossible to respond with a "no" answer to the final question. So you ask, "Then you'd like to be one of our lucky customers?" By accepting the "yes" pattern, the buyer will be more inclined to fall into agreement with your final request. The same technique could be useful in a meeting as a persuader gets the group members to agree with all but the final point in favor of the change in work schedules, for instance. They agree that flexibility is good, that more free time for workers is good, and so on. They are almost bound by the need to be consistent to agree that the change is a good one. A politician might ask if we want to lower jobless rates, if we

---

6.   These and many other tactics are, mentioned in texts and books of advice for persuaders. For example, see the following, which mentions many of the tactics noted here: Clyde J. Faries, "Teaching Rhetorical Criticism: It's Our Responsibility," *Journal of the Illinois Speech and Theatre Association*, Vol. 33 (Spring 1977), pp. 7–15. See also Ernest G. Bormann, William L. Howell, Ralph G. Nichols, and George L. Shapiro, *Interpersonal Communication in the Modern Organization* (Englewood Cliffs, N.J.: Prentice-Hall, 1969) pp. 233–241.

want to stop high fuel imports, and if we want to cut inflation. It follows then that we may be inclined to favor that politician's plan of action to combat the weakness in the status quo.

Persuaders can and do use this technique to slowly lead their target group or person through stages to a final "yes" answer to the request for purchases, change, or votes. Persuadees need to be alert to this tactic so they do not get trapped into making unwise choices just because they agree with parts of the whole pitch.

Don't Ask If, Ask Which

Suppose you run a small company. You want to ask an elderly department head to take early retirement. This is a common problem in all organizations. Now suppose your persuadee is evasive. He is not available when you phone. He finds excuses to avoid conferences. He refuses to discuss a retirement date. You need to get some kind of action. So you use the don't-ask-if, ask-which technique. This tactic asks the person to make a choice. There is no option other than the ones given. In the retirement situation, you say, "I need to have a meeting with you. Is Tuesday better or Wednesday?" There is no room for an answer like "I don't want to meet at all." The person can try to shift ground by saying, "Neither of those is good." This can easily be met with the same tactic. You ask, "Which day this week is good then?" You will eventually nail down a definite day. You can follow with "Your office or mine?" or "Two o' clock or three?" and thus force the action. Once the meeting is set, the tactic can go on as you ask if this June is better or would July be a good time to retire. There may be need for an interim step such as "Have you thought about retirement or is that something you haven't considered?" This sets the stage for your suggestion.

Salespersons often use this tactic, asking, "Which suit is best on you—the brown or the blue?" They follow with "Would you like a matching shirt and tie or just the suit for now?" Politicians ask "Who do you want to lead this great state, a party hack or myself?" TV and print ads often ask "Which wax cleans best—Pledge or the lemon oil brand X?"

Though the don't-ask-if, ask-which tactic can be very manipulative, it has the value of forcing action when buyers, voters, or others are stubborn and try to avoid making decisions. Persuadees need to watch for this tactic in order to avoid being trapped into a poor decision.

Answer a Question with a Question

A tactic that some persons use to throw you off guard is to respond to a request by asking a question. For example, they say, "Why do you think I would like to do that?" or "What gave you that idea?" or a similar response. We are expecting them to come to the point, to make a statement that relates to the discussion or the request. This throws us off pace and may leave us speechless for a moment. Then the initiative is gone. What is a good counter to this approach? The tactic of answering a question with a question is useful here. For example, a sales prospect responds to a sales pitch about a new car with a question, saying, "Aren't new cars awfully high priced these days?" The salesperson sputters, unable to say "yes" or "no." Cars are high priced but to admit this weakens the sales pitch. The best tactic for the seller is to ask, "What do you mean by high priced?" or "In relation to what? A new house or your tax bills?" The buyer must answer the question in some way; but the initiative is back with the salesperson, who has the added advantage of having time to think. Politicians often use this tactic. A voter at a rally asks, "Why is the treaty a good one for us if we own the canal anyway?" The politician counters with "What do you mean by the word 'own'?" and is back in the driver's seat. The tactic is not often seen in the ad world, but you do run into it sometimes. The ad says, "People have been asking why Mr. Coffee is better. We ask why are they willing to throw away flavor."

This tactic is most useful in question-and-answer sessions and when the target person or group uses the tactic of asking to throw us off pace. It has the advantage of shifting the initiative and giving you time to think. I recently used the tactic when questioned about a meeting that was held while the person I was trying to persuade was out of town. He asked if there had been such a meeting, suggesting that it was somehow held behind his back. My response to the query was, "Do you think there was something wrong about that?" I forced him into accusing me of being unfair or coming up with a reason for his suspicion. We do not often see this tactic used against us unless we are using the question to stymie those who are trying to persuade us. The person who uses the question to throw persuaders off is more frequent. Persuaders need to know how to deal with the questioning tactic. "Answer one with one" is the best advice.

Getting Partial Commitment

Evangelists often close their pitch by asking members in the tent or auditorium to bow their heads and close their eyes for prayer. This gets a partial commitment from all the audience. The preacher then asks in the prayer for the Lord to enter the hearts of all and can then ask those who want God to come into their lives to raise their hands or to stand up. This is a second act by which persons commit to part of the request. The final request may then be "Those of you with your hands up come to the front and be saved." The tactic is seen elsewhere, too. A sales pitch may include asking if you could afford to give up one pack of cigarettes a week to help put the Great Books series into your home. This willingness to commit oneself to a part of the deal can be continued until the sale is made. Ads offer a free sample of the product. You try it and have taken the first step in the purchase process. You get a free taste of cheese or sausage or yogurt in the supermarket and you will be more likely to commit yourself to buying the product. A politician can ask you to sign a petition to put his or her name on the ballot. The act is a form of commitment to that politician. Bumper stickers or buttons are used in campaigns to get people to commit themselves in part to the candidate. If they wear the button or put the sticker on, there is a good chance that they will vote for the candidate.

This tactic resembles the yes-yes technique but uses acts instead of words to lead the persuadee to the final request. Persuaders can use it with neutral or negative audiences. We need to watch ourselves as we make commitments. It is possible that we are being led to a major decision that is not the one we would make if it were the only thing we had to decide.

Ask More, so They Settle for Less

This tactic tries to set a price or level in people's minds. It is higher than what the source really wants so that when the persuader backs off, the buyers or voters feel as if they are getting a special offer. For example, suppose I bring in a set of test scores to my class and write on the chalkboard the curve that the computer suggests. Now I pass back the answer sheets; students moan because the curve is so high. Then I say that since I am so kind and sweet, I am making my own curve and write it on the board. It is a lower curve. Students cheer and sigh with relief. Then I tell them that the one-to-three-point essay can be added on without changing the curve. I am now the front runner for Teacher of the Year. I set a high expectation. Then I back off from that high level and the students believe they are getting a bargain. In truth, my curve, even with the added points, may be stringent, but when it is compared with the machine curve, I am Santa Claus. Government officials often use this tactic as they ask for more appropriations than they expect they will get or propose a more stringent bill than they expect to get. The whole sales field is built on the notion that you can mark down prices.

Persuaders can use this tactic when they have a hard product or goal to sell. Better to ask for more than your audience will stand for, so that in compromising, you will persuade. Audiences need to watch for this tactic and test the source's real bottom line.

Planting

This device uses one of the five senses to open a channel to the memory. We want the target group or person to recall our product, idea, or candidate. Memory responds best, it seems, to messages that have sense data as raw material. Thus the key factors are sight, sound, smell, taste, and feel. For instance, take the classic series of ads for bathroom tissue. Which is the softest tissue on the shelves? Why, of course it is Charmin. How do we know this and what makes us respond as one to the question? The source cleverly used the sense of touch to plant the Charmin message in our minds. We know that Mr. Whipple is always caught red-handed squeezing the stuff because it is so soft. The appeal to the sense of touch and the unique personage of Mr. Whipple created a long-lasting image in our mind. The source could appeal to the sense of smell instead. Then Mr. Whipple would be caught sniffing the packages of perfume-laden Charmin. Or the sense of sight might be used as Mr. Whipple is dazzled by the bright whites of Charmin. Candidates try to relate with audiences by referring to their local foods, reminding them that they have eaten Iowa corn or Maine lobster. Sight is also used. The candidate tells of the beauty of the Blue Ridge country. Sound might be useful if a candidate mentioned the deafening sounds of the drop forge to union steel workers. In each situation, the senses would be the key factor in getting the message planted in the voter's memory. In informal contexts, how might you make your points "stick" by using the tactic of planting?

Getting an I.O.U.

Sometimes called the swap or trade-off tactic, the technique of getting an I.O.U. aims to get your listeners to feel as if they owe you something. For instance, the insurance rep spends several hours doing a complex assets and debts analysis for a buyer. The goal is to prove to the buyer that he or she needs more insurance. The sales rep then spends hours explaining the figures to the husband and wife, perhaps taking them out to lunch or dinner. By the end of all the special treatment, the couple may feel that they really *ought* to buy something, even though they may not need it or cannot afford it. They need to cancel out the obligation—the I.O.U.—that was built. Hare Krishna members used this tactic at an airport until police made them stop. They were giving away a costly book that details their beliefs. If you took the "free" book, you felt duty-bound to listen to the Krishna pitch. After all, they had been nice enough to give you the free gift. Many door-to-door sales schemes use the same tactic. The seller may give you a vegetable brush, a sample of hand lotion, a plastic letter opener, or a set of steak knives to force you into an I.O.U. In order to clear the debt, you feel obligated to listen to the pitch. Ads sometimes include free offers that try to build the swap or I.O.U. tactic.

Persuaders find this tactic useful when it is hard to make a first contact with buyers, voters, or joiners. We need to note when a source tries to get us into debt through free gifts, samples, or offers of help. The old adage that "there's no such thing as a free lunch" is a pretty good warning in our doublespeak world. All these techniques and others offer sources many routes to success when the goal is to persuade others to action. As you develop your skills to persuade, you can try some of the tactics cited here and some of the others that you will meet. As a persuadee, you need to observe these and other tactics in use, often in sales but also in advertising and politics.

A REVIEW AND CONCLUSION

We all have to persuade at some point. The problem we have when we try to persuade is that we are careless when we go at it. We do not spend enough time planning how our format will affect the message. We do not often spend much time developing our forms of support and thinking about which would be most useful. We do not spend enough time trying to control factors in delivery. We need to use *source factors* like posture, eye contact, and so forth. *Channel factors* are subject to our control. *Receiver factors* can be used to get the target group involved in its own persuasion. As you are called on to persuade, use these skills in preparing. Rely on the kind of audience analysis that the receiver-oriented approach teaches—listen to your audience in order to *get messages out of them, not into them.*

Questions for Further Thought

1. Where does humor fit into the persuasion process? Give examples of sources who use humor. Does it relate to the audience? How?

2. What are the demographic factors you can locate for the persons in your class? In your dorm? In your church? Elsewhere?

3. What is a task-oriented message? Give examples from ads in which persuaders have done a good job of this. Where have they failed?

4. What are the forms of organization discussed above? How do they differ from the forms of support? What might be other ways to organize a message?

5. What are the factors in credibility? Name a person who really has each of them. Find an ad that relies on each of them. Share these in class.

6. What factors in delivery are most often used by our President when he wants to persuade? By your teacher? By your parents? By your special friends? What factors are not useful with these persons?

Experiences in Persuasion

1. Attend a persuasive meeting on your campus. There are numbers of them—Campus Crusade, transcendental meditation, political rallies, and so forth. Identify the demographic profile of the audience. See if the persuader seems to be sensing the same things you do. Study the speaker's organization, forms of support, style, and delivery. Focus on strengths and weaknesses. Report back on your experience to the class.

2. Do the same thing as in project 1 above, but for a set of magazine ads (for example, the Pepsi ads as they run in different magazines).

3. Buy a magazine that you usually do not read. Carefully look at the ads, at the letters to the editor, at the articles, at the cover, at the editorials, and at the features. Judging from these things, describe the target audience.

4. View a TV program you do not often watch. Using factors like the spots tied to the show, type of program, complexity of plot, development of character or setting, and so forth, describe the target audience.

5. Identify a persuasive presentation which you will face (for example, the job interview). Go through the steps outlined here—analyze your target, consider format, locate sources of support, work on style, plan your delivery. Prepare a report on your project or actually try to persuade.

6. Become a print persuader by writing a letter to the editor of your campus or home-town paper. Go through the steps outlined in this chapter and in project 5 above. Send the letter off to the paper.

Media in
Persuasion 8

The most common kind of persuasion that we receive is advertising—in TV and radio spot commercials and in print ads. As noted before most college freshmen have seen more than 22,000 hours of TV programming and more than 350,000 spots.[1] Not only are the spots forms of persuasion, but often the programs are, too. We live in a world in which media messages are common. The careful receiver needs to be alert to ways in which advertisers use the power of the media to achieve their goals. Researchers have only started to study the processes by which we receive and use media in our lives. Results are either speculative or sketchy. One thing is clear, however, and that is that the mass media are the most effective ways to persuade people of certain things. Mass media persuade us to buy products, to vote, and to take up causes. Why is this? One reason may be that since there is no real feedback in mass message systems (you cannot question, applaud, or respond), certain ploys work here that will not work in an open arena. Viewers, listeners, and readers may assume there is no way to respond to a program, a column, or to an ad. Without an easy way to feed their distaste back to the source of the message, they either ignore it or switch to another channel, paper, or magazine. In this chapter we will look at ways in which media may work. We will also discuss some common appeals that lend themselves to mass media. These should begin to alert you to the doublespeak that is used when persuaders employ mass media.

---

1.   David Burmeister, "The Language of Deceit" in *Language and Public Policy* ed. by Hugh Rank (Urbana, Ill.: National Council of Teachers of English, 1974) p. 40.

SCHWARTZ'S PERSPECTIVES ON MEDIA USE

We have mentioned Tony Schwartz in earlier chapters. His theory and book *The Responsive Chord*[2] have both been picked up and used by sources ranging from a presidential media staff to hundreds of firms and ad agencies selling anything from baby powder to barrels of booze. He offers two competing models of the way media work to persuade. The *evoked recall* or *resonance* model is one, and the *transportation* or *teaching* model is the other. Schwartz favors the first approach and offers reasons why.

The evoked recall or resonance approach works on the idea that it is better to get a message out of the receiver than to try to put one into him. In other words, it relies on the set of experiences and memories that people have stored in themselves. The basic tactic in getting these data out is to cue them in some way. Using this approach, persuaders might want to think of the kinds of problems people have with, say, a stalled car. Often a stall occurs when we are most rushed. The stall is sometimes a result of some minor bit of repair that we neglected. Maybe it was ice in the gas line or a dirty air filter. Knowing that the potential buyer of the product—the Amoco Motor Club Card—has been through at least one stall, the source can build a message around the feelings you have when your car stalls. Actors in an ad can show frustration. They can signal the anxiety you felt when you knew that the stall would make you late. The music or score can heighten the feelings. The voice-over can come on in a soothing way at the end to say, "When you've got to be there, Amoco gets you there." Schwartz observes that most experiential meaning is not cued symbolically since it is not stored as a symbol. Instead it is stored as a feeling—a sense of ease or dis-ease. The best way to cue these feelings out is drama. The source acts out the feeling in the listener's head. Many times the cuing is done by music, color, sound effects, the actor's face, tone of voice, acoustics, or some other message.

The Verbal Script

Of course, this idea runs counter to what many ad agencies believe. It is also counter to much of the theory about persuasion that keys in on being specific, logical, and clever with words. That view only looks at the verbal script, which *is* the message. Ad agencies test their ads, and do just that.

---

2.   Tony Schwartz, *The Responsive Chord* (Garden City, N.Y.: Anchor Press/Doubleday, 1973).

They ask people to look at ads and then to respond recalling the words, numbers, and names that are in the ad. Rarely are viewers asked about their feelings or about the characters in the ads. It is often a quirk of fate that brings out data like the persons who resented their suitcase because it survived a plane crash. It was luck that the Leo Burnett agency found that viewers feared for the average-sized people in the valley of the Jolly Green Giant in commercials that showed the giant moving around.

The Sound Script

The TV spot is more than just its verbal script. It includes a sound script—the things you hear that are not words. For instance, the good feelings we have about keg parties can be cued out by the sounds of a keg being tapped. As we hear the thunk of the tap being punched through the cork, the spin of the wing nut bolting down the tap, and the gurgle of the first mug being filled, the good times come back. Then it is fairly easy to add words: "We've got beer in a can that's as good as beer from a keg—Hamm's Draft in the new aluminum can." The can is shaped like a barrel or keg to reinforce the good feelings most people have about past keg parties. So the sound script can be a key means of cuing feelings out.

The Sight Script

The sight script is also important as a source of such cues. The sight of the Hamm's beer can in a keglike shape is a good example, as is the packing of certain cleaners in drum-shaped bottles to give the feeling of heavy-duty power. There are other ways by which the sight script can cue feelings out of us. Camera angle often has a cuing value. A low angle that "looks up" to the leader somewhat distorts size and "says" that this person is one to be looked up to—a cut above most people. A wide-angle shot with crowds of people thronging to see the leader and shouting salutes sends the message that this is a great leader of a great movement. Hitler used this technique in the famous Nazi propaganda film *Triumph of the Will.* It was outlawed in Germany for many years after World War II due to its power to raise the emotions and feelings. Close-up or zoom-in shots of persons "say" that we need to get a closer look, find out what kind of stuff they are made of and what sort of persons they are. Editing can call out feelings, which can then be used to persuade. Many news films of battle situations depend on clever editing to build a sense of action. They use quick cuts from one action shot to another. Tanks shoot across the screen. Then we cut to planes diving. Then we cut to troops running across a field firing all the way, and so on. The quick cut makes the viewer feel that there is a lot of effective action. It looks like "the good guys" are making raceway progress across the land of "the bad guys." Of course anyone in the Army knows the truth in the old maxim about the Army's way of doing things—hurry up and wait. The quick cut can build the same kind of sense of action in other contexts. We see a snowmobile leaping across the screen and cutting through a snowdrift. Then we cut to a downhill racer carving a trail in new snow. We are ready to hear about "Lake Geneva— where winter isn't going to get you down."

Other aspects of the sight script keep getting messages out of us. Many newscasts depict a newsroom atmosphere. The teletypes clatter, people rush around the set carrying pieces of paper meant to be news flashes, and so on. Walter Cronkite and Roger Mudd are then superimposed on the set from another studio giving the visual impression that they are in the middle of the hustle and bustle. You get the impression that you won't miss any news if you stay tuned to that channel. The background shots for candidates can be part of the sight script and can prompt out feelings, too. A TV producer during the 1976 campaign argued that he could not feature the candidates at a roundtable meeting: "We couldn't figure a way to do it on television. What do you show, people sitting around a table?"[3] The same thing happens on spot ads and even entertainment programs. Feelings are cued out of viewers through the background setting. These and many more elements in a visual script can be used to evoke or recall feelings, the real stuff of persuasion, according to Schwartz. As we receive media messages, we need to be alert to the verbal script or the substance of the message, and also to the sound and sight scripts and their varied messages—the messages of color, camera angle and movement, background, sound effects, and musical score.[4]

McLUHAN'S PERSPECTIVE ON MEDIA USE

Marshall McLuhan is another theorist who has studied media use in our times. His ideas in many ways are like those of Schwartz. In fact, the two are friends and often draw on one another for examples and insights. McLuhan feels that we relate to media in two ways. He says every medium is an extension of one of our senses or body parts.[5] Media do certain

3. Quoted in "And That's the Way It Was?—Television Covers the 1976 Presidential Campaign" by David L. Swanson, *Quarterly Journal of Speech*, Vol. 63 (October 1977), p. 245.

4. A fuller discussion of how to criticize those elements is found in "Media Metaphors: Two Perspectives for the Rhetorical Criticism of TV Commercials," a paper presented by Charles U. Larson at the Annual Spring Symposium at the University of Minnesota, May 1976.

5. For a full discussion of these ideas, see *Understanding Media: The Extensions of Man*, by Marshall McLuhan (New York: Signet Books, 1964).

things to our self-image, regardless of the message content. So just watching TV will have effects on you. McLuhan focuses his ideas around two key words—"hot" and "cool"—which are useful in describing media and media messages.

Hot Media

"Hot" refers to media and messages that have high fidelity or definition, in McLuhan's words. These media are easy to perceive. Their images are well drawn or recorded. We do not have to work to get the image or the sound. It is sort of like the difference between the old wind-up phonograph that scratched out the sounds of the 1920s and the quad sound that makes you feel as if you are right in the middle of the orchestra. The quad set-up is hot because it has high fidelity or definition. It is easy to perceive. Messages have the same kind of quality. Hot messages are clear, distinct, easy to understand or get. We do not have to work at them. A good example might be the advertiser who comes on during the late movie and tries the hard sell about three rooms of carpeting for only $399.99. The message is distinct and comes through crystal clear. This is a hot message. Or consider the hot politician who comes on strong and does not pull any punches but blurts out his message in simple words. George Wallace and Ronald Reagan would be past examples of hot speakers. Both men have spoken in a kind of gut-level language. It has often turned many voters off, though it does appeal to certain sets of people. This is the kind of politician who, Schwartz says, will "blow out" viewer fuses. Howard Cosell, the controversial but able sportscaster, does not seem to be a very pleasant guy. He is a hot message, too. The persuader presents hot messages by means of both hot and cool media, and conflicts occur. McLuhan says that TV is not a hot medium since it has such low fidelity. Only half the screen is active at any moment. Half the lines are on and half are off at any moment. Now we put Howard Cosell on TV, the cool medium. Who should appear with him? Would we pick another hot person or a cool one? *Monday Night Football* seems to suggest that a cool one works best. Dandy Don Meredeth and Frank Gifford have been matched with Cosell—perhaps to cool down Howard's hot personality. When Cosell hosted his own cool variety show without any co-host, it flopped.

Cool Media

Conversely, cool media have low fidelity or definition. We have to work to process these messages. We have to put together the half images we see on TV. We have to imagine a lot of sound quality into the wind-up Victrola. Low-fidelity sounds come out of a telephone. What kinds of messages are best for these media? McLuhan says that cool media breed cool messages,

Medium	Source of Information	Definition	Participation	Type of Medium
Television	Lighted dots	Low	High	Cool
Books	Completed letters	High	Low	Hot
Cartoons	Dots on paper	Low	High	Cool
Photographs	Image on film	High	Low	Hot
Telephone	Low-fidelity sound wave	Low	High	Cool
Movies	Moving image on film	High	Low	Hot
Telegraph	Dots and dashes in sound	Low	High	Cool
Stereo	High-fidelity sound wave	High	Low	Hot

Figure 8-1 *Hot and Cool Media.*

ones that are vague and ill defined. Thus he sees the politician of the TV-dominated future being abstract, fuzzy, shaggy around the edges. There is no need for this type to say everything at gut level. Instead, this type lets the voter fill in or put together a meaning or image. If McLuhan is right, we should have seen a growth in image politics since the theory was first presented in 1964. That is exactly what has happened. The politicians who seem to catch on are those with an easy-going, never-clear approach. They are abstract to the voter, not distinct. Likewise we ought to be seeing more TV commercials that rely less on words or scripts than on giving a mood or feeling. Then the viewer can add to or subtract from what he watches to get a final meaning. Think of the many commercials that do this through the use of music or sets or lighting. We hear the sounds of a Broadway-musical love ballad. Then we see a well-dressed man and woman slowly walking down the stairs at the Opera House. He asks the doorman to signal for his car. Up drives a Volkswagen Rabbit. Only then do we hear the voice-over tell us that the "VW is in good taste anytime, anywhere." We fill in or add to the message we have received.

So in today's world, we need to be alert to how we add to cool media and cool messages. We need to note the media mix that results when hot media carry cool messages and vice versa. Being aware even if it is only on a part-time basis, can help us to sense doublespeak in the mass-media world. Refer to Figure 8-1 for examples of hot and cool media.

LANGUAGE USE IN MEDIA

We have been looking at how the media work with images. This focus leaves out concern for the use of words in media messages. We know that symbols are the basic raw material of persuasion. We know words are central carriers of symbolic meaning. So we need to look at how clever persuaders can use words and at how these work in mass-media messages. Carl Wrighter, a former adman, in his book *I Can Sell You Anything*[6] focuses on some of the key words that he thinks are used to deceive us. He calls them *weasel words* because they allow the persuaders to seem to say something without ever really saying it. These words let sources weasel their way out of a promise. Let us look at a few of these. They are key tip-offs to the kind of pitch we need to guard against.

"Helps"

The word "helps" is a clever one. It seems to offer aid or perhaps even a cure. We hear that Listerine mouthwash *helps* prevent colds. Even if you get a cold, it *helps* you feel better right away. What is the promise here? Can you expect that you will feel better in a few days if you use Listerine? If you did, could you say your improvement was due to the *help* Listerine gave? These questions point up the problem with a word like "helps." We need to be alert to this often-used weasel word. Ads for products use it. Politicians promise that they will *help* get this country moving again. Those who try to advance a certain idea or ideology promise that boycotting a certain chain store will *help* establish new hiring policies that will include minorities.

"Like"

Another weasel word used in mass-media ads is the word "like." For instance, there on the TV screen is poor Mrs. Housewife. Her house is so dingy and drab. She wonders if hubby will come home or will he go out with the boys instead? Then out of a bottle of floor and wall cleaner comes a white tornado. We hear that Kleenstuf cleans *like* a white tornado. Now how does a tornado of any color clean? Does it scrub, brush, mop, or scour? Further, do white tornadoes clean better or worse than red ones? You can easily see the deception that can be floated with a word that has as many loopholes as the word "like." In newscasts, we hear that this or that event is *like* some event in the past. Abuse in prisons is brushed off because that is what prisons are *like*. Charlie's Angels are supposed to be *like* young women all over the world. Soap operas claim to be *like* real life.

Perhaps that is the secret to so many of the words we see and hear in print and broadcast ads. They are loaded with escape hatches so they can promise without really giving. Think of the many promises that are given

---

6.   Carl Wrighter, *I Can Sell You Anything* (New York: Ballantine Books, 1972).

with the word "like." A certain stereo component will create sound that will make your listening moments almost *like* being there. A prepared food tastes just *like* homemade. A jug wine tastes *like* the expensive French wines. A facial cream acts *like* "a thousand busy fingers massaging at your face."

"Virtually"

The weasel word "virtually" resembles "like" except that it seems to promise even more. The new cotton chamois shirts are *virtually* indestructible. Anyone want to bet?—try putting them into the furnace or through the table saw. Leatherette feels *virtually* like cowhide. As noted earlier, Cascade leaves your dishes and glassware *virtually* spotless. The promise seems so specific. There is only a tiny loophole. That loophole widens as much as is needed when the consumer says that the chamois shirt wore out after several months' wear or when we find out there are a few spots here and there on the dishes and stemware. If the product did what is claimed, the word "virtually" would not be needed. The same thing applies to the politician who asks for support for his program that will *virtually* wipe out discrimination. This weasel word appears in fund appeals, too. The fund is *virtually* within sight of its goal for the new year, so give a little more.

"As Much As"

The weasel words "as much as" tell you *the most* you can expect from a product and then suggest that *the most* will be everyday. Many thought that the policy of publishing Environmental Protection Agency (E.P.A.) mileage estimates in every auto ad would assure honesty. The estimates were what you could expect under best conditions—perfect roads, good weather, fine tuning of the engine, and so forth. You were promised *as much as* 38 miles per gallon in city driving in a Dodge Colt, but you were not *promised* 38 miles per gallon.

A politician promises to cut taxes by *as much as* 20 percent. We find that this applies to few people. The newscast says there will be *as much as* 10 inches of snow. We hear that *as much as* 40 percent of the town was destroyed. All these uses of this weasel phrase aim to maximize the drama of the promise or event to get us to fall for the flimflam.

"Stronger," "Faster," or "Better"

"Anacin fights pain *better* than ordinary aspirin." The impact of that claim lies in the comparison being made. What we are *not* told is how much better or better in what ways. The makers of Anacin might answer,

"One tenth of 1 percent better." They could say "...better because it melts quickly." However, they persuade us because the message limits our options. We can compare Anacin only with all other *ordinary* aspirins. In what way are they ordinary? Instead of having a choice of ten we now have a choice between two: Anacin and the others. So the weaseling has two impacts. It intensifies the advantages of one brand. At the same time, it limits the options that we consider. The candidate says that a program for health insurance is *better*. All other programs are lumped into a single category just as Anacin does with all ordinary aspirin tablets.

"Everyone" says that we have a *better* system of government. In what ways? Compared with what? These are the questions to ask. Entertainment programs imply that it is *better* to be sexy, rich, into sports, and so on. Why? In what ways? Compared with what?

Wrighter discusses several other weasel words in his book. You will be able to identify many others as you focus on media messages. A good way to find them is to search for words that sound like promises. They often have loopholes—"Feels like . . ." or "It is literally . . ." or "Can be effective in . . ." or "Easier than . . ." and many others. We need to be alert not only to weasel words but also to other uses of language that imply a promise while hiding a loophole.

DECEPTIVE CLAIMS IN MEDIA

Another kind of deception to which we are exposed in media ads is found in the claims that are made. We discussed content claims in Chapter 4 and spent most of our time looking at how the claim was supported and at the logic behind it. Now we need to focus on the wording of the claim. Clever sources use claims to attract our attention and to prompt us to buy, to vote, or to adopt certain practices. Let us look at several kinds of such claims.[7]

The Irrelevant Claim

Some persuaders use media messages to make claims that sound impressive but are really irrelevant if you look at them closely. For instance, we see Andy Granatelli pick up a screwdriver with his thumb and forefinger. That is easy until he coats the tool with STP. Now it is impossible for Andy to pick it up. Looks neat, doesn't it? That must be some stuff! Look at the claim more carefully..There are no lies here—Strongman Andy

---

7.   See Wrighter, Chapter 3, "A Baker's Dirty Dozen of Claims," pp. 41–76.

really cannot pick up the screwdriver if it is coated with STP. However, the truth that is shown is irrelevant to whether STP will protect your engine and give it new life. We are asked to associate the dramatic media test of STP with the need for lubricating our car. The irrelevant claim has power if we make the association.

You will be exposed to such claims whenever you turn on your TV, open a magazine, or tune in your radio. The basic tactic is to make a truthful claim that has little to do with the purpose of our product, plan for change, or idea. Then we dramatize the claim in such a way that the people link the claim with our product, candidate, or movement. The key to spotting such a claim as that of Figure 8-2 is to ask yourself why you would want to have quality X? Why would you want a slippery screw-driver? What is unnatural in scotch whisky? If there is a reason for having the quality, then ask if there is reason to believe that all scotches do not have the same quality, for example. Are there any scotches that do not use naturally fermented grain to make alcohol? If the answer is "no" to either question, then you have hit on an irrelevant claim.

The Question Claim

Wrighter notes a kind of claim that we often see beamed at us through media. This is the claim that seems to ask an obvious question. The obvi-ous answer to it would imply purchasing a product or voting for a candi-date. In New York in 1970, James Buckley had a slogan: "Isn't It Time We Had a Senator?" The question is one that everyone would have to answer with "yes." *Anytime* is the time to have a senator. Buckley's opponent, incumbent Senator Charles Goodell, could have responded to the Buckley slogan with another slogan like "We *Have* a Senator for the Times." The impact of this kind of claim comes from its ability to get us into a yes-yes pattern. We answer the persuader's question with "yes" or by buying or by voting. "Yes, it's time we had a senator; yes I'll vote for Buckley" is the yes-yes pattern in that example. Enough voters had a yes-yes response that Buckley was elected. Whether you see it or hear it, the question mark is a tip-off to the yes-yes tactic or the question claim.

The Advantage Claim

Wrighter noted the claim which seems to offer some advantage for a product or idea. Mother's noodles claim to be fortified in a certain way. This is a supposed advantage over all other brands. We are asked to assume that the fortification with vitamins is good and that it is exclusive to the Mother's product. Neither of these assumptions is 100 percent true. Telling people that they can put their own fresh eggs into the cake mix is

Figure 8-2 Consider the claim made for J & B scotch whisky. The word use here is clever. What things make us feel good about the word "natural"? What in the message gives us a feeling of nature? (Courtesy E. T. Howard Company, Inc., © 1977 Paddington Corporation, N. Y.)

After investing all this in a car, isn't it worth investing $3.95 in a can of oil?

$3.95 might seem like a big investment—even for a good premium oil. But then, Mobil 1 synthetic motor oil is much more than just a good premium oil.

What can you expect from an oil change with Mobil 1?

For one thing, you won't have to change it so often. 15,000 miles (or one year, whichever comes first) compared to the usual 4,000-6,000. (If your car is still under warranty, however, you should change your oil in accordance with warranty requirements.)

Mobil 1 even protects your engine better than premium oils do. To prove it, we ran Mobil 1 for 15,000 long, unending miles. Then we tested it. The used Mobil 1 still protected the engine as well as premium motor oil that was brand new.

It can give you better mileage, too. Because it reduces friction better, it will take the average car up to 10 extra miles on each tankful of gas. And it starts delivering better mileage from the first time you use it.

And because it doesn't evaporate as quickly as premium oils, you'll use less oil with Mobil 1. (Provided, of course, that your engine is in good mechanical condition.)

Finally, it won't thin out the way ordinary premium oils do in a hot engine in summer. And Mobil 1 stays thin enough to help your engine start easier in winters as cold as 35° below zero.

At $3.95 or even more, is a can of Mobil 1 a big investment? Not when you consider the size of your returns.

The oil that saves you gas ...saves you oil changes.

Mobil 1 is available in Canada through Imperial Oil stations.

Figure 8-3 *What is the yes-yes in this ad for Mobil 1? (Courtesy Mobil Oil Corporation.)*

no advantage at all. It just increases the cost of the cake. Some regulations force all product sellers to fortify certain foods. Compare the levels of vitamins in several types of breakfast cereal. You will discover that they are all about the same. Most of the goodness comes from the milk and not the cereal. Thus there is no advantage in Corn Chex's ballyhoo on their box that they are "Fortified with 6 Important Vitamins and Minerals!" These are advantages that aren't.

Some politicians stress their humble beginnings. We discussed the strategy behind this in Chapter 6. Let us look at it as an advantage claim. That is what the persuader is doing—telling us that there is an advantage in coming from humble roots. Well, it might have been an advantage for Honest Abe Lincoln. However, he might have done even better had he gone to Harvard Law School. In fact, Lincoln was not a great lawyer. He was always a junior partner in the law firms he joined. The humble early childhood of Richard Nixon may have made him insecure enough to want to overdo his 1972 campaign. Humble beginnings may have led to the bugging and dirty tricks and other acts that finally ruined the man. Likewise, the candidates may share the same advantage with every other person in the running. Most politicians are able to point to a career outside the political arena. So the advantage claim is leaky on two grounds. There is no need for the advantage and all competitors share the same advantage.

The Hazy Claim

This claim is one that confuses the buyer or voter. If persuaders can confuse you, you will follow their advice just to be on the safe side. Consider the ad for Dannon Yogurt shown in Figure 8-4. It confuses the reader by refusing to promise a chance at long life and then by making the promise that there might be a chance after all. As you read more of the ad copy, you see that the only health claim Dannon can make is that their yogurt, unlike some others (how many? off brands? so what?), has active cultures. The consumer does not know whether it is good to eat Dannon Yogurt, yogurt of any kind, or no yogurt. Out of this confusion, Dannon persuades through its slogan: "If you don't always eat right, Dannon Yogurt is the right thing to eat." We ought to ask "Why is it right?" "Who says?" and "With what proof?" when a hazy claim appears.

Again, we can see this claim widely used in the world of politics. A politician says that he supports the economic policies of free trade and protective tariffs. These policies are 180 degrees apart. The result for voters is confusion. If voters watch images, the problem becomes worse. What does it prove if a politician kisses babies or plays baseball or talks about the price of pork? These activities do not tell us much about an elected official's ability to construct policies on education, leisure time, or farm prices. They are likely to confuse the voter and draw attention away

Dannon® Yogurt may not help you live as long as Soviet Georgians. But it couldn't hurt.

Bagrat Topagua, age 89.

His mother.

There are two curious things about the people of Soviet Georgia. A large part of their diet is yogurt. And a large number of them live to be well over 100.

Of course, many factors affect longevity, and we are not saying Dannon Yogurt will help you live longer. But we will say that all-natural Dannon is high in nutrients, low in fat, reasonable in calories. And quite satisfying at lunch or as a snack.

Another thing about Dannon. It contains active yogurt cultures (many pre-mixed or Swiss style brands don't). They make yogurt one of the easiest foods to digest and have been credited with other healthful benefits.

Which is why we've been advising this: If you don't always eat right, Dannon Yogurt is the right thing to eat.

By the way, Bagrat Topagua thought Dannon was "dzelian kargia." Which means he loved it.

Dannon Milk Products, 22-11 38th Ave. Long Island City, N.Y. 11101.

Figure 8-4 *The hazy claims about longevity and yogurt may confuse the persuadee enough to try the product to be on the safe side. (Courtesy Dannon Milk Products.)*

from the issues. The unclear or hazy claim leaves you not really sure what is being claimed because the source is never clear about it. This is designed to draw attention away from the real nature of the product or candidate.

The Magic Claim

Wrighter calls this the mysterious claim because it refers to a mysterious ingredient or device that makes a better product. I prefer the idea of magic instead because most of these ingredients or devices are not touted as spooky or mysterious. We are told that there is a drop of retsyn in each Clorets tablet. The retsyn is just salad oil that helps bind the tablet together. However, we are told that retsyn has magic power to destroy bad breath. Or we are told that Shell has the special stuff called platformate in it, which results in greater mileage. We get a demonstration that is like the stunt in which a magician pulls a rabbit from a hat. Two identical cars are hooked up to identical bottles of gasoline that contain exactly the same amount of fuel. This set-up is like the wizard asking a spectator to check out his silk hat to see if there is anything in it. The two cars are then driven at identical speeds until one runs out of gas and the other goes on farther. Which car had the platformate? You guessed it—the one that went farthest. That result is like the rabbit being magically pulled out of the hat. You are told that a certain model's dress should look purple on your TV screen and another's hair should look red and certain flowers shown us by another model should look bronze. If they do not, then you really are not getting the kind of color you deserve. RCA's new color gun can give it to you. It is designed to spread color signals to more of the special receiver modules fixed on an RCA screen. The model flicks a switch and the camera zooms in. Magically the colors are true. The dress is purple. (Cut to next model.) The hair is red. (Cut to last model.) The flowers are true bronze. The mysterious claim is sometimes used by religious evangelists, too. If you really believe and do your converting in our magic way, then you, too, can be saved. That is the standard format for such appeals. Various groups insert their own dogma, relics, or rites. Each touts its own belief in a kind of magical act that yields salvation. Politicians do not usually brag about any magical quality but sometimes create a mysterious atmosphere around one of their ideas. For instance, the President requests prime time from the TV networks. Then we hear his announcement concerning energy. Then a leak reveals that he intends to replace his energy secretary. The mystery is built up, but there is nothing magical about replacing a cabinet officer. When running for the presidency in 1968, Nixon referred to a "secret plan" he had for ending the Vietnam war. He refused to show it or discuss it. He said the enemy would then know what to expect. He would begin to reveal his plan after being elected. This tactic did not go over very well. It was like the child saying to a playmate, "Open your mouth and close your eyes, and I'll give you something to make you wise." Then the kid puts dirt or worse in the victim's mouth. When you hear that something magic will happen if we follow a certain course of action or that there is a secret ingredient in a given product, you can bet that nothing too special exists. If they had a real secret ingredient, they would not tell about it. Spies might find out what it is and sell the recipe to the competition. So if there is turtle oil in a face cream, the oil might be a good binder and not a wrinkle fighter.

Many other kinds of claims are made through the mass media. Wrighter's book points out some. You will discover others as you begin to evaluate the mass-media messages you receive. The important thing to do is to maintain a critical attitude. Ask key questions of the claim.

AGENDA SETTING BY THE MEDIA

Mass-media theorists talk about the ability of the media to set the agenda for the nation, state, or locality. In other words, *mass media do not tell us what to think; they tell us what to think about.* There is some truth in this theory. How do mass media get us to attend to certain issues and not others?

Suppose that you were in charge of programming at a network. You want to push some idea—say, the meatless diet. What kinds of things could you do to promote your idea? You could run a series of documentaries on personal health. One of them could focus on nutrition and the value of meatless diets. That way your idea would be hidden in the series as a whole, but you could get your message across. Then you might refuse ads for meat products. You might have a show for gourmet cooks and use a vegetarian natural-foods advocate to host the show. Cooking shows do not get much of the market, but it might be worth a try. You could also try an editorial. Probably the single most useful thing to do would be to get your newsstaff to investigate the slaughterhouses across the state and nation. Tell them to highlight stories in which food poisoning or contamination came from meat. All these tactics would help get people ready for your meatless ideas. None of them would be very useful in getting people to change from meat-eating to vegetarian habits. That has to be done more overtly, in situations where fewer people are being persuaded. You would get people to think about the vegetarian way versus meat menus. In other words, you would tell people what to think about, not what to think. You put meat eating on the public agenda. Let us look at some of the tactics that help set our agendas.

Humor

The cartoon shown in Figure 8-5 relies on knowledge of classical mythology and of the ecological crisis. The Roman god Mercury is central. Mercury, the messenger of the gods, was a speedy guy and hence was thought to have wings on his heels. Mercury is also the name of a metal. The metal mercury is used in many industrial processes like paper making. It is often dumped into streams and lakes where it sinks to the bottom. There it poisons fish and finally humans if they eat the fish. Contrast the Mercury cartoon with the one in Figure 8-6, which focuses on Social Security. The second cartoon sets an agenda for us. The cartoon is based on the Old Testament. Carter is shown as Moses parting the waters of the Red Ink Sea to send his people to their promised land. The average foreigner would probably not get the point of this cartoon. A foreign person would probably understand the humor in mercury poisoning. The financial state of Social Security is known to citizens of the United States. Foreign persons would not know this. So when humor is used to set agenda, it requires some inside knowledge of the issue. Humor is often aimed at persons who are well informed and well read. Perhaps that is why the agenda-setting humor in newspapers is mostly hidden away on the editorial pages. It may also be why we see so little political humor on TV. Supposedly the networks target their programs for a 12-year-old mentality; such viewers are not informed on the issues. So political humor fails just as it fails with foreign persons.

Though humor can be used to put an item on the nation's agenda, it works only with persons who are opinion leaders. If we want to reach a more general audience, other means will have to be used.

FRANK AND ERNEST   by Bob Thaves

Figure 8-5 *Although a person needs to know something about Mercury to get the point of this cartoon, the knowledge is not inside information. (Reprinted by permission of NEA.)*

Figure 8-6 *This cartoon requires some sophisticated knowledge about the finances of Social Security, as well as common knowledge about the Bible. This use of humor helps to set the agenda for government. (Reprinted courtesy of the Chicago Tribune.)*

Editorial Comment

In most of the mass media, editorials are used from time to time to put issues on the public agenda. During one week in 1978, these issues were brought up in the newspaper I read: mandatory retirement at age 70, the plight of the black family, the higher education budget in Illinois, U.S. withdrawal from the International Labor Organization; secrecy and perjury and CIA officers, the need to disband Illinois' "navy," the SALT talks, the effect of union demands on the British pound, and the conservative/liberal splits in both major parties. Of course, not all these items are going on the public agenda. Editorials nominate items for our agenda. They also often take positions that are pro or con. The humor in cartoons does not do this, though it could. Editorials, however, are extremely potent in either limiting or expanding the number of issues that will be considered by the general public. During Watergate, for example, almost every issue of every newspaper and every weekly newsmagazine had at least one comment on the scandal. That limited the items for the agenda. It forced

Watergate issues onto the agenda. It also forced other items to a backburner position. Such backburner issues as energy, the economy, and many others were probably as important as the scandal. Nixon's argument that he was impeached in the press had some validity if we look at the power of the mass media to set the nation's agenda. Again, editorials appeal to elite, well-read, and well-informed groups. How might the mass media do some agenda setting with everyday, noninformed, nonreading audiences?

Dramatizing

We have discussed the power of drama in several places. It also is a potent device that the mass media use to set agendas and to gain support for certain agenda items. Dramatic evening news programs or headlines focus our attention. We hear or read about political bribes. This information leads to sentiment for further investigation and later follow-up reports. Public feeling runs against the politicians. In a final stage, perhaps the drama results in resignation of officials or court cases. The key factor that keeps attention focused is the reported drama of the situation. In 1977, a New York City man killed a number of young couples in their parked cars. He was nicknamed the .44-Magnum Killer in news accounts. Later he was called Son of Sam. Before his arrest, the press focused on the killer, his choice of weapon, the similarities among his victims, his letters warning of his need to spill blood, and so forth. Son of Sam became a major item on the New York City agenda and on the agenda of the nation as well. The drama of the killings and of the mental problems of the killer turned everyone into a detective looking for the .44-Magnum Killer. The citizens of New York City became a vigilante force. This is how the killer was finally caught. Some people reported descriptions of a car that had been parked near the murder sites. It belonged to a man who had been reported as a suspect by neighbors. He looked like the artist's drawings made from victim and witness descriptions. The news media led the successful search for Son of Sam. They injected a lot of drama into the number-one agenda item.

Another thing we need to do as receivers is to look carefully at the dramas that are played out in the evening newscasts and in the daily headlines. Sometimes they will build agenda items that need attention. Sometimes they will overdramatize a problem and make us use undue effort to solve it. Perhaps the Son of Sam case shifted attention from the scores of other murders that occur each year in New York City. Sometimes they may focus us on problems that do not deserve agenda status. Anita Bryant was pushed into the national limelight when she supported a certain ordinance in one city in Florida; it banned homosexual teachers.

At other times, the media may ignore certain problems and never dramatize them, even though they need to be looked at. Various aspects of the energy problem were covered in the media for years before the 1973 Arab oil boycott riveted attention on energy as an agenda item. When we see dramas beginning to unfold in the print and broadcast media, we need to ask why and at what cost (that is, what other problems will thus not get our concerned attention?).

Of course, drama is the stock-in-trade of the entertainment programs that we see on TV and hear on radio. Here the dramas are simple and require less critical viewing. They may persuade us to follow a certain lifestyle or to adopt certain slang expressions. However, they rarely set agendas for us. The more important thing which these dramatizations do is to provide us with role models. They show us day in and day out that crime does not pay, that attractive people succeed, that wives and mothers are at home in the kitchen and laundry while fathers fly the friendly skies, and so on and on and on. These messages may have a more enduring effect on society than all the various policy questions that the news programs put on our various local and national agendas.

ROLE-MODELING AND MEDIA

In earlier times people learned to model themselves after the patterns shown by those with whom they worked or lived. Girls learned to be good housewives by watching their mothers. Boys learned to be farmers by watching their fathers and the other farmers in the community. Today, the media exert a much more potent force on role-modeling than the world around us does.

As we enter into the many contexts in which we work and play, we are forced to adopt various roles. These roles are patterns of acting and talking that signal many meanings to persons around us. We act like a stuffy teacher and that sends messages to students that lead them to treat us as stuffy. We come on as the hale, hearty, extrovert type, and people expect us to have good jokes, to be easy to talk with, and so on. These roles shift from place to place and time to time. I do not often swear in church, but I am quite good at it on a canoe trip. You act the humble student when you are trying to get the teacher to let you do extra credit to make up for the low grade on the midterm test.

We adopt such roles in two ways. First, we may take on a certain role because the scene or setting demands it of us. For example, certain roles are called for at funerals while others are called for at weddings. These are *assigned roles*. A President may suffer a personal tragedy but should not show its effects too obviously in public. The scene assigns him the role of leader, and shows of emotion are not called for in leaders. At other times, the setting may demand a role that we do not accept, and we choose another role. For example, a pro-football player should be tough and burly. He should make a show of proving that he is all man. Big, tough, burly he-men don't hurt and they don't cry. The scene of the football field assigns this role. However, suppose that players know that a teammate is dying of some disease, as was the case with the Chicago Bears a number of years ago. Now the tough guys show emotions and cry at the end of the final game of the stricken player's final season. These actions come from roles dictated by the players, not the scene. These can be called *assumed roles*. They are taken at the will of the role-player and often run counter to the demands of the scene. If you return to Burke's dramatic pentad (see Chapter 2), the assigned role is a result of the scene:agent ratio and is a situation in which the scene dominates. The assumed role flows out of the same ratio but here the agent dominates. Again and again through all our lives, we choose between these two options—the assumed and the assigned roles. We have varying degrees of success and failure in playing roles, and we learn from them. How do we learn which roles are called for and which are not?

Here is where mass media come in. Unlike our ancestors, even our grandparents, who lived in earlier times when role assignments or assumptions were fairly simple, we live in a complex society. We cannot predict the scenes we will act in. In a few years, some of you will be working in jobs and professions that do not exist today. It is impossible for us to foresee, let alone prepare for, all the potential roles that we may be asked to fill in our own communities. Our grandparents learned roles from people around them. We learn about roles from mass media. Ask yourself what a working mother is like? Your responses may come from watching your own working mother, but they will also come from the role-models of working mothers you have seen and heard through mass-media messages. You will identify certain characters in ads or in situation comedies or in certain other TV and radio programs as models. You read newspaper or magazine stories featuring working mothers and your role-model grows.

This is why the critics of the mass media are so concerned about programs, ads, and other messages that feature sex or violence. Suzanne Somers is a good example. When she was first featured on the sitcom *Three's Company* she skyrocketed to fame. Some thought her shape had something to do with the rise to fame. Women's groups objected to featuring her body in almost every episode of the series. They argued that a role-model that featured large breasts was being sold through the mass media to millions of young girls. Along with many others, the Dirty Harry films have also been accused of fostering equally bad role-models. In every film, Harry shot a dozen or so persons with his .44-magnum pistol.

Remember the .44-Magnum Killer noted earlier in this chapter? Some blamed his choice of weapons on the role-model provided by the Dirty Harry movies.

How does a child learn about the social graces? Again, the mass media play a part. Children learn from the media that successful people drink cocktails, lust, smoke, and sometimes do unethical things. So role-models train us to act in certain ways long after we have forgotten that we have ever seen the model. Thus, in a mass-media age, we need to be on guard so that all roles do not become assigned ones—assigned to us by the role-models to which we are exposed daily through TV, radio, newspapers, billboards, and so on. The critical persuadee needs to be aware that ads are not the only persuasive messages in mass media. Role-models are acted out and sometimes even prescribed to us in all the communications media.

Finally we can note briefly that dramatization is often a key factor in mass-media advertisements. The dramas are endless, even though they follow very similar patterns (a person who is down and out buys the product and makes good, or conversely a person is doing well and does not buy the product and ends up a loser). We have seen thousands of washday dramas where dirt gets defeated and hundreds of marriages that have been brightened up by a new kind of prepared food or a certain kind of perfume or foot powder.

SUBLIMINAL PERSUASION AND THE MEDIA

Subliminal persuasion is a controversial topic. The idea behind this means of persuading is to present a message that is either so brief or so disguised that it is not consciously processed by the receivers. For example, the soundtrack of the film *Jaws* supposedly had screams recorded at the precise points where the film makers expected real screams from the viewers. The subliminal cue or recorded scream triggered screams in the theatre audiences. Of course, persons who saw the show told their friends about how many people screamed during the film, thus advertising it better than any newspaper, radio, or TV ad could ever do. In other instances, hazy messages are included in films, photos, and soundtracks. These enter our subconscious mind and prompt us to action.

This idea of subliminally persuading an audience has been tested. In one of its early trials, the words "buy popcorn" were momentarily inserted in several frames of a movie. Audiences stormed the popcorn stand when the supply was sold out. The message registered in the viewer's subconscious, where it created a compulsion to buy popcorn. Finally, the frustrated viewer *had* to act. At another time, viewers were exposed to a hidden message to call a certain phone number. The lines were supposedly busy for days and callers reported that they felt compelled to call that number even though they did not even know what it was for. The technique seemed to be so powerful that it was barred from use.

Recently the controversy was heightened by Wilson Bryan Key, an advertising researcher and college professor. Key decided to look at the possibility that messages could be "imbedded" into the visuals used in magazine advertising. He was struck by the need to touch up by airbrush in certain magazine advertisements. For example, Key notes that most liquor ads need airbrushing because the ice cubes in the glasses melt under the hot lights needed for magazine-quality photos. As long as the persuaders were airbrushing in the ice cubes, Key reasoned, why wouldn't they consider airbrushing in a subtle message like the words "buy" or "good"? Now, most magazine ads in major weekly or monthly publications cost tens of thousands of dollars. Given the investment, the persuader needs to get maximum impact for the advertising dollar. We know that man's basic needs are the most motivating and that themes of sex and combat are central in most persons' fantasy worlds.

Operating from those premises, Key felt that it was likely that ad designers would try to imbed into ads sexual messages to arouse readers. He tested his hypothesis with a Gilbey's gin ad in which the word "SEX" seemed to be airbrushed into the ice cubes and in which other parts of the layout continued the seduction theme. He thought he detected phallic symbols, reflections that depicted various stages in seduction, and so on. Now, seeing these vague airbrushed words and symbols might all have been in Key's head, so he tested 1,000 people by showing them the ad and asking them to put into words the feelings they had while looking at the ad. None of the 1,000 were told what to look for, and none had heard of or knew of subliminal techniques. Although 38 percent did not respond at all, the remaining 62 percent reported that the ad made them feel "sensual," "aroused," "romantic," "sexy," and even "horny" in several cases.[8] It is possible that this finding was accidental, but Key claims to have replicated the test with several ads with similar results. It is also possible that the advertiser does not consciously put subliminal messages into his ads—that they are accidental. I suppose it really does not matter as long as there are receiver effects. The point of persuasion is to get people to change their behavior or beliefs. We assume that any changes ought to be in source-intended ways, but the effect can be accidental and not related to the source. Of course, if the advertisers really were trying to persuade

---

8. Wilson Bryan Key, *Subliminal Seduction: Ad Media's Manipulation of a Not So Innocent America* (New York: Signet Books, 1973), p. 4. The book also has several sample ads in which Key claims to have identified "imbeds."

by manipulating the subconscious, that would raise some ethical issues, as we shall see in the following chapter. However, if an advertising agency did use subliminal techniques, they would probably deny it, as many agencies have done since the publication of Key's book. So whether the messages are there as a strategy of the source or not, the message has effects that correlate with Key's hypothesis that symbolic imbeds (usually sexually oriented) have impact on audiences. Key advises us to become critical receivers by looking beyond the surface message in any ad and searching for elements in the background, in the lighting, in the potential symbolic messages that could be generated. That will alert you to an ad's hidden meaning and may train you as an "imbed spotter." He says that the ad copy, layout, and characters should tip you off to any potential imbeds. Whether you see the imbedded sex symbols or not, you can get cued to possible subliminal persuasion by looking at ads more critically and by trying to determine what they suggest without saying.

There are several sides to the subliminal controversy. The ad people say they never use the stuff, and persons like Key say that our world is loaded with subliminal seducers. Interested observers also differ. Some say that Key is like the man who responded with "sex" in a Rorschach test to every inkblot presented by the psychiatrist. When accused of being preoccupied with sex, the patient countered that it was the doctor who collected all the dirty pictures. My position is that if it can be done (that is, if you can persuade through subliminal messages—sexual or otherwise), then someone is probably doing it. In a world where persuasion bombards us so often, we need to be on guard for any kind of persuasion that might occur. Taking a second, hard look at ads for imbedded messages cannot hurt us. We will be almost guaranteed of being less likely to fall for as many pitches. We can learn about the kinds of things that are put into ads that persuade us on a conscious level—background objects, furniture styles, the kind of jewelry that the models wear, and so forth.

NEWS MANIPULATION AND PERSUASION

In his book *Don't Blame the People,* Robert Cirino makes the point that there is a news industry in our country and that its business is to do business with business.[9] In other words its self-interest lies in the news that insures the status quo. After all, the media stand to profit from the success of their clients and customers. Does news manipulation really

9.   Robert Cirino, *Don't Blame the People* (Los Angeles: Diversity Press, 1971).

occur or are people like Cirino supersensitive and paranoid about the power of the networks, the wire services, and the major newspapers and newsmagazines? Any answer to that question only leads to debate between those who espouse a free press and free speech and those who denounce the profit system. A better way to react to the question of news fixing is to say, "There may be cover-up, shading, and other ways to shape the news." If there are, persuadees ought to acquaint themselves with the possible tactics that can make or unmake news. That will allow us to have an extra safeguard against possible "hidden persuasion" in news programs. Let us look at some of these tactics and at our news system.

There are basically three wire services to which you are exposed in mass-media news programs or reports. They are United Press International (U.P.I.), The Associated Press (A.P.), and Reuters. These three channels pour out most of the news you hear and read. Go through your daily newspaper and see how many stories are run from any of the services. You will find that most of the items come from the central three wire services. That means that, in a way, we are all getting the same news. There is nothing wrong with that, as long as the news is accurate and as long as the key news items get printed or broadcast. That is the problem. The key items are not always the ones on the front page, as we noted with agenda setting. The problem is worse with broadcast news. The evening news on TV is only about twenty-two minutes of news. Furthermore, the messages are sent through the aural/oral channel. We speak and listen at speeds much slower than those used for reading. The speech speed on broadcast news is about 125 words per minute or less. That means that you will hear a maximum of about 3,000 words of news, weather, sports, and editorial comment on the half-hour nightly news. If you read at a speed of, say, 400 words per minute *you could read what you hear in about seven or eight minutes!* Clearly, a lot is going to pass you by if you rely on only TV or radio. So the problem has two facets—the centralization of news and the short supply of it even if it is fair. Beyond the problem of supply is the more serious problem of shading the news, which happens more often than most of us realize.

Cirino observes that if the poor and hungry in this country controlled CBS, ABC, NBC, the *New York Times,* and so forth, hunger would be a major daily news item. Hunger simply is not what we hear or read about night after night. How is it that problems like this slip by without notice?

Ignoring

One tactic is simply to ignore the news item and not print or broadcast it at all or to hide it away on obscure inside pages. A good example cited by Cirino is the information about the Kennedy assassination. Available data indicated that things were not so simple as the Warren Report said. Mark Lane's book *Rush to Judgment,* which was the first to really get media exposure on the killing and on the idea of a conspiracy, was ignored by mass media for several years. In fact, it took Lane nearly fifteen months to find a publisher for it. For months before publication, he was refused interviews by the news industry or if he was interviewed the interviews were never reported.[10] So a critical receiver of mass-media news needs to look at what is hidden on inside pages and to wonder about what is not even exposed at all. You ought to learn to rely on many sources for your news—papers, radio, TV, news weeklies, and so on, and to look for the underplayed stories as well as at the headlines.

Sponsorship

Another thing to look at is who sponsors the news and what kind of play does that business or group get. It is easy to turn aside a story on smoking if 20 percent of your income is from ads placed by tobacco companies. This is a more long-term kind of news research that receivers need to do. We need to keep track of the kind of treatment advertisers get from the paper or station. Few media outlets wanted to feature Ralph Nader's report on the unsafe Corvair. It was not just chance that General Motors spent heavily on advertising in all those media.

The Pseudo-event

Daniel Boorstin first coined the term "pseudoevent." It means creating news where there was none. Business has done it for years. For instance, it is not really newsworthy that on a certain day the new models of autos are available. It certainly does not deserve front-page space or time on the evening news. Yet, year after year, the auto companies ballyhoo this date with press releases, billboards, luncheons for reporters, and ads. As a result, many papers and stations do human interest stories on the new models. Announcement of a stock dividend or a contract settlement can also be a pseudo-event. Mass movements hitchhiked on this idea by creating events such as rallies, bra burnings, strikes, vigils, and so on. Only then did the news industry really take note of the movements—and only then did criticism of the news programs start. Even the military knows how to use the pseudo-event. Most military units have persons called Public Information Officers who handle public relations for their units. They send news releases telling of new weapons, planes, awards, and so on. The press is invited to see the test flight or the parade or the maneuvers and thus an event is made into news.

---

10.   Cirino, p. 284.

Bias

We have mentioned two kinds of bias already. The first bias is in the source of the news or the wire services, networks, and key papers that control the flow of news. A second kind of bias is in the selection of news or agenda setting. But there are other kinds of news bias of which receivers need to be aware. A skillful journalist can interview with bias and can thus shade and slant the result. As the controversial black leader Malcolm X put it: "I don't care what points I made . . . it practically never gets printed the way I said it."[11] Some journalists lead interviewees into topics where they can be trapped. Mike Wallace of CBS once asked a media advisor to Democrats, "Then you're a gun for hire?" How do you answer that? If you say "yes," you look sleazy. If you say "no," Wallace can follow up and ask if you get money for advising candidates. It is the old tactic of demanding a "yes" or "no" answer to the question "Have you stopped beating your wife?"

Another kind of bias is in appearing to be unbiased. We hold a news show and bill it as a documentary—*60 Minutes* or *Issues and Answers.* Then we control the content of the show and come off getting the persuasion done while appearing fair and decent. Why are some persons featured on these shows and not others? Why do some questions get asked and not others? These are questions that receivers need to ask about the news features.

Bias can also be seen in photo selection and captions. Richard Nixon was never popular with news media people, including photographers and picture editors. Published photos often showed him in poor poses. Sometimes he was caught glancing at his watch as if to brush off the important persons he was talking to. His nose got good play from various camera angles as though the press wanted to remind the reader of what happened to Pinocchio. In a cut of film featuring a campaign walk by Robert Kennedy on the streets of New York, the cheering of the crowd was deleted and booing was dubbed in. The film editor's goal was to show Kennedy as a controversial candidate. Clever captions can do the same kind of persuading. A photo on a coal strike for instance might be captioned "Miners Warm Up While Nation Freezes," thus giving the union a black eye. *Time* once captioned a photo of a black civil rights leader with the words "As qualified as Attila the Hun," thereby reducing his ethos.[12]

Finally, the language of camera angle and movement and editing can create bias. If we see a person from a low camera angle, that figure appears larger than life. Long shots persuade us to believe in great size. Zoom-ins ask us to take a closer look—things are not as they seem. Quick-cut edit-

---

11.   Cirino, p. 147.
12.   Cirino, p. 170.

ing gives the effect of great speed and activity. Montage superimposes two conflicting images—say strikers and strikebreakers or angry housewives and angry farmers. Though the people pictured are not actually angry at one another, the montage tends to persuade us of the conflict. There are other ways in which bias in news coverage can be created by the news industry. Ask controversial persons about their news coverage, and they will tell you that you ought to believe half of what you see and less of what you hear and read.

Propaganda Devices

Many propaganda devices create bias. They are often used in the news business. For instance, every election year we see the technique called bandwagon used in news stories to show that Candidate X is the front-runner or that candidate Y's campaign is running out of steam. This invites us to get on the X bandwagon before the Y bandwagon falls apart. The media oblige candidates by showing them in the "plain folks" situations. We see the office seeker chatting with housewives, guessing the weight of a prize sow, and playing softball or touch football. All these media events build the image of a plain, ordinary man running for office. The media often feature announcements by office holders that they are endorsing one candidate or another. That is the technique called testimonial, and it gives publicity to both endorser and endorsed. You will notice more of these propaganda devices in the news as you become more and more critical and observant of the news you get—and curious about the news you do not get.

The point here is not to convince you that all news is false or even slanted but to get you to take a second, more critical look. Knowing that the news industry is in business to do business with business can help you to guard against what may be unfair news practice.

A REVIEW AND CONCLUSION

We began this chapter with statistics that the average eighteen-year-old American has seen 22,000 hours of television and 350,000 commercials. Remember that TV is just one media channel being used for persuasion. Most of us are affected by billboard persuasion. Films persuade us; magazines and newspapers frequently persuade us through their ads and their stories and editorials and cartoons. Further, labels, bumper stickers, T-shirts, and other paraphernalia seem to be increasingly used for persuading. Although on the average, Americans buy less than one third of a book per person per year (we don't know if they are ever read), books may sometimes persuade us.[13] All in all, we live in a highly persuasive, media-rich environment. We cannot hope to provide you in this book with enough tools to filter out all these messages, and maybe that would not be good anyway. You need to be persuaded about some things, and media persuasion is sometimes the best way to get information about your choices. One thing that we all can do, though, to protect ourselves from all persuasive attempts made by the media is to begin to look beyond the surface meanings in media messages. Look for the responsive chords that are being plucked and decide whether the messages that elicit them are hot or cool. Look for the agenda items that are being set up. Identify the deceptive language and claims being used by persuaders. Finally, you might want to consider the possibility of the subliminal messages imbedded in media. This chapter is just the tip of the iceberg—you will want to research the role of media in persuasion much further.

Questions for Further Thought

1. What kinds of things that are in you could be evoked by a persuader and then tied to his product, idea, or candidate? Think of favorite experiences you have had that could be tied to a product. Or try to recall some unpleasant experiences that could be used. What about your responses to certain songs? Could they be tied to products, candidates, or ideas? How?

2. What is a hot medium? Give an example. Why is it hot? What kinds of messages seem to go best on a hot medium or doesn't there seem to be a pattern?

3. Why is television a cool medium? What kinds of responses do people have when you disturb their TV watching? Does that suggest high or low involvement? Why?

4. What is now on the political agenda for the nation? For your state? For your local government? What about on campus—has the campus newspaper or radio station set an agenda for the administration or for the student government?

5. What kind of language is being used in ads you see or hear? Can you identify any deceptive use of language there? If so, give examples.

6. When Folger's claims to be the coffee that is "mountain grown," what kind of claim are they making?

---

13.   Schwartz, p. 6.

7. When Goodyear calls its snow tire "The Gripper," what kind of claim is being made or imprinted?

8. When Top Job ballyhoos its "Ammonia D" as an ingredient, what kind of claim is being made? Give other examples of this kind of claim.

9. What is subliminal persuasion? Can you identify some examples of subliminal messages?

Experiences in Persuasion

1. Write up a media persuasion logbook, keeping track of how many persuasive messages you process in the space of one day and which medium is used by you as a persuadee most often. Identify the message that is most effective during that day. See if it is reinforced through several channels. Try to determine how that message is working on you.

2. Collect samples of the various kinds of language deceivers discussed in this chapter. You may use magazine ads, speech excerpts, editorials, cartoons, and so forth, as your examples.

3. Make a similar collection demonstrating the various kinds of claims that persuaders can make through the mass media.

4. Read Carl Wrighter's book *I Can Sell You Anything* and report to the class on the other language deceivers he discusses. Tell about the various kinds of demonstration that can be conducted by persuaders in order to get you to buy.

5. Read either of Wilson Bryan Key's books on subliminal persuasion (*Subliminal Seduction* or *Media Sexploitation*)[14] and make a project in which you report to the class on the issue. For example you might want to prepare a scrapbook containing examples of subliminal seduction or prepare a slide show. You may want to report in a paper on the views of both sides of the controversy—those who believe subliminal persuasion is occurring and those who do not.

6. Develop a campaign for getting an item of concern on the agenda of your college or university administration. Report to the class or go ahead and conduct your campaign and observe and report the results.

---

14. Key, *Subliminal Seduction* (cited in Footnote 8) and *Media Sexploitation* (New York: Signet Books, The New American Library, 1976).

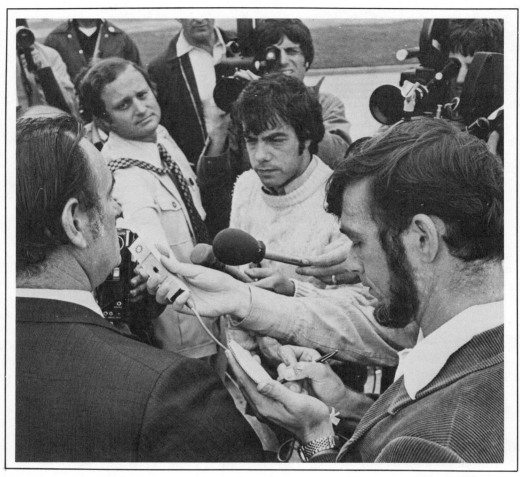

Perspectives on Ethics in Persuasion

Richard L. Johannesen
Northern Illinois University

9

Figure 9-1 *Woody Allen on American ethics. (© King Features Syndicate Inc. 1977.)*

I magine that you are an audience member listening to a speaker, call him Mr. Bronson. His aim is to persuade you to contribute money to the cancer research program of a major medical research center. Suppose that, with one exception, all the evidence, reasoning, and motivational appeals he employs are valid and above ethical suspicion. However, at one point in his speech, Mr. Bronson *consciously* chooses to use a *false* set of statistics to scare you into believing that, during your lifetime, there is a much greater probability of your getting some form of cancer than there actually is.

To promote analysis of the ethics of this hypothetical persuasive situation, consider these issues: If you, or the society at large, view Mr. Bronson's persuasive end or goal as worth while, does the worth of his end justify his use of false statistics as one means to achieve that end? Does the fact that he consciously chose to use false statistics make a difference in your evaluation? If he used the false statistics out of ignorance, or out of failure to check his sources, how might your ethical judgment be altered? Should he be condemned as an unethical person, as an unethical speaker, or in this instance for use of a specific unethical technique?

Carefully consider the standards, and the reasons behind those standards, that you would employ to make your ethical judgment of Mr. Bronson. Are the standards purely pragmatic? In other words, should he avoid the false statistics because he might get caught? Are they societal in origin? If he gets caught, his credibility as a representative would be weakened with this and future audiences. Or his getting caught might weaken the credibility of other cancer society representatives. Should he be ethically criticized for violating an implied agreement between you and him? You might not expect a representative of a famous research institute to use questionable techniques and thus you would be especially vulnerable. Finally, should his conscious use of false statistics be considered unethical because you are denied accurate, relevant information you need to make an intelligent decision on a public issue?

As receivers and senders of persuasion, we have the responsibility to uphold appropriate ethical standards for persuasion, to encourage freedom of inquiry and expression, and to promote the health of public debate as crucial to democratic decision making.[1] To achieve these goals, we must understand their complexity and recognize the difficulty of achieving them.

The process of persuasion involves your presenting good reasons to people for a specific choice among probable alternatives. Whether you are a candidate seeking votes, an elected official urging citizen adoption of a governmental policy, a protestor demanding reform by the Establishment, an advertiser appealing to consumers to purchase a product, a citizen urging others to accept your belief as sound, or a student advocating a change in your school's educational programs, alternatives are present and you marshal logical and psychological supports for the choice of specific alternatives.

Receivers of persuasive messages evaluate them according to standards they perceive as relevant. For example: Is the message interesting and directly relevant to my concerns? Am I clearly understanding the message as intended by the persuader? What is the persuader's purpose?

---

1.   For a much more extensive exploration of the perspectives, standards, and issues discussed in this chapter and identification of relevant resource materials, see Richard L. Johannesen, *Ethics in Human Communication* (Columbus, Ohio: Charles E. Merrill Publishing Co., 1975). Copyright 1977 by Richard L. Johannesen. Reprinted 1978 by Avery Publishing Group, Inc., Wayne, New Jersey. The present chapter, in whole or in part, may not be reproduced without written permission from the publisher and from the author.

Do I perceive the persuader as a credible source on this subject (expert, competent, trustworthy, experienced, sincere, honest, concerned)? Has the persuader presented sufficient evidence and reasoning for me to accept the message as reasonable (workable, practical, efficient, and so forth)?

As a receiver do I see a legitimate connection between the persuader's message and my related needs, motives, and goals? Is the persuader's message consistent with my related beliefs and attitudes? Is the message consistent with my relevant values, my conceptions of the good or desirable? As a receiver do I feel that the nonverbal elements of the persuader's message reinforce or conflict with the verbal aspects? How do I perceive the persuader's view of my personal worth and abilities? What role does the persuader's message play in some larger, continuous campaign of persuasion? To what degree are the persuader's techniques, appeals, arguments, and purpose ethical?

Ethical issues focus on value judgments concerning right and wrong, goodness and badness, in human conduct. Persuasion, as one type of human behavior, always contains *potential* ethical issues because (1) it involves one person, or a group of persons, attempting to influence other people by altering their beliefs, attitudes, values, and overt actions; (2) it involves conscious choices among ends sought and rhetorical means used to achieve the ends; and (3) it necessarily involves a potential judge (any or all of the receivers, the persuader, or an independent observer).

How, as receivers and senders of persuasion, you evaluate the ethics of a persuasive instance will differ, depending upon the ethical standards you are using. You may even choose to ignore ethical judgment entirely. One of several justifications often is used to avoid direct analysis and resolution of ethical issues in persuasion: (1) Everyone knows this appeal or tactic obviously is unethical, so there is nothing to talk about; (2) since only success matters, ethics are irrelevant to persuasion; and (3) after all, ethical judgments are only matters of our individual personal opinion anyway so there are no final answers.

Nevertheless, potential ethical questions are there, regardless of how they are answered. Whether you wish it or not, consumers of persuasion generally will judge, formally or informally, your effort in part by *their* relevant ethical criteria. If for none other than the pragmatic reason of enhancing chances of success, you would do well to consider ethical standards held by the audience.

As receivers of persuasion, we must realize that accurate understanding of a persuader's message may be hindered by our attempt to impose our ethical standards on him or her. Our immediate, "gut-level" ethical judgments may cause us to distort the intended meaning. Only after reaching an accurate understanding of the persuader's ideas can we reasonably evaluate the ethics of his or her communicative strategies and purposes.

In making judgments of the ethics of our own communication and of the communication to which we are exposed, our aim should be specific rather than vague assessments and carefully considered rather than "gut-level" reactions. The quality of judgment of ethics of persuasion usually would be improved (1) by *specifying exactly* what ethical criteria, standards, or perspectives we are applying; (2) by justifying the *reasonableness and relevancy* of these standards; and (3) by indicating in what respects the persuasion evaluated *fails to measure up* to the standards.

In this post-Watergate era of mounting public distrust of truthfulness of public communication, we must combat the growing assumption that most public communication always is untrustworthy. Just because a communication is of a certain type or comes from a certain source (government, candidate, news media, advertiser), it must not automatically, without evaluation, be rejected as tainted or untruthful. Clearly, we must always exercise caution in acceptance and care in evaluation, as emphasized throughout this book. Using the best evidence available to us, we may arrive at our best judgment. However, to condemn a message as untruthful or unethical solely because it stems from a suspect source and before directly assessing it is to exhibit decision-making behavior detrimental to our political, social, and economic system. Rejection of the message, if such be the judgment, must come after, not before, our evaluation of it. As with a defendant in the courtroom, public communication must be presumed ethically innocent until we, or experts we acknowledge, have proved it guilty. However, when techniques of persuasion do weaken or undermine the confidence and trust necessary for intelligent public decision making, they can be condemned as unethical.

SOME ETHICAL PERSPECTIVES

We shall briefly explain six major ethical perspectives as potential viewpoints for analyzing ethical issues in persuasion. As categories, these perspectives are not exhaustive, mutually exclusive of one another, or given in any order of precedence.

As receivers of persuasion, we can employ one or a combination of such perspectives to evaluate the ethical level of a persuader's use of language (such as metaphors, ambiguity, and what Richard M. Weaver labels God terms and Devil terms—see Chapter 2 of this book) or of evidence and reasoning (such as what Stephen Toulmin calls data, warrant, backing, reservation, qualifier, and claim—see Chapter 4). We also can utilize them to assess the ethics of psychological techniques, such as appeals to needs and values, the stimulation and resolution of dissonance and imbalance, or the appeal to widely held cultural images and myths—all discussed in earlier chapters. The persuasive tactics of campaigns and social movements also can (indeed must) be subjected to ethical scrutiny.

Religious Perspectives

Religious perspectives stem from the moral guidelines and the "thou-shalt-nots" embodied in the ideology and sacred literature of various religions. For instance, the Bible warns against use of lies, slander, and bearing false witness. Taoist religion stresses empathy and insight, rather than reason and logic, as roads to truth. Citing facts and demonstrating logical conclusions are minimized in Taoism in favor of feeling and intuition. These and other religiously derived criteria could be used to assess the ethics of persuasion.

Human Nature Perspectives

These perspectives probe the *essence* of human nature by asking what makes a human fundamentally human. Unique characteristics of human nature that set us apart from "lower" forms of life are identified. Such characteristics then can be used as standards for judging the ethics of persuasion. Among some of the characteristics that have been suggested are capacity to reason, capacity to create and utilize symbols, capacity for mutual appreciative understanding, and capacity to make value judgments. The assumption is that uniquely human attributes should be promoted, thereby promoting fulfillment of maximum individual potential. A determination could be made of the degree to which a persuader's appeals and techniques either foster or undermine the development of a fundamental human characteristic. A technique that *dehumanizes*, that makes a person less than human, would be unethical. Whatever the political, religious, or cultural context, a person would be assumed to possess certain uniquely human attributes worthy of promotion through communication.

Political Perspectives

The implicit or explicit values and procedures accepted as crucial to the health and growth of a particular political-governmental system are the focus of political perspectives. Once these essential values are identified for that political system, they can be used for evaluating the ethics of persuasive means and ends within that system. The assumption is that public communication should foster achievement of these values; persuasive techniques that retard, subvert, or circumvent these basic political values would be condemned as unethical. Different political systems usually embody differing values leading to differing ethical judgments. Within the context of American representative democracy, for example, various analysts pinpoint values and procedures they deem fundamental to healthy functioning of our political system, and, thus, values that can guide ethical scrutiny of persuasion therein. Such values and procedures might include enhancement of citizen capacity to reach rational decisions, access to channels of public communication, access to relevant and accurate information on public issues, maximization of freedom of choice, toleration of dissent, honesty in presenting motivations and consequences, and fairness in presenting evidence and alternatives.

Situational Perspectives

To make ethical judgments, situational perspectives focus *regularly* and *primarily* on the elements of the specific persuasive situation at hand. Virtually all perspectives (those mentioned here and others) make some allowances, on occasion, for the modified application of ethical criteria due to special circumstances. However, an extreme situational perspective *routinely* makes judgments *only* in light of *each different context.* Criteria from broad political, human nature, religious, or other perspectives are minimized; absolute and universal standards are avoided. Among the concrete contextual factors that may be relevant to making a purely situational ethical evaluation are (1) the role or function of the persuader for the audience, (2) expectations held by receivers concerning such matters as appropriateness and reasonableness, (3) degree of receiver awareness of the persuader's techniques, (4) goals and values held by the receivers, (5) degree of urgency for implementation of the persuader's proposal, and (6) ethical standards for communication held by receivers. From an extreme situational perspective, it might be argued that an acknowledged leader in a time of clear crisis has a responsibility to rally support and thus could employ so-called emotional appeals that circumvent human processes of rational, reflective decision making. Or it might be argued that a persuader may ethically employ techniques such as innuendo, guilt by association, and unfounded name-calling as long as the receivers both recognize and approve of those methods.

Legal Perspectives

Legal perspectives would take the general position that illegal communication behavior also is unethical. That which is not specifically illegal is viewed as ethical. Such an approach certainly has the advantage of allowing simple ethical decisions. We would need only to measure persuasive techniques against current laws and regulations to determine whether a technique is ethical. We might, for example, turn for ethical guidance to the regulations governing advertising set forth by the Federal Trade Commission or the Federal Communications Commission. However, we also must consider to what degree legal perspectives lead to oversimplified, superficial judgments of complex persuasive situations.

Dialogical Perspectives

Dialogical perspectives emerge from current scholarship on the nature of communication as dialogue rather than as monologue.[2] Such perspectives contend that the attitudes toward each other among participants in a communication situation are an index of the ethical level of that communication. Some attitudes are held to be more fully human, humane, and facilitative of personal self-fulfillment than are other attitudes.

Communication as dialogue is characterized by such attitudes as honesty, concern for the welfare and improvement of others, trust, genuineness, open-mindedness, equality, mutual respect, empathy, humility, directness, lack of pretense, nonmanipulative intent, sincerity, encouragement of free expression, and acceptance of others as individuals with intrinsic worth regardless of difference over belief or behavior. Communication as monologue, in contrast, is marked by such qualities as deception, superiority, exploitation, dogmatism, domination, insincerity, pretense, personal self-display, self-aggrandizement, judgmentalism that stifles free expression, coercion, possessiveness, condescension, self-defensiveness, and viewing others as objects to be manipulated. In the case of persuasion, then, the techniques and presentation of the persuader would be scrutinized to determine the degree to which they reveal an ethical dialogical attitude or an unethical monological attitude toward receivers.

SOME FUNDAMENTAL ETHICAL ISSUES

With the above six ethical perspectives (religious, human nature, political, situational, legal, dialogical), we can confront a variety of questions that underscore difficult issues relevant to ethical problems in persuasion. As receivers constantly bombarded with a variety of verbal and nonverbal

---

2.   For a general analysis of communication as dialogue and monologue, see Richard L. Johannesen, "The Emerging Concept of Communication as Dialogue," *Quarterly Journal of Speech*, Vol. 57 (December 1971), pp. 373–382.

persuasive messages, we continually face resolution of one or another of these fundamental issues.

To what degree should ethical criteria for assessing persuasion be either absolute, universal, and inflexible or relative, context-bound, and flexible? Surely the more absolute our criteria are, the easier it is to render simple, clear-cut judgments. However, in matters of human behavior and public decision making, the ethics of persuasive ends and means are seldom simple. In making ethical evaluations of persuasion, we probably should avoid snap judgments, carefully examine the relevant circumstances, determine the perspectives most appropriate to the instance, and consider the welfare of all involved.

Do the ends justify the means? Does the necessity of achieving a goal widely acknowledged as worthwhile justify the use of ethically questionable techniques? To say that the end does not *always* justify the means is different from saying that ends *never* justify means. The persuasive goal is probably best considered as one of a number of potentially applicable criteria, from among which the most appropriate standards (perspectives) are selected. Under some circumstances, such as threat to physical survival, the goal of personal security—temporarily—may take precedence over other criteria. In general, however, we can best make mature ethical assessments by evaluating the ethics of persuasive techniques apart from the worth of the persuasive goal. We can strive to judge the ethics of techniques and ends separately. In some cases we may find ethical persuasive devices employed to achieve an unethical goal. In other cases unethical techniques may be aimed at an entirely ethical goal.

Are all so-called "emotional appeals" inherently unethical? Although a countertrend seems to be emerging, as reflected by encounter groups and sensitivity training, our culture traditionally has viewed with suspicion the expression of or capitalization on emotion. The Aristotelian heritage in rhetorical theory has perpetuated the primacy of logic over emotion in selecting ethical persuasive strategies. However, one point that has emerged from behavioral science research on persuasion is that receivers of persuasive messages find it difficult to categorize appeals or supporting materials as either emotional or logical in exactly the same manner as the persuader intends them. Differing audiences may view the same appeal differently. A given technique, such as a set of statistics indicating the high probability of falling victim to cancer during one's lifetime, may be perceived as possessing both logical and emotional components.

Since neither logical nor emotional appeals are inherently unethical, but depend largely on manner and circumstance of usage, the need to dichotomize persuasive appeals into logical and emotional categories is not very great. If you do wish to evaluate the ethics of a persuasive technique that you perceive as emotional appeal, the following guideline is suggested. Assuming that the appeal is ethical in light of other relevant perspectives, the emotional device is ethical if it is undergirded by a substructure of sound evidence and reasoning to support it. Presentation of this substructure could accompany the appeal in the persuasive message or the substructure could exist apart from the message and should be produced upon the request of a critic. The emotional appeal is ethical if you are asked to view it not as proof for justification but as the expression of the persuader's internal emotional state. Generally, the emotional appeal is unethical when it functions as pseudoproof giving the appearance of evidence or if it functions to short-circuit your capacity for free, informed, responsible choice.

Does sincerity of intent release a persuader from ethical responsibility relative to means and effects? Could we say that if Adolf Hitler's fellow Germans judged him to be sincere, his fellow citizens could not assess the ethics of his persuasion? In such cases, evaluations probably are best carried out if we appraise sincerity and ethics separately. Thus, for example, a persuader sincere in his or her intent may be found to utilize an unethical strategy.

Is intentional use of ambiguity ethical? Clear communication of intended meaning usually is one major aim of an ethical communicator, whether that person seeks to enhance receiver understanding or seeks to influence belief, attitude, or action. Textbooks on oral and written communication typically warn against ambiguity and vagueness; often they directly or indirectly take the position that intentional ambiguity is an unethical communication tactic. In some situations, however, persuaders may feel that the intentional creation of ambiguity or vagueness is necessary, accepted, expected as normal, and even ethically justified.

Such might be the case at times, for example, in religious discourse, in some advertising, in international diplomatic negotiations, or in labor-management bargaining. A persuader might feel that ambiguity is justified ethically in order to heighten receiver attention through puzzlement, to promote maximum psychological participation of receivers by letting them create relevant meanings, to satisfy receiver expectation of ambiguity as a norm for a certain type of communication, or to promote maximum latitude for revision of position in later dealings with opponents or constituents (avoidance of being locked-in to a single position). In some advertising, for instance, intentional ambiguity seems to be understood as such by consumers and even accepted by them. Consider possible ethical implications of the advertisement for Noxema Shaving Cream which urged (accompanied by a beautiful woman watching a man shave in rhythm with strip-tease music): "Take it off. Take it *all* off." Or what about the "sexy" woman in the after-shave cologne advertisement who says, "All my men wear English Leather, or they wear *nothing at all*." Consider whether intentional ambiguity should uniformly and always be condemned as unethical.

The foregoing questions highlight only some of the complex issues involved in determining the ethics of persuasion. Several additional areas of concern—such as propaganda and the demagogue, political persuasion, and commercial advertising—will be discussed at greater length.

ETHICS, PROPAGANDA, AND THE DEMAGOGUE

Is propaganda unethical? The answer to this question in part depends on how propaganda is defined. Numerous, often widely divergent, definitions abound. Originally the term "propaganda" was associated with the efforts of the Roman Catholic Church to persuade people to accept the Church's doctrine. Such efforts were institutionalized in 1622 by Pope Gregory XV when he created the Sacred Congregation for Propagating the Faith. The word "propaganda" soon came to designate not only institutions seeking to propagate a doctrine but also the doctrine itself and the communication techniques employed.

Today one cluster of definitions of propaganda presents a *neutral* position toward the ethical nature of propaganda. A definition combining the key elements of such neutral views might be: Propaganda is a *campaign of mass persuasion*. According to this view, propaganda represents an organized, continuous effort to persuade a mass audience primarily using the mass media.[3] Propaganda thus would include advertising and public relations efforts; national political election campaigns; the persuasive campaigns of some social reform movements; and the organized efforts of national governments to win friends abroad, maintain domestic morale, and undermine an opponent's morale both in hot and cold war. Such a view stresses communication channels and audiences and categorizes propaganda as one species of persuasion. Just as persuasion may be sound or unsound, ethical or unethical, so too may propaganda.

Another cluster of definitions of propaganda takes a *negative* stance toward the ethical nature of propaganda. Definitions in this cluster probably typify the view held by many average American citizens. A definition combining the key elements of such negative views might be: Propaganda is the intentional use of suggestion, irrelevant emotional appeals, and

---

3. For example see Terrence H. Qualter, *Propaganda and Psychological Warfare* (New York: Random House, 1962), Chapter 1; Paul Kecskemeti, "Propaganda," in Ithiel de Sola Pool, Wilbur Schramm, Frederick W. Frey, Nathan Maccoby, and Edwin B. Parker, eds., *Handbook of Communication* (Chicago: Rand McNally, 1973), pp. 844–870.

pseudoproof to circumvent human rational decision-making processes.[4] Such a view stresses communication techniques and sees propaganda as *inherently* unethical.

Are the traditional propaganda devices always to be viewed as unethical? Textbooks in such fields as journalism, speech communication, and social psychology often discuss the traditional list: name-calling, glittering generality, transfer, testimonial, plain folks, card-stacking, and bandwagon. Such a list does not constitute a sure-fire guide, a "handy-dandy" checklist, for exposure of unethical persuasion. The ethics of at least some of these techniques depends on how they are employed in a given context. Let us examine, for instance, the devices of name-calling and of plain folks.

Name-calling involves labeling a person, group, or idea with terms carrying extremely negative or evil meanings. Whether calling an opponent a "card-carrying Communist" would be ethical or unethical would be determined in part by whether the opponent *actually was* a formal, registered member of the Communist Party.

The *plain folks* technique stresses humble origins and modest backgrounds shared by the communicator and audience. The persuader emphasizes to the audience, although usually not in these words, that "we're all just plain folks." In his whistle-stop speeches to predominantly rural, Republican audiences during the 1948 presidential campaign, Democrat Harry Truman typically used the plain folks appeal to establish common ground in introductions of his speeches. He used the device to accomplish one of the purposes of the introductory segment of most speeches—namely, establishment of rapport; he did not rely on it for proof in the main body of his speeches. If a politician relied primarily on the plain folks appeal as pseudoproof in *justifying* the policy he or she advocated, such usage could be condemned as unethical. Furthermore, Truman really was the kind of person who could legitimately capitalize on his actual plain folks background. A politician of more privileged and patrician background, such as Edward Kennedy, could be condemned for using an unethical technique *if* he were to appeal to farmers and factory workers by saying "you and I are just plain folks."

Today the label "demagogue" frequently is used to render a negative ethical judgment of a communicator. Too often the label is left only vaguely defined; the criteria we are to use to evaluate a person as a demagogue are unspecified. In ancient Greece, a demagogue simply was a leader or orator who championed the cause of the common people.

---

4.   For example see W. H. Werkmeister, *An Introduction to Critical Thinking*, rev. ed. (Lincoln, Neb.: Johnson, 1957), Chapter 4; Stuart Chase, *Guides to Straight Thinking* (New York: Harper & Row, 1956), Chapters 20 and 21.

In the following description of Governor George Wallace of Alabama, what characteristics are suggested as marks of a demagogue? To what extent should we agree with them as appropriate criteria for judging a demagogue? Should we accept as valid the linkages between each characteristic and the public figure used to illustrate it? Would *you* label Wallace as a demagogue?

> *He is the quintessential demagogue, combining the missionary zeal of a Barry Goldwater, the raw pursuit of power of a Kennedy, the expansive populism of a Huey Long, the chameleon-like adaptability of a Nixon, and the disarmingly blunt, or somewhat crude, appeal of an Archie Bunker.*[5]

You now are invited to consider the following five characteristics collectively as possible appropriate guides for determining to what degree a persuader merits the label "demagogue."[6]

1. A demagogue wields popular or mass leadership over an extensive number of people.

2. A demagogue exerts primary influence through the medium of the spoken word—through public speaking, whether directly to an audience or by means of radio or television.

3. A demagogue relies heavily on propaganda defined in the negative sense of intentional use of suggestion, irrelevant emotional appeals, and pseudoproof to circumvent human rational decision-making processes.

4. A demagogue capitalizes on the availability of a major contemporary social issue or problem.

5. A demagogue is hypocritical; the social cause serves as a front or persuasive leverage point while the actual primary motive is selfish interest and personal gain.

Several cautions are in order in applying these guidelines. A persuader may reflect each of these characteristics to a greater or lesser de-

---

5.   Stephan Lesher, "The New Image of George Wallace," Chicago *Tribune*, January 2, 1972, Sec. 1A, p. 1.

6.   The basic formulation from which these guidelines have been adapted first was suggested to me by Professor William Conboy of the University of Kansas. These five characteristics generally are compatible with the standard scholarly attempts to define a demagogue. For instance, Reinhard Luthin, *American Demagogues*, reprinted ed. (Gloucester, Mass.: Peter Smith, 1959), pp. ix, 3, 302–319; Barnet Baskerville, "Joseph McCarthy: Briefcase Demagogue," reprinted in Haig A. Bosmajian, ed., *The Rhetoric of the Speaker* (New York: D.C. Heath, 1967), p. 64.

gree and only in certain instances. A persuader might fulfill only several of these criteria (such as items 1, 2, and 4) and yet not be called a demagogue; characteristics 3 and 5 seem to be central to a conception of a demagogue. How easily and accurately can we usually determine a persuader's *actual* motivations? Should we limit the notion of a demagogue solely to the political arena?

ETHICAL STANDARDS FOR POLITICAL PERSUASION

Directly or indirectly, we daily are exposed to political and governmental persuasion in varied forms. The President appeals on national television for public support of a diplomatic treaty. A senator argues in Congress against ratification of a treaty. A government bureaucrat announces a new regulation and presents reasons to justify it. A federal official contends that information requested by a citizen-action group cannot be revealed for national security reasons. At any given moment, somewhere a national, state, or local politician is campaigning for election. At a city council meeting, a citizen protests a proposed property tax rate increase. What ethical criteria should we apply to judge the many kinds of political-governmental persuasion? We shall consider a number of potential sets of criteria in the hope that among them you will find ones especially useful in your own life.

Thomas Nilsen offers one version of what we earlier in this chapter described as a political perspective for judging the ethics of persuasion.[7] Values essential to the healthy functioning of American representative democracy are the intrinsic worth of the human personality, reason as an instrument of individual and societal development, self-determination as the means to individual fulfillment, and human realization of individual potentialities. Necessary democratic procedures include unrestricted debate and discussion; varied forms of public address, parliamentary procedure, and legal procedure; freedom of inquiry, criticism, and choice; and publicly defined rules of evidence and tests of reasoning.

From this basis Nilsen develops ethical guidelines, not fixed criteria, for a view which he labels "significant choice." The ethical touchstone, he believes, should be "the degree of free, informed, and critical choice"

---

7.   Thomas R. Nilsen's viewpoint of "significant choice" is elaborated in his *Ethics of Speech Communication*, 2d ed. (Indianapolis: Bobbs-Merrill Publishing Co., 1974); and Nilsen, "Free Speech, Persuasion and the Democratic Process," *Quarterly Journal of Speech*, Vol. 44 (October 1958), pp. 235–243.

which is fostered by communication on matters significant to us. Ethical communication techniques are those which foster significant choice.

It is choice making that is voluntary, free from physical or mental coercion. It is choice based on the best information available when the decision must be made. It includes knowledge of various alternatives and the possible long- and short-term consequences of each. It includes awareness of the motivations of those who want to influence, the values they serve, the goals they seek. Voluntary choice also means an awareness of the forces operating within ourselves. . . .

In public discourse, where relationships are relatively impersonal and the issues public, the good is served by communications that preserve and strengthen the processes of democracy, that provide adequate information, diversity of views, and knowledge of alternative choices and their possible consequences. It is served by communications that provide significant debate, applying rational thought to controversial issues, recognizing at the same time the importance and relevance of feeling and personal commitment. Further, the good is served by communications that foster freedom of expression and constructive criticism, that set an example of quality in speech content, in language usage, and in fair play and civility. . . .

The ethical issues are whether the information presented is the most relevant available and is as complete as the particular circumstances make feasible. Further, since selection of material is inevitable, it must be made clear to the listeners what principles of selection are operating, what biases or special interests characterize the speaker, and what purposes are being served by the information given. Definitions must be adequate; statistical units must be defined and the assumptions underlying their use made explicit. The listeners must not be led to believe that they are getting a more complete and accurate picture than they really are. In addition, the subject must be placed in the proper perspective as far as its individual and social importance is concerned. In brief, the speaker must provide for the listener as adequate a grasp of the truth of the situation as is reasonably possible under the circumstances.[8]

What he believes are "some simple moral principles that are readily identifiable and should be easily practiced" are advocated by Robert Oliver. As you consider this or similar lists of ethical standards, speculate on what exceptions there might be where a standard would, at least tem-

---

8.   Nilsen, *Ethics of Speech Communication*, pp. 45, 18, 72.

porarily, be set aside in favor of some other ethical standard. Also, what are possible meanings for such terms as distort, misrepresent, falsify, deceive, and conceal?

1. Do not falsify or misrepresent evidence.

2. Do not speak with assurance on a subject about which you are actually uninformed.

3. Do not seek approval from your audience for a policy or a program by linking it in their minds with powerful values (such as patriotism or sympathy) with which it has no actual connection.

4. Avoid confusing the minds of the audience about the worthiness of a point of view by smear attacks on the leadership associated with it.

5. Do not delude yourself into feeling that the end justifies the means.

6. If you are advocating a proposal due to self-interest or allegiance to a particular organization, do not conceal that fact and pretend an objectivity you do not possess.

7. Do not advocate for an audience something in which you yourself do not believe.[9]

To alert receivers of persuasion to techniques that should be examined as possibly unethical, Wayne Thompson suggests a series of "warning signals."

1. The speaker who may have a selfish interest in the product or proposal.

2. The speaker who tries too hard to be ingratiating, plain folks, or "honest John."

3. The message that abounds in loaded language and emotional appeals.

4. The vague testimonial, such as "statistics prove" or "unbiased scientific tests show."

5. The message that presses for an immediate decision.

6. The message that translates straightforward statistics into comparisons and dramatizations without clarifying the changes.

---

9. Robert T. Oliver, *The Psychology of Persuasive Speech*, 2d ed. (New York: Longmans, Green, 1957), pp. 20–34.

7. The speaker who engages in frequent name-calling or who spends much of his or her time in expressing approval of vague but attractive generalizations.

8. The message that overuses ideas that the listener would like to hear.

9. The speaker who oversimplifies the problem and who urges the listener to make an either-or choice.[10]

Some guidelines for evaluating the ethical responsibility of governmental communication have been developed by Dennis Gouran.

1. The deliberate falsification of information released to the public, especially under circumstances involving the general welfare, is inappropriate and irresponsible.

2. The classification of government documents for the purpose of deceiving or otherwise keeping the public uninformed on matters affecting private citizens' well-being is inappropriate and irresponsible.

3. The deliberate use of official news sources for the purpose of obscuring embarrassing and deceitful governmental acts is inappropriate and irresponsible.

4. Criticism of the press for the purpose of assuring that governmental acts are viewed only in favorable terms is inappropriate and irresponsible.

5. Deliberate attempts by governmental agents to suppress or otherwise interfere with an individual's legitimate exercise of free expression within the limits defined by our courts are inappropriate and irresponsible.

6. Overt and covert governmental acts designed to misrepresent a political candidate's, or any other citizen's, character or position or to violate said individual's rights are inappropriate and irresponsible.

7. Language employed by governmental figures for the purpose of deliberately obscuring the activity or idea it represents is inappropriate and irresponsible.[11]

For the 1976 presidential campaign, Common Cause, a national citizens lobbying group, proposed a set of standards that easily might aid in

---

10.   Wayne N. Thompson, *The Process of Persuasion* (New York: Harper & Row, 1975), p. 472.

11.   For a detailed discussion of the guidelines, see Dennis Gouran, "Guidelines for the Analysis of Responsibility in Governmental Communication," in Daniel Dieterich, ed., *Teaching About Doublespeak* (Urbana, Ill.: National Council of Teachers of English, 1976), pp. 20–31.

assessing the ethics of any political candidate's campaign. According to their criteria, an ethical candidate exhibits the following behavior:

1. Engages in unrehearsed communication with voters, including participation in open hearings and forums with other candidates on the same platform, where the public is given opportunities to express their concerns, ask questions, and follow up on their questions

2. Holds press conferences at least monthly throughout the campaign, and in every state where contesting a primary, at which reporters and broadcasters are freely permitted to ask questions and follow-up questions

3. Discusses issues which are high on the list of the people's concerns, as evidenced, for example, by national public opinion polls; clarifies alternatives and tradeoffs in a way that sets forth the real choices involved for the nation; and makes clear to the American people what choices he or she would make if elected to office

4. Makes public all information relating to a given poll if releasing or leaking any part of a campaign poll (including when and where the poll was conducted, by whom, a description of the sample of the population polled, as well as all questions and responses)

5. Allows interviews by a broad spectrum of TV, radio and newspaper reporters, including single interviewer formats which provide maximum opportunity for in-depth questions

6. Takes full public responsibility for all aspects of his or her campaign, including responsibility for campaign finance activities, campaign practices of staff, and campaign statements of principal spokespersons

7. Makes public a statement of personal financial holdings, including assets and debts, sources of income, honoraria, gifts, and other financial transactions over $1,000, covering candidate, spouse and dependent children

8. Does not use taxpayer-supported services of any public office now held—such as staff, transportation or free mailing privileges—for campaign purposes, except as required for personal security reasons

9. Uses only advertising which stresses the record and viewpoint on issues of the candidates

The Fair Campaign Practices Committee, a national nonpartisan watch-dog organization that monitors campaigns, urges political candidates to sign the following Code of Fair Campaign Practices:

1. I shall conduct my campaign in the best American tradition, discussing the issues as I see them, presenting my record and policies with sincerity and frankness, and criticizing without fear or favor the record and policies of my opponent and his party which merit such criticism.

2. I shall defend and uphold the right of every qualified American voter to full and equal participation in the electoral process.

3. I shall condemn the use of personal vilification, character defamation, whispering campaigns, libel, slander, or scurrilous attacks on any candidate or his personal or family life.

4. I shall condemn the use of campaign material of any sort which misrepresents, distorts, or otherwise falsifies the facts regarding any candidate, as well as the use of malicious or unfounded accusations against any candidate which aim at creating or exploiting doubts, without justification, as to his loyalty.

5. I shall condemn any appeal to prejudice based on race, sex, creed, or national origin.

6. I shall condemn any dishonest or unethical practice which tends to corrupt or undermine our American system of free elections or which hampers or prevents the full and free expression of the will of the voters.

7. I shall immediately and publicly repudiate support from any individual or group which resorts, on behalf of my candidacy or in opposition to that of my opponent, to the methods and tactics which I condemn.

The following Code of Ethics for Political Campaign Advertising was adopted by the American Association of Advertising Agencies in 1968.

1. The advertising agency should not represent any candidate who has not signed or who does not observe the Code of Fair Campaign Practices of the Fair Campaign Practices Committee, endorsed by the A.A.A.A.

2. The agency should not knowingly misrepresent the views or stated record of any candidates nor quote them out of proper context.

3. The agency should not prepare any material which unfairly or prejudicially exploits the race, creed, or national origin of any candidate.

4. The agency should take care to avoid unsubstantiated charges and accusations, especially those deliberately made too late in the campaign for opposing candidates to answer.

5. The agency should stand as an independent judge of fair campaign practices, rather than automatically yield to the wishes of the candidate or his authorized representatives.

6. The agency should not indulge in any practices which might be deceptive or misleading in word, photographs, film, or sound.

Frequently political candidates are condemned for stressing "image" over "issues" in their campaigns. Traditionally, so-called image-oriented campaigns are viewed as ethically suspect. However a contrasting view should be considered.[12] Some scholars argue that issues and stands on issues are too transitory and too complex for voters to make dependable judgments. For example, an issue vital today often soon fades to be replaced by one unforeseen during the campaign. Or issues may have to be created if none loom large in the public mind at the inflexible time when the campaign occurs. Instead, suggest some scholars, voters should assess the basic dimensions of the candidate's image (personal qualities) as a better basis for evaluations. In the long run, the key questions would be: Does the candidate's past record demonstrate strength of character, decisiveness of action, openness to relevant information and alternative viewpoints, thoroughness in studying a problem, respect for intelligence of others, and the ability to lead through public and private communication?

ETHICAL STANDARDS FOR COMMERCIAL ADVERTISING

Consumers, academic experts, and advertisers themselves clearly do not agree on any one set of ethical standards as appropriate for assessing commercial advertising. Here we will simply survey some of the widely varied criteria that have been suggested. Among them you may find guidelines that you feel will aid your own assessments.

Using a kind of religious perspective, John McMillan contends that the first responsibility of an advertiser is not to either business or society but rather to God and to principles higher than self, society, or business.[13] Thus, advertisers are responsible to multiple neighbors—to owners, employees, clients, customers, and the general public. Second, they have

---

12.   See for example, Dan F. Hahn and Ruth M. Gonchar, "Political Myth: The Image and the Issue," *Today's Speech*, Vol. 20 (Summer 1972), pp. 57–65; James David Barber, *The Presidential Character: Predicting Performance in the White House* (Englewood Cliffs, N.J.: Prentice-Hall, 1972), Chapter 1.

13.   John E. McMillan, "Ethics and Advertising," in John S. Wright and Daniel S. Warner, eds., *Speaking of Advertising* (New York: McGraw-Hill, 1963), pp. 453–458.

a responsibility for objective truth. Third, they are responsible for preparing advertising messages with a sense of respect for their audience. Finally, argues McMillan, advertisers are responsible for seeking product improvements.

Several writers on the ethics of advertising suggest the applicability of perspectives rooted in the essence of human nature. Thomas Garrett contends that a person becomes more truly human in proportion as his or her behavior becomes more conscious and reflective.[14] Because of the human capacity for reason and because of the equally distinctive fact of human dependence on other people for development of potential, Garrett suggests there are several ethical obligations. As humans we are obliged, among other things, to behave rationally ourselves, to help others behave rationally, and to provide truthful information. Suggestive advertising, in Garrett's view, is that which seeks to bypass human powers of reason or to some degree render them inoperative. Such advertising is unethical not just because it uses emotional appeal, Garrett feels, but because it demeans a fundamental human attribute and makes people less than human.

Clarence Walton observes that some critics employ a philosophical model that identifies three components of human nature as vital elements to be considered in evaluating the ethics of marketing practices: (1) human capability for rational judgment, (2) human capacity for exercising free options among defined alternatives, and (3) human motivation to serve primarily selfish interests or to serve the welfare of others.[15] By extending the implications of such a framework, advertising and marketing tactics could be judged by the degree to which they undermine the human capacity for rational decision, constrict free choice among alternatives, and foster largely selfish interests.

Theodore Levitt uses a human nature position to *defend* advertising techniques often viewed by others as ethically suspect. While admitting that the line between distortion and falsehood is difficult to establish, his central argument is that "embellishment and distortion are among advertising's legitimate and socially desirable purposes; and that illegitimacy in advertising consists only of falsification with larcenous intent." Levitt grounds his defense in a "pervasive, . . . *universal*, characteristic of human nature—the human audience *demands* symbolic interpretation of everything it sees and knows. If it doesn't get it, it will return a verdict of 'no interest.'" Because Levitt sees humans essentially as symbolizers, as converters of raw sensory experience through symbolic interpretation to

---

14.   Thomas M. Garrett, S.J., *An Introduction to Some Ethical Problems of Modern American Advertising* (Rome: Gregorian University Press, 1961), pp. 39–47.

15.   Clarence C. Walton, "Ethical Theory, Societal Expectations and Marketing Practices," in John S. Wright and Daniel S. Warner, eds., *Speaking of Advertising* (New York: McGraw-Hill, 1963), pp. 359–373.

satisfy needs, he can justify "legitimate" embellishment and distortion. He contends:

> Many of the so-called distortions of advertising, product design, and packaging may be viewed as a paradigm of the many responses that man makes to the conditions of survival in the environment. Without distortion, embellishment, and elaboration, life would be drab, dull, anguished, and at its existential worst.[16]

Sometimes advertisers adopt what we earlier in the chapter called legal perspectives in which ethicality is equated with legality. However, Harold Williams observes, concerning the ethics of advertising:

> What is legal and what is ethical are not synonymous, and neither are what is legal and what is honest. We tend to resort to legality often as our guideline. This is in effect what happens often when we turn to the lawyers for confirmation that a course of action is an appropriate one.
>
> We must recognize that we are getting a legal opinion, but not necessarily an ethical or moral one. The public, the public advocates, and many of the legislative and administrative authorities recognize it even if we do not.[17]

Typically, commercial advertising has been viewed as persuasion that argues a case or demonstrates a claim concerning the actual nature or merits of a product. To such attempts at arguing the quality of a product, many of the traditional ethical standards for "truthfulness" and "rationality" have been applied. For instance, are the evidence and the reasoning supporting the claim clear, accurate, relevant, and sufficient in quantity? Are the emotional and motivational appeals directly relevant to the product?

The American Association of Advertising Agencies, in a code of ethics revised in 1962, went beyond simple obedience to the laws and regulations governing advertising to broaden and extend "the ethical application of high ethical standards." As you read the following standards, consider their degree of adequacy, the degree to which they still are rele-

---

16.   Theodore Levitt, "The Morality (?) of Advertising," reprinted in John S. Wright and John E. Mertes, eds., *Advertising's Role in Society* (St. Paul, Minn.: West Publishing Co., 1974), pp. 278–289.

17.   Harold M. Williams, "What Do We Do Now, Boss? Marketing and Advertising," *Vital Speeches of the Day*, Vol. 40 (February 15, 1974), pp. 285–288.

vant and appropriate today, and the extent to which they presently are followed by advertisers. Association members agree to avoid intentionally producing advertising that contains:

1. False or misleading statements or exaggerations, visual or verbal.

2. Testimonials that do not reflect the real choice of a competent witness.

3. Price claims that are misleading.

4. Comparisons that unfairly disparage a competitive product or service.

5. Claims insufficiently supported or that distort the true meaning or practicable application of statements made by professional or scientific authority.

6. Statements, suggestions, or pictures offensive to public decency.

The American Advertising Federation suggests the following Advertising Code of American Business.

1. Advertising shall tell the truth, and shall reveal significant facts, the concealment of which would mislead the public.

2. Advertising agencies and advertisers shall be willing to provide substantiation of claims made.

3. Advertising shall be free of statements, illustrations, or implications that are offensive to good taste or public decency.

4. Advertising shall offer merchandise or service on its merits, and refrain from attacking competitors unfairly or disparaging their products, services, or methods of doing business.

5. Advertising shall offer only merchandise or services that are readily available for purchase at the advertised price.

6. Advertising of guarantees and warranties shall be explicit. Advertising of any guarantee or warranty shall clearly and conspicuously disclose its nature and extent, the manner in which the guarantor or warrantor will perform, and the identity of the guarantor or warrantor.

7. Advertising shall avoid price or savings claims that are false or misleading or that do not offer provable bargains or savings.

8. Advertising shall avoid the use of exaggerated or unprovable claims.

9. Advertising containing testimonials shall be limited to those of competent witnesses who are reflecting a real and honest choice.

What if ethical standards of truthfulness and rationality are *irrelevant* to most commercial advertising? What if the primary purpose of most ads is *not* to prove a claim? Then what ethical standards we apply may stem from whatever alternative view of the nature and purpose of advertising we do hold. Some advertisements function primarily to capture and sustain consumer attention, to announce a product, to create consumer awareness of the name of a product.[18] What ethical criteria are most appropriate for such attention-getting ads?

Lawrence W. Rosenfield views commercial advertising as a type of poetic game.[19] Here techniques of making the commonplace significant, of aesthetically pleasing structure, of connotation, and of ambiguity all combine to invite consumers to participate in a recreational, emotionally satisfying experience. If there is such a thing as commercial "advertising-as-poetic," what ethical standards should we use to judge this kind of poetry?

Finally, consider again Tony Schwartz's resonance theory of electronic media persuasion discussed earlier in Chapter 8.[20] As part of his view he argues that because our conceptions of truth, honesty, and clarity are a product of our print-oriented culture, these conceptions are appropriate in judging the content of printed messages. In contrast, he contends that the "question of truth is largely irrelevant when dealing with electronic media content." In assessing the ethics of advertising by means of electronic media, Schwartz feels that the Federal Trade Commission should focus not on truth and clarity of content but on effects of the advertisement on receivers. He laments, however, that at present "we have no generally agreed-upon social values and/or rules that can be readily applied in judging whether the effects of electronic communication are beneficial, acceptable, or harmful." Schwartz summarizes his argument by concluding that

> truth is a print ethic, not a standard for ethical behavior in electronic communication. In addition, the influence of electronic media on print advertising (particularly the substitution of photographic techniques for copy to achieve an effect) raises the question of whether truth is any longer an issue in magazine or newspaper ads.[21]

---

18.   See, for example, Lawrence W. Rosenfield, Laurie Schultz Hayes, and Thomas S. Frentz, *The Communicative Experience* (Boston: Allyn and Bacon, 1976), pp. 310–312, 324.

19.   Rosenfield, pp. 254–283.

20.   Tony Schwartz, *The Responsive Chord* (Garden City, N.Y.: Anchor Books, 1974), pp. 1–18, 23–25, 92–97. See also Rosenfield, pp. 313–323.

21.   Schwartz, pp. 18–22, 31, 33, 79, 97.

A CASE STUDY: RICHARD NIXON'S FIRST TELEVISED ADDRESS ON WATERGATE

On April 30, 1973, in simultaneous broadcasts over the three major television networks, President Richard M. Nixon delivered his first speech concerning the break-in at the Democratic National Headquarters located in the Watergate apartment complex in Washington and concerning the subsequent cover-up of that event. This speech could be subjected to analysis to determine its ethical level; you are encouraged to go beyond (and take issue with) the points to be made here. A full text of the speech, or an audio or video recording, should be consulted as a basis for analysis.[22]

Nixon's first Watergate speech could be examined from various ethical perspectives and lists of criteria discussed throughout this book. For example, whether important from political or human nature perspectives, to what degree did the means used by him in the speech promote or undermine the human capacity to reason logically? What kinds of dialogical or monological attitudes of speaker toward audience were reflected in the speech? What elements in the immediate speech situation and occasion might suggest appropriate criteria for judging the ethics of the message? To what degree or in what ways did the speech promote or undermine public confidence in truthfulness of public communication?

At one point Nixon said: "I will not place the blame on subordinates, on people whose zeal exceeded their judgment and who may have done wrong in a cause they deeply believed to be right." Here Nixon seems to be arguing that we should allow sincerity of intent, no matter the suspect ethics of the means used to achieve that intent, to significantly soften our ethical judgment. Do you agree? Should sincerity of intent and degree of ethics be judged separately?

Nixon's Watergate speech could be examined by applying the "significant choice" political perspective developed by Thomas Nilsen and discussed previously in this chapter. As applied by Nilsen to public communication, techniques are ethical to the degree that they foster "free, informed, critical choice" in citizen decision making. Ethical communication presents complete, relevant, accurate information, assesses long- and short-term consequences of alternatives, reveals the communicator's

---

22. For a complete text of Nixon's speech, see *Vital Speeches of the Day*, Vol. 39 (May 15, 1973), pp. 450–452; or Waldo Braden, ed., *Representative American Speeches, 1972–1973* (New York: H.W. Wilson, 1973), pp. 50–59. For an ethical case study of Nixon's 1972 presidential campaign, see Karen Rasmussen, "Nixon and the Strategy of Avoidance," *Central States Speech Journal*, Vol. 24 (Fall 1973), pp. 193–202.

motivations and values, and avoids misleading receivers into believing that they are getting a more accurate and complete picture than they really are. We shall apply and extend Nilsen's "significant choice" viewpoint in suggesting various judgmental considerations.

Advance publicity by the Administration created a citizen expectation that the speech would present the basic facts and Nixon's complete explanation of the Watergate situation. In the speech itself, Nixon says he will address two central questions: "How could it have happened?" "Who is to blame?" Here was an opportunity to promote free, informed, critical decision in the citizenry by providing the information necessary for them to form a reasoned opinion. Instead Nixon presented less than the needed relevant information, left some basic questions unanswered, and sought sympathy for himself personally through diversionary appeals and emotional images. Nixon utilized some ethically questionable communication tactics which, intentionally or not, had the effect of beclouding and confusing citizen assessment of information on Watergate.

What are we to make of such items as these? Nixon addresses us from the Lincoln Room of the White House with a sculptured head of *Honest* Abe visible in the background. At one point focus is shifted from an explanation of Watergate to discussion of supposedly more important "work to be done" toward promoting peace: the approaching visit of West Germany's Chancellor Brandt, the American-Russian arms reduction and nuclear limitation negotiations, the maintenance of peace in the Middle East, and even the domestic task of controlling inflation.

Nixon pictures himself, on Christmas Eve, during his "terrible personal ordeal of the renewed bombing of North Vietnam," setting aside family matters to write out his goals for his second term. These goals, it turns out, are the usual, stereotypical ones endorsed by virtually every American President; and their relevance to Watergate is left unclear. How relevant to an explanation of Watergate is the fact that he first heard about the break-in while "in Florida trying to get a few days' rest after my visit to Moscow"? How relevant is the fact that upon his second Inauguration he gave each member of his senior White House staff a calendar indicating the number of days remaining in the Administration? Are there any ethical implications we should attach to his conclusion? "God Bless America. God bless each and every one of you." We have suggested, then, that an application of the "significant choice" political perspective could lead to the negative ethical judgment that some of Nixon's communication techniques undermined free, informed, critical citizen response.[23]

---

23.   Some of these insights concerning the ethics of Nixon's address are adapted from a graduate course research paper by Kathryn Bentley McRary, "Ethical Implications in Richard M. Nixon's April 30, 1973, Watergate Speech," Northern Illinois University, Department of Speech Communication, 1973.

A REVIEW AND CONCLUSION

The process of persuasion demands that you make choices about the methods and content you will use in influencing receivers to accept the alternative you advocate. These choices involve issues of desirability and of personal and societal good. What ethical standards are you to use in making or judging these choices among techniques, contents, and purposes? What should be the ethical responsibility of a persuader in contemporary American society?

Obviously, answers to these questions have not been clearly or universally established. However, the questions are ones we must face squarely. In this chapter, we have explored some perspectives, issues, and examples useful in evaluating the ethics of persuasion. Our interest in the nature and effectiveness of persuasive techniques must not overshadow our concern for the ethical use of such techniques. We must examine not only *how* to, but also *whether* to, use persuasive techniques. The issue of "whether to" is both one of audience adaptation and one of ethics. We should formulate meaningful ethical guidelines, not inflexible rules, for our own persuasive behavior and for use in evaluating the persuasion to which we are exposed. It is hoped that we will share the sincere concern for ethical communication expressed by the late Secretary General of the United Nations, Dag Hammarskjöld, in his book *Markings*:

> *Respect for the Word—to employ it with scrupulous care and an incorruptible heartfelt love of truth—is essential if there is to be any growth in a society or in the human race.*
>
> *To misuse the word is to show contempt for man. It undermines the bridges and poisons the wells. It causes Man to regress down the long path of his evolution.*[24]

Questions for Further Thought

1. Why are potential ethical issues inherent in every persuasive situation?

2. Can you briefly and clearly explain the nature of the six perspectives suggested for possible application in judging the ethics of persuasion?

---

24.   Dag Hammarskjöld, *Markings* (New York: Alfred A. Knopf. 1964), p. 112.

3. Should criteria for assessing ethics of persuasion be absolute or relative?

4. To what degree can a worthy end justify use of unethical persuasive techniques?

5. When might intentional use of ambiguity be ethically justified?

6. In what ways may some of the traditional propaganda devices not be inherently unethical?

7. To what degree are all emotional appeals unethical?

8. To what degree does sincerity of intent free a persuader from ethical responsibilities toward receivers?

9. What standards do *you* believe are most appropriate for judging the ethics of political-governmental persuasion?

10. What ethical criteria do *you* feel should be used to evaluate commercial advertising?

Experiences in Persuasion

1. Develop a written rationale for including or excluding *tastefulness* as an ethical standard for judging persuasion. Are appeals in advertisements or campaign persuasion labeled as being in poor taste also to be condemned as unethical?

2. With the most recent national presidential campaign as your focus, hold a small-group discussion of four to six people in which you assess the persuasive ethics of the major candidates. Be sure you clearly identify the ethical perspectives and standards you employ.

3. In Saul Alinsky's *Rules for Radicals*,[25] read pages 24 to 47 and then present your assessment of the soundness of his suggested ethical guidelines. As an alternative, read pages 125 to 164 and present your evaluation of the ethics of the tactics he discusses.

4. Read a chapter in Bruce Felknor's *Dirty Politics*[26] and give your assessment of the ethics of the political campaigning practices described in that chapter.

5. Select a chapter on a twentieth-century politician in Reinhard Luthin's *American Demagogues*.[27] Based on your reading of that

---

25.   Saul Alinsky, *Rules for Radicals* (New York: Random House, 1971).

26.   Bruce Felknor, *Dirty Politics* (New York: W. W. Norton & Co., 1966).

27.   Richard Luthin, *American Demagogues* (Boston: Beacon Press, 1954; reprinted Russell and Russell, 1968).

chapter, present your evaluation of the persuasive ethics of that politician.

6. Read Chapter 4 on propaganda devices in W. H. Werkmeister's *An Introduction to Critical Thinking* (rev. ed., 1957).[28] Select three propaganda devices and describe how they might be unethical or *ethical* in two different situations or from two different ethical perspectives.

7. Write your reply to the following questions concerning the ethics of advertising: (1) What is the morality of encouraging housewives to be nonrational and impulsive in buying the family food? (2) What is the morality of playing upon hidden weaknesses, such as aggressive feelings, dread of nonconformity, infantile hangovers, and sexual yearnings, to sell products? (3) What is the morality of manipulating small children to pressure their parents to buy products? (4) What is the morality of encouraging a public attitude of wastefulness toward national resources by promoting the planned "psychological obsolescence" (out-of-style view) of products already in use?[29]

---

28. Werkmeister (cited in Footnote 4).

29. Questions are adapted from Vance Packard, *The Hidden Persuaders* (New York: Pocket Books, 1958), Chapter 24.

The Role of the Persuadee
in a Mass Society 10

OUR ACHILLES' HEELS
    Identity Searching
    The Broken Fantasy
    Rebirth Hopes
    The TV Brainwash
ALL'S NOT LOST—YET

Several years ago, a researcher tried to identify how persuasion was being taught in a large Midwestern state. He conducted two surveys. The first was to identify how much time, either in a whole course or in units of study, was being devoted to the study of persuasion. His results were based on response from state universities and junior colleges. They were chilling. Only one third of the colleges and universities even offered a course on persuasion. Only one third of this small number required the courses of communication majors. In other words, not much time was being devoted to the study of persuasion. It clearly was not seen as something essential to our citizenry. His second study grew out of the challenge issued by the National Council of Teachers of English to teach students to become experts at spotting doublespeak. He wrote to teachers of these very few persuasion courses to see how much time they devoted to the training of receiver skills—how to be persuaded without being manipulated. Only one fourth to one third of the classes devoted a major emphasis to topics like political persuasion or advertising. Most of the textbooks did not cover these topics either, and some did not deal with mass media at all. He noted that this was at a time when the dangers of political skullduggery à la Watergate were well known and when advertising budgets totalled nearly $30 billion each year. The only bright spot he found was that most courses did devote time to the study of faulty logic and logical fallacies.[1]

1.　　Daniel Dieterich, "Training College Students as Critical Receivers of Public Persuasion" in *Teaching About Doublespeak* ed. by Daniel Dieterich (Urbana, Ill.: National Council of Teachers of English, 1976), p. 192. Dieterich's work is based on his dissertation, "The Training of College Students in Illinois as Critical Receivers of Public Persuasion" University of Illinois, Champaign-Urbana, 1976.

OUR ACHILLES' HEELS

It is not surprising, then, that so many consumers, voters, and joiners are easily fooled by the clever flimflam that surrounds them. The ad people know their buying habits. The politicians seem to be well tuned to their responsive chords at election time. The Reverend Moons of the world know how to attract followers. Most consumers, voters, and joiners are old hands at being tricked, and the strange thing is that they rarely do anything about it. Why? We all have our own answers to that question. Most people would include in their answers some reference to the way the world has changed in the very recent past. They refer to such things as TV, videotape, computers, and other tools of persuasion. What they would really be talking about would be the mass society in which we live.

What is a mass society and what does it do to us? For one thing, it deprives us of much of the privacy we used to have. Somewhere there is a credit file on almost every person. In it are data on the number of credit cards you own and use, how well you meet payments on bills, and other data. At the same time that we lose privacy in a mass society, we also tend to lose individuality. We share much information simply because we are all exposed to the same basic data bank through the mass media. These shared data make us more like one another than in earlier times. We all get the same basic news each day, even though it might be from different networks or wire services. Persuaders treat us as members of market segments, not as individual human beings.

Identity Searching

A new school of advertising theory called *positioning* maintains that a product need only have name recognition to be successful. The theory assumes that each buyer is nothing more than a brand-recall device and not a thinking and responding human being. People who feel less and less private and who see themselves treated as though they are only ciphers in a mass will react in some way to those feelings. They become skeptical about the world they live in. They seek out ways to express their individuality. If Maslow is right (see Chapter 3), they will seek out ways in which they can belong and can self-actualize. All those actions reduce the feelings of estrangement that come from being faceless and nameless members of some market target dreamed up in an ad agency.

This action is natural. Who wants to be faceless and nameless? We want to be noticed and appreciated. Remember the industrial research that showed that workers rated being listened to, being appreciated and fellow workers higher than wages, fringe benefits, and work conditions?

Those data show the same thing—a desire to be more than a Social Security number. However, this presents a real problem. How do we assert our individuality? Persuaders try to sell us many ways. We can buy identity—perhaps a Thunderbird or a motorcycle. We can join groups to get identity—the Y.M.C.A., a fraternity or a sorority. We can take action to assert ourselves—help in politics, be a leader. We can join the new religion, the Neo-Nazis, or some other group. However, all these options are dwarfed in relation to the tremendous power of the mass media to mold us. A single billboard can persuade more persons than all the door-to-door soliciting that a single person can do. For example, in spite of a large mass movement in favor of women's rights, with its hopes of changing the role of women from sex objects to equals with men, our TV programs reflect a continuing interest in women as things, not persons. The "jiggly" programming typical of the late 1970s (shows that star sexy, well-built Charlie's Angels or Suzanne Somers of "Three's Company," for instance) is good evidence of that. Those shows were not just for leering males; they drew more female viewers than male viewers. The mass-media image of woman as a sex object seems to be getting stronger not weaker, much to the dismay of activists in the Women's Liberation Movement. The same kind of case could be made for other things— increased smoking despite the ban on TV tobacco commercials, increased violence and crime, and so forth. We are helpless when compared with the mass media. It is as though the media and mass culture drive us and not we them. So we become skeptical and try to escape mass anonymity by becoming involved in the world around us.

That is a good place to begin as critical receivers of persuasion— skeptical but involved. We have tried to fine-tune critical skills by assuming that you are already skeptical about the persuasion world in which you live and that you want to be involved in that world in spite of your skepticism. However, there still are dangers.

Broken Fantasy

As we have already noted, the nature of our TV programming seems destined to produce skepticism. Whenever you interrupt the viewers' fantasy worlds to tell them to buy some product or to believe that a character called "Mother Nature" is fooled by Chiffon margarine or that a cartoon bear in Hamm's country is really a bumbler, you are also bound to create a skeptical reaction. One group of critics put it this way:

> The constant exposure to this shower of matter—half-true, true, or even true, but always simplified, always loud, always self-serving— induces a peculiar mixture of gullibility and cynicism that is close to

neurosis. It is not an attitude that is well adapted for distinguishing between bullshine and brass tacks, rhetoric and reality.[2]

Thus, not only does the form of our TV programming encourage a skeptical reaction, but so does the content. We are asked to believe the ridiculous in the midst of the serious. At the same time, the serious and imagined fantasy or show we believe in is shattered by constant interruption for ads, thereby further convincing us that little is real or sincere.

These feelings of doubt are bound to affect us in other ways. Like the trend to become involved in TV, which prompts us to engage in the real world, the doubt caused by the TV world is bound to spill over outside that fantasy world. Not surprisingly, we find that, in the past ten years, people seem to have become less sure of themselves. You can pick up almost any contemporary magazine and find several articles dealing with this problem. How to deal with depression. When to get into sensitivity groups. What to do when your husband leaves you. The problem is further underscored when you look at other developments of the technological age. For example, most of us get a lot of third-class mail that tries to induce us to buy various products. In almost every one of these pieces of mail, there is a "personal" letter in which our names and address have been printed in order to fool us into believing that we are one of a select few chosen to receive the letter. We are aware that the world is rapidly becoming polluted beyond redemption—the seas, the land, the air—yet no one seems to be able to do anything about it. Another example of this sense of helplessness is in job hunting. At least in the late 1970s, that passport to success—a college degree—no longer guaranteed that you would find a job and be happy. The college degree often proved a detriment in getting a job. The evening news on any night of the year underscores the cynical and doubting frame of mind we have been describing. If the politicians are not being exposed for gypping the public, there is a new source of pollution or someone is going on strike or another airplane is hijacked or a sniper is picking people off in a large city. So skepticism is a by-product of the TV age as well as of mass society.

Rebirth Hopes

There are dangers that may go along with this atmosphere of doubt and skepticism. Theodore Roszak noted some of them in his book *Unfinished Animal*. In the midst of a dehumanizing and alienation-producing mass

2. Lewis Chester, Godfrey Hodgeson, and Bruce Page, *An American Melodrama: The Presidential Campaign of 1968* (New York: The Viking Press, 1969), p. 47. This observation is particularly interesting since the authors are British and perhaps more objective in viewing American culture.

society, people seek out ways to have a kind of rebirth, he says. This explains the many therapies that have blossomed—Esalen, primal therapy, gestalt. The rebirth is seen in the sensations that people seek out—drugs, quad-sound, thrill movies, occult religions, and so forth. The danger lies in our need to have a new beginning and being dissatisfied with our old self. This need is a prime target for persuaders. Focus on the many TV spots that you see. Nearly all of them have as a basic theme the idea that you will be a new and better person if you decide to use the product. Use Ultra Ban and you will find true love. There's a Ford in your future. Phillips 66—the performance company—is interested in our environment. Roszak notes that "Every totalitarian mass movement of modern times has borrowed and perverted the psychology of rebirth for its own purposes."[3] He predicts the possibility of a world controlled by those who sell us new identities. They might be political persuaders promising a new rebirth for our national goals. They might be promising a new rebirth of personality, attractiveness, or energy once you use a certain product. Roszak says we would be "a global wasteland where only an ensconced, bandit elite of corporate profiteers, commissars and technocrats, together with their armed defenders and reliable clients enjoy the dwindling riches of the Earth, while the impoverished billions starve without even clean air in which to draw their last breath."[4] So there is a real reason to become a critical consumer of persuasion if Roszak is right in his predictions and observations.

The TV Brainwash

On another front, we have even more to fear in a mass society. Jerry Mander, a researcher into the effects of TV, became aware of several factors that sent chills down his spine.[5] When TV first became available we assumed that it would make all of us better educated, more involved in our world and government, and likely to improve ourselves. The models and images that we saw daily could be the patterns we might follow. Instead, "people's patterns of discernment were becoming dulled . . . many viewers took programs to be real!" For instance, when the program was on the air, Dr. Marcus Welby received 250,000 requests for medical advice. Mander noted further that "80 million viewers were sitting separately in dark rooms engaged in exactly the same activity at the same

---

3.   Theodore Roszak, *Unfinished Animal* (New York: Harper & Row, 1975), p. 40.

4.   Roszak, p. 178.

5.   Jerry Mander, "Arguments for the Elimination of Television," in *Penthouse*, March 1978, pp. 54–58.

time . . . it was as if we sat in isolation booths unable to exchange any responses about what we were all going through together."

This TV jag was bad enough to Mander, but his fears really increased when he learned that the Pentagon had proposed to President Nixon that every TV set in the country be fitted with a gadget that would turn on the set and turn it to the appropriate channel whenever the President wished, night or day. Though the Administration turned down the proposal because people might "misinterpret the intentions" of the project, the fact that the gadget existed and was being considered for use was scary. The "Big Brother Is Watching" world of George Orwell's novel 1984 seemed just around the corner in Mander's mind.

He delved further into the effects of TV. What he discovered did not allay his fears. He learned that in 1975, researchers in Australia found that during TV viewing our normal thought processes slow down and even stop. We lose our critical ability to some degree. As they noted, "television not only destroys the capacity of the viewer to attend; it also, by taking over a complex of direct and indirect neural pathways, decreases vigilance." Their brainwave research showed that the left half of the brain, which does critical thinking, integrates data, and prepares us to act, slows down during TV viewing. TV viewing is really sleep teaching, if these data are valid. It trains us to *not* think or to *not* react. It is the Ultimate Brainwash. The Australian results have been replicated by several researchers in this country. As we watch TV, the alpha or slow brain waves increase, while the beta or fast brain waves decrease. As Mander puts it: "TV does not educate; it implants . . . there is no way to change it."

Put all these trends together and we are faced with an almost impossible task as receivers. We are molded by mass society to doubt everything. We feel isolated and dehumanized and are thus easy prey for clever persuaders. We want to have a kind of rebirth or renewal experience and that also makes us open to being persuaded. The prime message carrier of our times—our seven-hours-a-day companion—makes zombies or robots of us all. As good old Professor Harold Hill of *The Music Man* might have said, "There's trouble, my friends, right here in River City. Yes, I said trouble and that starts with T and that rhymes with V and that stands for TV!" And the many other media of our mass culture.

ALL'S NOT LOST—YET

A few years ago, Kenneth Boulding, author of *The Image*, noted in an interview that one of the major problems in our society is not a loss of confidence but the deterioration of legitimacy. He argues that, with the development of nuclear missiles, the "unconditional viability of the national state" (that is, legitimacy) is destroyed.

> *If you don't have what we call internal legitimacy—which is the equivalent of morale or self-confidence or nerve—you obviously can't function. . . . And you can't function without external legitimacy, without having people accept the role structure and the authority structure and so on. . . . The erosion of legitimacy is a profound problem in society but we mustn't overestimate it.*[6]

He goes on to argue that though much of this loss of legitimacy or believability can be attributed to the effects of mass society and to the information explosion, the case is not hopeless. Information, he says, is not knowledge—"knowledge . . . is attained much more by a loss of information than by the gain of it."[7] In other words, though things seem to be out of control and depersonalized we can control them by becoming involved in the world of persuasion around us. The ultimate error would be to allow our cynicism and skepticism to cause us either to accept all persuasion without question or to reject all persuasion as manipulation. We need to be persuaded in a mass society, but persuasion should occur only after we have critically lost or reviewed some of the data sent us. In the same interview cited above, Boulding replied to a question about how he could remain optimistic in spite of all of the fears expressed by himself and others concerning the problems of the future. He answered the question this way: "Your perception is accurate. The only unforgivable sin is despair, because that will justify itself. I believe man is very far from exhausting the potential of his extraordinary nervous system."[8]

We need to avoid despairing because the world seems so uncontrollable and uncertain. One of the ways to avoid that feeling is to become actively involved in the persuasion that is continually aimed at us. We need to become alert and critical persuadees so that we can responsibly practice the reception of persuasive messages. We hope that we have given you a few of the tools to let you succeed as you face the many persuaders in your world.

---

6. Robert W. Glasgow, "Aristocrats Have Always Been Sons of Bitches," (interview with Kenneth Boulding), *Psychology Today,* January 1973, pp. 61, 63.

7. Glasgow, pp. 63–64.

8. Glasgow, p. 87.

INDEX

285